JEREMIAH TOWER COOKS

JEREMIAH TOWER COOKS

250 RECIPES FROM AN AMERICAN MASTER

Jeremiah Tower   Paintings by Donald Sultan

STEWART TABORI & CHANG / NEW YORK

Published in 2002 by
Stewart, Tabori & Chang
A Company of La Martinière Groupe
115 West 18th Street
New York, NY 10011

Export Sales to all countries
except Canada, France, and
French-speaking Switzerland:
Thames and Hudson Ltd.
181A High Holborn
London WC1V 7QX
England

Canadian Distribution:
Canadian Manda Group
One Atlantic Avenue, Suite 105
Toronto, Ontario M6K 3E7
Canada

Library of Congress Cataloging-in-Publication Data

Tower, Jeremiah
    Jeremiah Tower Cooks: 250 recipes from an American master / by Jeremiah Tower
        p. cm.
    ISBN 1-58479-230-2
    1. Cookery, American--California style. I. Title

TX715.2.C34 T69 2002
641.59794--dc21   2002066827

The text of this book was composed in the typefaces Minion and The Sans
Edited by Gail Monaghan
Designed by Galen Smith with Allyson McFarlane and Kristine Ann Platou
Graphic Production by Kim Tyner

Printed in Japan.

10 9 8 7 6 5 4 3 2 1
First Printing

ACKNOWLEDGMENTS

I would like to thank: Mark Magowan, for giving me the opportunity to do this book; Leslie Stoker and Constance Herndon, for taking it on at Stewart, Tabori & Chang; my editor, Gail Monaghan, for her insistence on my writing a whole new book and for seeing it tirelessly all the way through the process; Donald Sultan, for understanding from the beginning how perfect his paintings are for the book; Jim Villas and Alex Birnbaum, for holding my hand every Tuesday night throughout the writing of the book; and, of course, my fearless agent and friend at IMG, Lisa Queen, without whom this book would never have seen the light of day or been as good.

TABLE OF
CONTENTS

INTRODUCTION

"NEW-OLD FOOD IN A NEW-NEW SETTING" IS HOW A HERO OF MINE, JOE BAUM, DESCRIBED the philosophy behind some of his restaurants, such as The Four Seasons, Windows on the World, and the recreated Rainbow Room. I've approached my own restaurants and my own cooking the same way. So when James Beard called my San Francisco restaurant Stars "a brilliant blend of old and new that has caught the spirit of the time," I was delighted.

When I thought about writing a new book on my cooking, I couldn't help but reflect that the ingredients and cooking techniques we had introduced in the 1970s and 1980s had now become mainstream. With an extraordinary range of fresh and exotic ingredients now available, the developments in American cooking have finally gone beyond restaurant chefs and into the home. The book, I realized, would be new-old material in a new-new setting because the changes we initiated remain fresh, even as they have taken their permanent place in our culinary tradition.

The new in this book, then, comes in celebrating the gloriously transformed world of American cooking. But I hold on to the old because without those things that have survived "the vicissitudes of fashion to make themselves sovereign and unignorable," as Michael Pollan wrote in *The Botany of Desire*, there would be no foundation for the new. So just as I've selected some recipes that are simple and easily prepared, my respect for the enduring classics propels me also to include more complicated dishes and more demanding techniques. Have fun making the "Fast and Easy" recipes such as the twenty-minute blueberry tart as well as revisiting more complex dishes, like a boned, breaded, and deep-fried sole "Colbert" filled with fragrantly flavored butter (see page 165). The soft and precious flavors and techniques of the past have given us a framework in which to use the riches of the present.

CHAPTER ONE

DELIGHTS *and* PREJUDICES

This chapter, Delights and Prejudices, is all about having one foot in the past and one in the present as we build a new American culinary tradition. My delight in opening a bay scallop, standing knee-deep in crystal Maine water and eating it right out of the shell, is as strong as my prejudice that our American culinary language must evolve at the same rate as our culinary discoveries, and that common sense, laced always with an appetite for life, should eventually prevail over the momentary pleasure of fashion.

Throughout this book, recipes are presented with head notes that include stories about the dishes and their ingredients. But this first chapter serves to introduce the way I think about food and cooking—everything from seasoning and equipment to culinary terminology. I'm aiming to help readers *understand* food and why we cook it the way we do—those things that lie at the root of what makes cooking and eating two of the great pleasures of life.

ERRORS AND IMPROVISATIONS

How bad can it get? Unless you confuse the sugar with the salt (or vice versa), or believe in the latest fad and put bananas in a red wine sauce meant for grilled salmon, you can recover from almost anything. If a soufflé falls, just scoop it out, put it in a buttered gratin dish, pour on a little cream, or custard if it's a sweet soufflé, shove it under the broiler, and call it your grandmother's pudding.

Above all, trust yourself. There are some things in recipe writing that are impossible to describe succinctly, such as when a pan is too hot, either with oil in it (for toasting dried chilies) or not (when toasting spices). "Heat until the pan is hot but not smoking" is imperfect because the moment you know with certainty that the pan is hot enough is when it is too hot and the oil has already begun to smoke. Learn to recognize that moment when the oil is getting ready to smoke, when it just starts to shimmer and move around in the pan. If you misjudge, simply take the pan off the heat for a minute. Trust your instincts and you will be fine.

I hope the recipes and dozens of variations in this book stimulate you to say, "I can do better than that," and then do it. Improvise and have fun.

COMMON SENSE

COOKING TIMES

Cooking times given in recipes are only an indication of how long something will take to cook. The temperature of the food as it goes into the pot or oven, the calibration of the oven, the condition of the burners, the type of fuel used (propane or city gas or electric), even the altitude above sea level—all of these cause variations in cooking times. So use the given times, but for perfect results, start to check the dish up to ten minutes before the recipe says it will be ready, and be prepared to go ten minutes more.

"OPTIONAL" VERSUS "VARIATIONS"

"Optional" is a word that recipe writers love to put next to any ingredient that looks as if it might cause the reader some discomfort or anxiety. I have chosen not to use the term because I know the reader can figure out that if a secondary ingredient—a garnish or one flavor among many—is out of season, too expensive, or unavailable, it can be omitted and the dish can be cooked anyway without a huge problem.

If the dish is french-style scrambled eggs with black truffles (page 35) and you don't have any truffles, then obviously the alarm goes off—if you don't have the truffles, don't make the dish. But in the case of a recipe that includes variations, such as meringues with longans (page 268), you will find that when longans are out of season, you may substitute rhubarb or cherries, which are from a different season than longans, or use anise-flavored mascarpone, which is available all year long.

ROOM TEMPERATURE

"Room temperature" means what it says, and at the same time, it does not. Since a lot of foods taste better when not cold (as in not directly from the refrigerator), room temperature is specified. But this does not mean the 100-degree temperature of a kitchen in Singapore in the summer—rather, it implies around 70 degrees.

SALT AND PEPPER TO TASTE

Well, of course, use salt and pepper "to taste." Meaning season the food with the best-quality salt and freshly ground, toasted white or black pepper (or a pepper mix, such as the one on page 39) so that it tastes good. I did not find it necessary to repeat the phrase every time salt and pepper are mentioned. If you are using an electric spice mill to grind the pepper, remember that you should sieve the ground pepper to separate the fine powder from the larger particles, but use them separately.

SEASON

"Season" means to sprinkle with salt and freshly ground white or black pepper, or whatever spices are called for in the list of ingredients.

EUROPEAN WORDS VERSUS ENGLISH OR AMERICAN

English has long been a mongrel language, strongly marked by just about every other tongue in Europe. With America's thriving immigrant communities, the English spoken here is even more of a mixed bag—and therein lies much of its vitality.

For American cooks, much of our vocabulary comes directly from the French—a logical enough development given our love and acceptance of their principles of cooking. But I do think the time has come for America to recognize that we have our own distinct cuisine and its own young language. Today, culinary students are not necessarily taught by European chefs and the best food in this country is often being cooked by a new generation of American-born and American-trained chefs. Perhaps it's about time for our vocabulary to catch up with our cooking.

I bring up this issue primarily as a point of discussion, in an effort to ensure that Americans who were not raised in the European culinary tradition have access to terminology that (put simply) makes sense. The old terms won't be replaced immediately, of course, but the question deserves serious consideration. We should have as much pride in our own culinary language as we have in America's achievements in the kitchen over the last thirty years.

Aromatic Vegetable Mix
(Mirepoix)

Called an "aromatic condiment," this mixture of carrot, onion, celery, and bay leaf is cooked with meats, vegetables (such as braised artichokes), and poultry, perfuming and flavoring them all.

Almost every cuisine has its own version: the *soffritto* in Italy (onions, tomatoes, herbs, and olive oil), the Puerto Rican and Caribbean versions (they add chopped salt pork, ham, and bell peppers), and the *sofregit* or *picada* of Catalonia (almonds, pine nuts, garlic, and parsley ground to a paste).

When the aromatic vegetable mix is to be left in the sauce or served with the dish, it should be cut up quite small, a matignon in French classic cooking. Brunoise is the same mix or a mixture of other vegetables like turnip, parsnip, and celery root, cut into ⅛-inch dice. Use a small dice if it is to be served with the final dish used in a short cooking phase (15 minutes), or when a new vegetable mix is cooked and added after the first one is sieved out of the cooking juices.

MAKES ABOUT 4 CUPS

1 pound	carrots, peeled and chopped
1 pound	yellow or white onions, chopped
1 pound	celery stalks, chopped
1	bay leaf, crumbled

Chop the vegetables as specified below, mix together, and add the bay leaf.

✦ for meat stocks:	2-inch pieces
✦ for poultry stocks:	1-inch pieces
✦ for fish stocks:	½-inch pieces
✦ for braising:	1-inch pieces
✦ for cooking with food in less than 30 minutes:	⅛-inch pieces

Blue (Bleu)

Would someone tell me what in America "a salad with bleu cheese" is? And why?

Cooking Juices (Au Jus)

Cooking juices that collect during the roasting, baking, or braising of meats, or those that end up on a board or platter of grilled meats often make the best sauce for the meats once the fats have been removed. However, the term on menus is still "au jus" (meaning "with the juices"), and is a term often quite comically pronounced by culinary students and cooks as "ajoo"—almost like a sneeze. Perhaps "served with its cooking juices" will do.

Cream (Crème)

Using the word "crème" on a menu written in English—as in "Indian Pudding with a Maple Syrup Crème"—is like holding your pinkie in the air when drinking tea.

Fat-Preserved Duck Legs
(Confit de Canard)

One of the simplest grand meals in the world is preserved duck legs (or goose, turkey, squab, pheasant, and so on) slowly cooked in their rendered fat and then preserved in it. It is also one of the easiest and simplest meals, because once the confit is made, making a finished dish with it takes only ten minutes in the oven or on the stovetop, broiler, or grill. Since preserved duck will last for weeks in the refrigerator, it is one of the ultimate fast foods.

Below is a recipe for four legs of duck, which will serve two to four, but it is better to cook more once you have decided to do the work. There is never enough duck fat rendered from a single duck, so I save up poultry fat and freeze it until I have enough for this cooking and preserving technique.

You also can buy rendered duck, goose, or chicken fat. Just make sure it is water-rendered and not baked (see page 30). If you buy whole ducks, use the legs for this recipe and the breasts for the recipe on pages 201, since you get the best results from the legs and breasts if you cook them separately.

SERVES 4

4	duck legs with thighs
1 cup	dry brine (see page 22)
8 cups	rendered duck fat

Rinse the duck under cold water and pat dry. Put the legs in a dish and rub each piece with the salt mixture. Pour the remaining salt on top of the duck, cover, and refrigerate for 24 hours, turning twice.

Preheat the oven to 230 degrees.

Wipe the salt off the duck pieces. Melt the rendered duck fat over low heat in a casserole just large enough to hold the duck and the fat. Add the pieces of duck, making sure they are thoroughly covered with the fat. Cover and bake until the duck is very tender when pierced with a skewer, about 1½ hours.

When the legs are cooked, take them out and cool on a wire rack over a pan.

Strain the fat remaining in the casserole and let it sit until the juices fall to the bottom of the container and the fat rises to the top. Carefully lift the fat out with a ladle, making sure you do not get any of the juices. These juices are a wonderful addition to sauces or soups and can be frozen for later use. If stored with the duck and fat, however, they will spoil.

Put the duck pieces in a sterilized preserving jar or crock and pour the fat over them, filling the jar until there is at least an inch of fat covering the duck. Cool in the refrigerator uncovered and then cover tightly.

Once the duck is entirely covered with fat, it will keep six months or more in the refrigerator, but its delicious taste and ease of preparation make it irresistible—I can never keep it that long without eating it. It has only to be cooked in a tablespoon of its fat, 15 minutes before serving time, to heat it through and crisp the skin (be sure to place it skin side down in the fat).

Gratin

I have found that most people think of a gratin as a dish cooked with cheese on top. Indeed, it can be topped with cheese, breadcrumbs, or both. But what the word means is "crust," referring to the thin finish that forms on the top of the dish (even though in the nineteenth century, the "gratin" was at the bottom of the dish) once it has been finished off in the oven or under a broiler. A gratin of vegetables or meat can be cooked from the raw state or made with leftovers in a shallow dish (a "gratin dish"), and it forms its own crust on top without the addition of breadcrumbs or cheese.

Gratin is a word that has become a part of standard American usage—we have even made other words like "gratineed"—so let's continue to use it as is.

Herb Bundle
(Bouquet Garni)

I can hear Richard Olney's voice as I write, since he gave us the most lucid and complete lecture about bouquet garni in Time-Life's *Good Cook* series, which I helped him write and recipe test in 1979. He would think my changing its name to herb bundle quite silly, but then maybe not, since his mind was never stuck in any mode except in a search for quality, simplicity, and proper scholarship.

Like the vegetable mix of carrot, onion, and celery that is added to stocks, stews, and braised dishes, this bundle of green (or the tough outer white) leek leaves, celery leaves, bay leaf, parsley, and thyme lends flavor and aromatic structure to cooking liquids. The herbs are tied together into a bundle that can be easily retrieved and discarded after the other ingredients are cooked. Like the vegetable mix, the herb bundle is an ensemble of flavors rather than the taste of any single ingredient. It is very difficult to judge the quantity of dried or fresh herbs to use for a long-cooking dish, but tied together as a bundle, the flavors of the herbs spread very slowly, so that over a few hours the flavors attenuate and refine.

Fresh or dried thyme lends support to most dishes in a way that does not overpower, but creates a base for all the other flavors. Other herbs can be included in the bundle if you want their particular flavors—you can adapt the herbs to your cooking and your mood. Marjoram, with its distinctive odor, will remain fairly dominant even after the cooking juices have been cleaned up and reduced into a sauce. So will tarragon, oregano, winter savory, hyssop (which adds a slightly bitter edge), and lovage (which riffs off the celery in the bundle, as does the leek off the onions in the vegetable mix).

MAKES 1 BUNDLE

4	green leek leaves, washed
1 stalk	celery
1	bay leaf
4 sprigs	fresh parsley
2 sprigs	fresh or dried thyme
2 sprigs	fresh chervil
1 sprig	fresh tarragon

Open up the leek leaves and wrap them around the remaining gathered-together ingredients to completely enclose them. Wrap the whole thing tightly in four or five rings of string.

Chop off the ends of the herb bundle, if only for the satisfaction of neatness. Note: You can prepare the herb bundle the day before and store it, very slightly damp, in a plastic bag in the refrigerator.

Hot-Water Bath (Bain Marie)

A hot-water bath is a pan full of hot water used either for keeping something warm or for providing cooking heat that is less hot than a double boiler. Cooking in a water bath protects delicate foods like custards and eggs from direct contact with the heat source or flame, so that they do not lose their emulsion, turn into scrambled eggs, disintegrate, or turn oily. Typical dishes to be cooked this way are custards, creams, egg dishes, some soufflés, and butter-egg sauces.

Double boilers tend to get too hot from the contained steam and have to be watched very carefully so they don't overheat whatever is in them. Scrambled eggs, for example, when prepared in the French manner (as they should always be), are cooked in a hot-water bath rather than in a double boiler.

Mixed Young Salad Greens (Mesclun)

In the early 1970s at Chez Panisse, I smuggled in seeds from France and had them grown for us, little edible greens and wild greens to make a mix of various leaves. The southern French word *mesclun* means just that, "a mix of wild greens." The concept, now ubiquitous and misunderstood, is one of the major culinary sins that can be laid at my feet.

I say "misunderstood" because, as mesclun began to appear in every supermarket and farmers' market, each purveyor thought that in order to get an edge on the competition, and because of America's undying belief that more is always better, they would dump into the mix any leaf that was colorful or new, regardless of whether or not it was desirable for the flavor, and certainly not because it was wild.

So mesclun is often no longer a subtle mix of leafy flavors but rather a riot of soft flavors (Bibb lettuces) paired with gross ones (kale), expressing a lack of understanding about which leaves taste better when immature rather than fully grown, and sporting the addition of leaves like red radicchio just for color, even though its flavor totally dominates the mix.

Part of the problem is the adoption of the word "mesclun," which has no meaning or reference in American culture, without the understanding that the mix was originally composed of those greens that showed up fresh in the spring to relieve the winter blues. When you specify "mixed young salad greens," everyone might understand what should be in the mix and what should not.

Grow and make your own young salad green mix, but be sure to include soft, fresh herb leaves and edible flowers, as was originally intended.

Mushroom Hash (*Duxelles*)

In culinary French, *duxelles* is a mixture of finely chopped mushrooms cooked in butter with minced shallots, sometimes fresh thyme, and finished with lemon juice, salt, and pepper. The mixture is never eaten by itself but, stuffed into almost anything, it works flavor miracles. Antonin Carême, in the first part of the nineteenth century, said it was a sauce, and then Auguste Escoffier, in the first part of the twentieth, said it was no longer a sauce but a dry preparation, the version we know today.

To me, *duxelles* is a hash.

MAKES ABOUT 1 CUP

1 pound	white mushrooms, chopped very fine
2	large shallots, peeled, finely chopped
3 tablespoons	unsalted butter
1 teaspoon	fresh thyme leaves, chopped
1½ teaspoons	freshly squeezed lemon juice
	Salt and freshly ground black pepper

Put the shallots, butter, and thyme in a pan with 2 tablespoons water. Cover and cook over low heat for 5 minutes.

Add the mushrooms, turn the heat to medium, and cook while constantly tossing or stirring for another 5 minutes. Add two pinches salt, turn the heat to high, and cook while stirring until the mushroom juices evaporate or are reabsorbed.

Remove from heat, add the lemon juice, and season.

Parsley, Garlic, and Lemon Zest Mix (*Persillade* and *Gremolata*)

I mention this mix of equal parts parsley and garlic, and the variation that adds an equal amount of grated lemon zest, because it is perhaps the least expensive and fastest way to add last-minute flavor and interest to vegetables, cooked meats, poultry, salads, and soups.

What is generally not known is that the garlic should be thoroughly pureed using a mortar and pestle before mixing with the chopped parsley. In this way, the fire and aftertaste of the raw garlic are diminished and the parsley is coated with the pureed garlic, resulting in a much more delicate flavor than if the garlic were minced.

Rocket (Arugula or *Roquette*)

This salad leaf of the plant *Eruca sativa* is one of my absolute favorites (as it has been for the Romans and many other cultures). It has the perfectly good English name of "rocket"—why not use it?

One finds it everywhere, with many different levels of quality and taste. The rule of thumb is that smaller leaves are better, although "baby" ones from some varieties can have no taste beyond a slightly soapy one. So taste before buying, and by all means grow your own. Dump a packet of seeds on the ground and up the rocket will come, seeding itself and coming back each year. If put in rich soil and watered, it will keep its milder personality.

Rocket flowers give a wonderful peppery taste and sweet perfume flavor to salads.

Cooking Terms and Phrases

Baby

As in vegetables, but it is time that some of them (like squash) become teenagers.

Fresh

"Fresh" has become everyone's cool mantra. As it should. But as we adopt the idea and practice it with our usual rushed American intensity, it is possible that we sometimes miss the point.

A few decades after we started this mantra in Berkeley, a chef who worked for me there misunderstood what we were looking for in freshness. He was from Singapore, where getting fresh fish other than garoupa was always a problem. Over the New Year's weekend, deliveries were to be terminated at least four days before the big night, but he had put fresh tuna on the menu. Somehow I didn't check that dish in the beginning of the evening and did not see or taste it until one in the morning when I sat down to eat. I smelled the fish on its way to the table while it was still a few feet away. I was horrified. "But it's fresh," he said, meaning that it had not been frozen. "But can you eat it?" I asked. "It would have been far better to use tuna that had been frozen right after it was caught than to use so-called fresh tuna, if this was the inevitable result."

In other words, fresh ingredients are supposed to produce a certain result and mean little or nothing as a concept when they don't.

Garnish (*Garniture*)

In that great French reference book from the beginning of the twentieth century, *Larousse gas-*

tronomique, there are hundreds of listings under garnishes. In Charles Ranhofer's monumental American cookbook, *The Epicurean* (1893), there are almost as many, but by 1972, James Beard, in his superb *American Cookery*, lists not a one. Perhaps it would have been better if he had, then maybe we would not have sprigs of fresh herbs sticking out of the top of every dish today. What are we supposed to do with these herb stems? Pluck off each little leaf of fresh thyme and scatter the leaves around the dish? If that is the case, the chef should have done it for us.

Let's decide that garnishes, from the old-fashioned chopped parsley or crayfish tails to the currently favored spiced salts and flavored oils and powders, should be edible and an integral part of the dish. They are not there just for visual stimulus but rather to enhance the flavors of the food as well. And, for the garnishes to accomplish this role successfully, let's also decide that they be put on or next to the food, leaving the rims of plates pristine and clear of any last-minute flurry from the kitchen. I ask also that all cooks eat some of the garnish themselves and make an honest, fad-free evaluation before using it, so that things like deep-fried angel hair leeks and artichoke leaves will never be seen again.

ICE BATH

You will see many recipes that call for an ice bath, usually for plunging vegetables into after they have been blanched or parboiled. I beg you to ignore this command (see also parboiling on page 25). It compromises fresh vegetables so much that you might as well save yourself the time and trouble and buy frozen ones instead, since the company packaging them has already blanched and iced the vegetables for you.

But I do think that a bowl full of ice and water (half and half) is the only way to go when you are making egg-thickened sauces, such as hollandaise or sabayon, because it instantly stops their cooking. An ice bath is also useful for cooling down delicately flavored vegetable soups and purees that would otherwise oxidize and keep cooking, consequently losing a lot of their fresh color and flavor. Simply place a metal bowl of the sauce, puree, or soup in a bowl half full of ice and water until cold.

KEEP IN A WARM PLACE

This command occurs in many of the recipes, and as I wrote this simple instruction so often, it occurred to me that what it means and how to do it are not so obvious as they might seem. I myself had a disaster once when the "warm place" was a turned-off electric wall oven (my first) and the insulation of the oven kept all the heat, in turning my beautiful medium-rare beef into a deep brown mess.

So here are some good "warm places:" on the open door of the turned off oven (keep dogs, cats, and children away); under the lid of a big Dutch oven or lobster pot; under a couple of layers of aluminum foil; in a microwave oven (if the dish cools off too much you can give it a quick blast of microwaves to heat it up); and in or over hot water, as with a chafing dish or hot-water bath (see page 16).

LATIN NAMES

I have included Latin names for wild mushrooms, fish and shellfish, tropical fruit, and anything picked from the wild.

Obviously there are health concerns with harvesting wild things such as mushrooms. The only way we can be absolutely clear about what is meant is to use the Latin botanical names, especially since the English or American names may change from region to region. Those regional changes seem to occur every hundred miles or so with fish and shellfish, so I believe that when using a word like "crayfish," for example, it is best to give the Latin name as well to avoid any confusion.

MAD SALAD

All of us in the 1980s thought we had invented everything, and this salad, whether called *fines gueules*, *folle*, *gourmande*, gourmet, or whatever, had several moments of fame. Unbeknownst to the public or most of the chefs, it just happened that this was to be only one of many such moments for this salad.

The basic idea of the Mad Salad dates back to Escoffier, who recorded a recipe in 1913 in *Le Carnet d'epicure* that calls for roasted partridge, truffles, crayfish tails, and celery, all dressed with olive oil, Dijon mustard, and a little tomato garnish. In the 1930s, Fernand Point took it one step further with his Salade Délice, which included those tiny green beans called *haricots verts*, sliced mushrooms, lots of truffles, foie gras, shallots, and chervil—which is how two of his star pupils, Paul Bocuse and Alain Chapel, were first introduced to it. And it was Bocuse, the leader of the young Turks of nouvelle cuisine, who took the salad into the 1970s, when it was picked up again by the Troisgros brothers and Michel Guérard.

Guérard makes his Salade Gourmande with green beans, asparagus tips, Treviso endive, shallots, foie gras, and lots of truffles. The Troisgros' Salade Riche is curly endive, Treviso endive, Bibb lettuce, crayfish tails, foie gras, truffles, chervil, nut oils, and a little tomato garnish.

I leave it up to you.

ORGANIC

Sometimes it seems that in America "organic produce" just means that the vegetables are unwashed and unrefrigerated. How many times have we seen expensive lettuces sitting on the shelf wilting away—but at least they are organic. The point is, who cares when the lettuce is in that condition?

Like "fresh," the use of the word "organic" is fraught with the peril of rushing to embrace a good concept without taking into consideration the result it is meant to produce. Organic does not mean only "free of dangerous chemicals and residual pesticides." Organic procedures play an important role in the creation of a sustainable agriculture and aquaculture, and when this approach is followed along with the use of heirloom varieties and seed banks, it is, in my book, the best path to quality of flavor and health.

SIMPLICITY

Food should be beautiful, but it should look like food all the same—and taste the way it looks. I could write another fifty pages trying to define this magic word, even when we all know the meaning. Do read the introductory section in Richard Olney's *Simple French Food* (1974) called "Simple Food."

Whether simple food is "classical" (a perfect beef tenderloin sauced with foie gras and black truffles), or "pure" (a game bird roasted on a spit and served with its own juices), or "rustic" (white beans cooked with wild boar pancetta and cipollini onions, as on page 225), it is always presented with the courage and discipline to leave well enough alone, letting the ingredients dictate their own conceit and not the cook's. Certainly the further a cooking style gets from the best that a great home cook can do, the more trouble the dish is in and the thinner the ice the cook is standing on.

Escoffier's command, *faites simple*, is (rightly) much quoted, and I always explained that phrase to my cooks and chefs by quoting my early hero Curnonsky, the "elected prince of gastronomes" in the

1920s and a champion of the simple cooking of the French. He broke French cooking into the categories of "Haute Cuisine," "French Family Cooking," "Regional Cooking," and "Impromptu Cooking," and it was he who first said that real cooking "is when things taste like themselves."

TECHNIQUES

BASTING

Everyone knows that basting a turkey is part of the endless battle to keep the white meat moist. But in basting poultry in the oven or on a spit, you are improving its flavor and appearance as well as its texture.

The contact of the outside of the meat with the hot basting fat helps the surface to brown more rapidly, searing the outside to keep in the moisture. And the juices in the basting liquid (add some stock or wine in the beginning) pick up the browned bits of meat and juice and deposit them back on the surface of the meat, again for flavor and color.

After beginning with fifteen minutes of high heat, you should turn the heat down and baste every ten minutes for the next three-quarters of the cooking time, then turn the heat down once again so the meat can start relaxing before it rests (see page 25).

BLANCHING (SEE ALSO PARBOILING)

Originally this word, from the French word for "white," referred to cooking vegetables that discolor after peeling (artichokes, salsify, celery root) *au blanc*, which means in water mixed with a little white flour and vinegar or lemon juice.

Sometimes meats like veal, rabbit, or frog were cooked very briefly this way too, both to keep the pale color of the meat and to remove any flavors considered strong.

The word in American cooking eventually became synonymous with the technique more correctly called "parboiling," which means putting vegetables in a lot of boiling salted water to start their cooking and set their color, then plunging them in ice water to cool. This procedure is also used for vegetables cooked in advance or prior to freezing, in order to preserve their color. It is a fairly nasty technique if you want a fresh vegetable taste.

BOILING IN SALTED WATER

For me, this is a far better way to cook vegetables than steaming them. If you take green beans, for example, the fastest (and therefore healthiest) method to cook them evenly is in boiling water, since they are surrounded by the water and cook at the same time. When they are stacked in a steamer, the steam gets to the parts of the beans not touching each other, and not to the areas in contact with other beans. For boiling to be the superior method, however, there has to be a lot of water (several quarts), so that it never goes off the boil.

Remember that the amount of salt used is in reverse proportion to the time the vegetables are in the water. The more time, the less salt, since the vegetables will progressively absorb the salt. But regardless of the amount, the water should always be detectably salty.

BONING

This is much easier than you think. All you have to do is remember that the process is one of moving a small and very sharp knife between the flesh and the bone carcass, and that if you are unsure of how the carcass works or what the shape is, use your fingers to explore (while the knife is on the table). In fact, a lot of poultry boning can be done with your fingers.

BRINING

Dry Brine or Duck Salt Marinade

MAKES ONE POUND

1 pound	kosher or sea salt
½ cup	sugar
6 sprigs	fresh thyme
6	bay leaves, torn apart
2 tablespoons	juniper berries, crushed
2 tablespoons	freshly ground coarse black pepper

Mix the ingredients together and store in a covered jar.

Dry Brining Times—Refrigerated

✦ Duck breast (whole) on the bone	6 hours
✦ Rib roast	2 days
✦ Whole fish (2–3 pounds)	2 hours
✦ Whole salmon	5 hours
✦ Lamb rack	6 hours

Wet Brine

MAKES ONE GALLON

1 gallon	water
1 cup	kosher or sea salt
½ cup	sugar
1 head	garlic, smashed
1 tablespoon	juniper berries, crushed
6 sprigs	fresh thyme
6	bay leaves, torn apart
4	dried red chilies, chopped
½ cup	fresh parsley, chopped

Heat the water, add all the ingredients, and stir until the salt and sugar are dissolved. Chill before using.

Wet Brining Times—Refrigerated

- Whole roasting chicken   24 hours
- Quail   1 hour
- Capon or large chicken breasts   2 hours
- 4- to 6-ounce portions of fish   1 hour
- Pork loin on the bone   12 hours
- Pork leg   48 hours
- Whole 15-pound turkey   24 hours

Pork Brining

In 1976 Jane Grigson's now classic book, *The Art of Making Sausages, Pâtés, and Other Charcuterie*, was published. Reading it then, I learned that if you brine pork for a day before cooking it, you are guaranteed moist and flavorful meat, as long as you don't overcook it. Remember, pork can be very slightly beige-pink and still be safe in terms of trichinosis, the trichinae being killed when the meat's internal temperature reaches 137 degrees.

The following method of brining allows us to consistently produce a perfect, thick double pork (or veal) chop that is flavorful, tender, and full of juices. The only meat not to use this method with is lamb, which benefits from dry brining only.

In this procedure, the pork is cooked enough initially to allow chops or medallions (boneless sections cut across the loin) to be cut and marinated. It is then reheated to finish the cooking process, with this second cooking taking less than half the time it would take to cook the meat from a raw state. This short cooking period means that the meat does not seize up and get tough, which would necessitate a long resting period.

SERVES 6

1	pork loin section with at least 8 ribs, chine bone removed
4 quarts	wet brine (see page 22)
4	bay leaves
1 tablespoon	allspice berries
1 tablespoon	dried thyme
2 tablespoons	freshly ground black pepper

Trim the loin so that there is only ¼-inch of fat on top. Mix the brine, bay leaves, allspice, and thyme. Put the loin in a pan just large enough to hold it and the liquid, and pour the brine over the pork to cover. Marinate overnight or at least 8 hours in the refrigerator.

When the pork is fully brined, remove it from the pan and wipe it dry. Season with the pepper.

Preheat the oven to 325 degrees.

Heat a sauté pan over high heat and sear the loin, browning it on all sides, about 5 minutes. Put the loin in a roasting pan just large enough to hold it and cook for 30 minutes. Remove the loin and let sit for 45 minutes.

At this point the loin is ready to be cut into portions, and for a second marination for an hour with fresh herbs or spices to develop and highlight the flavors in the meat. Then it is ready to finish the cooking.

Browning and Searing

The browning of meats and poultry (and sometimes vegetables) gives flavor to the meats and any stock in which they are to be cooked and, eventually, to any sauce made from those cooking liquids. While the meats are browning in fat, they are also being seared, so that when they are cooked later (as in braising), their juices are sealed inside.

Some points: the fat in which meat is seared and browned has to be removed from the pan before braising. So for fatty meats like short ribs, why use fat in the first place? Just season them and then brown and sear them on a rack in a 450-degree oven or under the broiler. After the meats are browned, do not put them on a flat surface like a pan or platter. If you do that, the seal is broken where the meat contacts the surface, and the juices leak out. Instead put them on a baking rack, and the juices that leak out are minimal. This tip is courtesy of Frank Stitt at the Highlands Bar & Grill in Birmingham, Alabama.

Chopping

In this book I have used the terms "finely chopped" (1/16-inch pieces), "chopped" (1/8-inch pieces), and "coarsely chopped" (1/4-inch pieces).

For fine chopping, when you want pieces all the same size, it is often useful to cut the pieces into sticks first with a slicing machine of some kind, a Japanese one or a mandoline. Then cut across the pile of sticks. You can also cut with a food processor or other machine, but only for large quantities. I don't like what happens to herbs and the onion family in a food processor (they seem to bleed a lot and take on even stronger flavors), so just plan to cut by hand using a sharp knife for ease and safety (see page 49).

Deglazing

Pour water, stock, or wine into a pan in which you have just cooked food after, and only after, you have wiped out all the fat, but leave the bits stuck to the pan to make "cooking juices" (see page 14), gravy, or a sauce.

Frenching

The term for cutting the meat off the bones on poultry breasts or meat chops, so that in presentation of the dish, the bone looks clean and is clean to pick up in one's fingers. The chicken breast usually has the first wing bone still attached and when frenched, the knuckle end of the bone is cut cleanly off and the meat on the inch-and-a-half of the bone leading up to the knuckle is scraped clean. With a chop the bone is cleaned all the way down to the rib or loin section of meat. It's a good thing.

Microwaving

One day in the perfect restaurant world, microwave ovens will be larger and stacked up on the cooking lines for reheating things like vegetable soups and braised meats. Microwave reheating changes the food less than any other method, preserving the fresh colors, perfumes, and flavors.

Parboiling (see also Blanching)

Parboiling means to cook something in a lot of boiling salted water for a short time, anywhere from a few seconds (fresh herb leaves) to five minutes (carrots). The vegetables or herbs are then plunged into an ice bath to refresh them, stopping the cooking and setting the color.

Parboiling is one of the nastier habits of restaurant cooking, but is not often questioned. The point is to have the vegetables cooked half or three quarters of the way in advance, to cut down on the time it takes to get the food to the customer. This is a horrible practice, because in reality, if you are organized and know how to set up the cooking line (hot-water faucets over the pots on the back burners, lots of extra pots coming to the boil so that the water is fresh and the cook does not have to wait for the new water to boil, and so on), there should be no delays, and most vegetables take no time to cook from the raw state anyway. The same goes for the home. Once the big pot of salted water is boiling, ten minutes for cooking, draining, and seasoning the vegetables is all the time it takes.

Pureeing

I like blenders—for milkshakes. The heat, oxidization, and violence they produce don't do most other foods much good. I think pureeing is best done by hand, through a sieve or hand-cranked food mill.

Try the following experiment: fill four cups with raspberries from one batch of fruit. Put one cup through a sieve by hand, put one through a food mill, and puree one in a food processor and one in a blender. Compare the purees: the hand-sieved puree has a bright color, a heady perfume of raspberries, a thick texture, and pure flavors. The blended berries are dull-colored, have very little fresh aroma, a thin, watery texture, and suppressed and oxidized flavors. The food processor method is in between.

The advantage of the hand food mill when pureeing vegetables for soup, for example, is that you can control the amount of liquid being used. The blender demands a certain minimum of liquid in order to operate properly, whether or not you want that amount of liquid in the finished product.

Resting

When meat and poultry are cooked in the oven (and, to a lesser extent, when they are spit-roasted or grilled) they tighten up, and if you slice into them as soon as they are finished cooking, the juices will flow out and the meat will be tough and taste dry as well.

Let the meat rest in a warm place (see page 19) for twenty to forty-five minutes so that the juices will be reabsorbed into the cells of the meat, keeping it moist and tender.

Stock-Making

Individual stock recipes are given in each chapter where applicable. The trick of the trade for clarifying a stock that has become cloudy is to add ice to it. If the stock has become cloudy and gray, throwing ice into it can shock it to give up the blood and albumin still stuck in suspension in the stock. This is strictly an emergency procedure; clarifying can also be accomplished by letting the stock sit overnight, removing the solidified fat, leaving the residue at the bottom, and then bringing the stock to a simmer rapidly, skimming all the time. Do not let it boil.

Sweating

This means cooking something, such as onions or a vegetable mix, over low heat, covered, with a little bit of moisture to prevent any browning or caramelization. This process starts the first cooking (or can complete it), while preserving all the flavors in the onions or other vegetables, which will then flavor other foods.

Toasting

Not bread here, but spices, including peppercorns. Toasting spices brings out the flavors of their aromatic oils and perfumes; it should be done right before using the spices.

Put the spices in a frying pan that will hold them in just one layer and heat gently until you smell the aromas coming off. If you see smoke, throw out the spices, turn down the heat and do it again in less time. Or you can put the spices on a sheet pan in a 375-degree oven for a few minutes, but I think the stove top allows for better supervision.

To Truss or Not to Truss

Many will claim that if you truss poultry before roasting or baking it, the bird will cook more evenly than if you did not. I am not sure about this.

What I do know is that a bird with its rear end hanging open is not as attractive on a platter at the table as one that has been cooked trussed. And I am certain that when cooked on a spit a bird must be trussed, otherwise it will hang on the spit unbalanced, cook unevenly, and ruin the rotisserie motor.

Don't drive yourself crazy trying to remember how to truss correctly. It is easy only for people who do it all the time. Just get that string out and find a way, without crossing the breast meat (which makes unsightly lines on the cooked bird), to hold the wings in place and keep the legs together and cover the cavity opening.

Fats

Amidst all the hysteria and confusion on the subject of fats in America (can anyone keep track of the latest theories about cholesterol?), all I can say about fats is that there are those that keep you alive from happiness, and those that kill you quick.

Your body will keep you informed about the happy ones, telling you whether you have just eaten healthy food or not, and you can help your body by not buying foods that are already packed with industrial emulsified fat. Adding fat in your cooking, like whisking a tablespoon of good butter or cream into a half cup of fish stock to make a sauce, will taste very good and leave your body feeling light, clear, and in a few hours, hungry again, a sign of healthy food and cooking procedures.

Eating improperly cooked food in which fats subjected to high heats (the fats left in the pan from a prime rib cooked in the oven, for example) have mistakenly been incorporated in the finished dish will leave you feeling heavy, unhappily satiated, and with a nagging reminder that maybe you should not have eaten that dish. Think about eating two hot dogs versus the same weight of lean beef in steak tartare, and the difference in how you feel two hours later.

Fats are all about what you buy, proper cooking techniques, moderation, and listening to your body.

BUTTER

Enjoy this most glorious of foods in moderation, and never eat it when it has been subjected to high heats. After you've cooked something in butter, drain the food for a second or two on paper towels and, if you are making a sauce in the pan, wipe the pan out thoroughly (without dislodging the wonderful bits stuck to the pan) to get rid of the cooked butter, then deglaze the pan (see page 24) and make your sauce by adding a tablespoon or two of fresh butter without ever letting it boil.

Treat yourself to French butter, or some of the new American ones made in the European style. They taste better, and their lower water content makes it easier to get the right consistency with sauces.

In this book I call for either "butter" or "unsalted butter" depending on the recipe. You may be confused as to why I call for unsalted butter and then salt the sauce. It is just a control issue—if you use salted butter to finish a sauce, it may oversalt the final product. With unsalted, you can always add more salt. But should you always use unsalted butter in cooking? You don't need to, so it's up to you.

CLARIFIED BUTTER

The main benefit of clarified butter is that it does not burn as easily as whole butter when heated.

Melt 1 pound of butter in the top of a double boiler or over very low heat. When completely melted, set it aside in a warm place for fifteen minutes. Skim all the foam off the top and discard. Then spoon off the clear yellow liquid (the clarified butter) and reserve it. Discard the milky liquid at the bottom or use it in mashed potatoes or other vegetables.

One pound of whole butter will yield ¾ cup clarified butter.

CREAM

Buy organic, and the best quality you can find.

DOUBLE CREAM

This is cream you thicken and enrich yourself, so that it has the body of whipped cream—for spooning over desserts and fruits without drowning them—and the taste of the best European and British creams.

MAKES 2 CUPS

1 cup	heavy cream
½ cup	mascarpone
¼ cup	buttermilk

Mix the ingredients together in a bowl until smooth, and let sit at room temperature for 8 hours. Refrigerate for 24 hours (or up to 3 days) before using.

OLIVE AND OTHER VEGETABLE OILS

Stick to canola, almond, very good quality peanut oil (probably French and in small bottles), sunflower, safflower, olive, or grapeseed oil. The commercial oils on the shelf of the supermarket I leave up to your own research. Just beware of stabilizers and other chemicals. Never use those commercial "fats" and oils for deep-frying, especially the butter-flavored ones.

When buying oils, choose them according to their use. As we embraced all extra virgin olive oils with passionate fervor, we thought the darker green the better, and Italian and unfiltered oils even better. The truth is in a question: would you pour raw green olive oil on a delicate butter lettuce? Of course the answer should be no. You would use a mild (but fully flavored) light yellow–colored extra virgin olive oil from the south of France. Or a good quality almond oil. Nut oils go very well with the whole endive and chicory family of greens, and canola is a good all-purpose cooking oil that does not cost a lot of money. When it is organic and cold-pressed, it can be magnificent. (See Resources page 280.)

FLAVORED OILS

Flavored oils are an easy way to add magic to a dish. Spoon a little cumin-scented oil over braised lamb shanks, for example, just before the plates go out to the table. It adds extra depth and a new dimension of tastes and flavors, which is all the more fascinating for not being immediately obvious. Further scent the cumin oil with a little orange- or rose-flower water, or mandarin orange zest, and the results are startlingly good.

These oils are inexpensive and easy to make. Their only problem is that they can easily turn rancid, so make the oils only as you need them. All the restaurant tricks like putting aspirin in the basil oil to keep it blindingly green or blanching green herbs to maintain their color should be avoided. Do not go for visuals only, since freshness of flavor is still the key with these flavored oils.

Use very good quality oils and choose the marriage of oil and flavoring wisely. With fresh herbs, I like olive oil; for spices, I like very good quality peanut oil—it works perfectly with cardamom and coriander; and for fresh-scented flowers such as jasmine and rose, I prefer almond oil.

So what flavorings should you use? A little vanilla bean with fresh kaffir lime leaves or lemon balances sweetness against tartness; kaffir lime leaves by themselves (warmed in a 300-degree oven for three minutes and put in almond or sunflower oil) for fish and chicken; fresh ginger by itself, or mixed with chili or vanilla; mint, chives, or chive flowers; spices like cinnamon used very sparingly with cumin and cardamom—well, the enjoyment of experimentation can go on forever.

In all cases, leave the flavoring in the oil only until the oil has the intensity you want, then sieve out and discard the flavoring agent(s). Remember that on food the oil will taste less strong than it does on your finger.

As for white truffle oil, it is a wonderful thing (when not rancid) but almost destroyed by its ubiquitousness. It is expensive, so you can make your own exotic oil—either perfect olive or safflower oil flavored with dried morels or cèpes/porcini, or one made with grilled portobello mushrooms (marinate them in garlic and thyme, grill them, soak them in olive oil for a week, drain off, save the oil, then eat the mushrooms on grilled bread with lots of chilled pink wine—and a few friends).

HERB OILS

There are two schools of thought regarding herb oils. One says to "blanch" (as in parboil) the herbs for ten seconds (basil) to thirty seconds (rosemary), then plunge them into ice water, squeeze them dry, put them in a blender, and then infuse the oil of choice (olive, grapeseed, canola, or almond) with the resulting puree. This produces a very nice, stable, and colorful infused oil for restaurants, perfect for filling squeeze bottles and putting little dots of oil on plates.

Of course, you can do this at home, but there is the alternative, if you have fresh herbs (thyme, tarragon, rosemary, chervil, parsley, hyssop, winter savory, fennel, mint, basil, or a combination). Cover them with olive oil in a jar or bottle and soak for three days. I prefer this method since I think the flavors are cleaner and more perfumed. You can also use just the stems if you have used the leaves in cooking, although you will need more stems than whole sprigs and it will take longer to infuse the oil.

JASMINE OR GINGER FLOWER
AND CARDAMOM-CHILI OIL

I love the combination of a powerful, tropical perfume triggered and balanced by the heat of chilies, with both flavors grounded in the base of a spice, as in fresh, new-crop Hawaiian pink ginger, garlic, and black pepper together. If using jasmine, just find a single stalk at the florist, or use gardenias as they do in China.

Use a light oil like almond, sunflower, or even canola, but make sure it is of good quality and fresh.

Sprinkle this oil on garlic-flavored creamy white beans accompanying a piece of salmon marinated in fresh basil, wrapped in bacon, and grilled (see page 170) and you will have discovered the excitement of easy yet spectacular cooking.

MAKES APPROXIMATELY 1 CUP

1 cup	almond oil
¼ cup	jasmine or ginger flowers, freshly picked
4	green cardamom pods, crushed and toasted
1	small serrano chili, seeded

Put the jasmine, cardamom seeds, and chili in a glass jar.

In a saucepan, warm the oil until it is just, and only just, getting hot. Immediately pour it into the jar. Stir together.

Cover and let macerate for 2 hours, or longer for more intensity.

Keep cool and use within a week.

MEYER LEMON OIL

I adore Meyer lemons but any good lemons will do. You can also use mandarin oranges, Rangpur limes, Key limes, *kalamansi* limes, or kumquats.

MAKES 1 CUP

6	Meyer lemons, zest only
1 cup	canola or almond oil
pinch	sea salt

Puree the lemon zest, oil, and salt in a food processor until smooth.

Transfer to a glass bowl or jar, cover, and refrigerate for 8 hours, then decant or spoon off the clear part of the oil, saving it in a covered jar or bottle in the refrigerator for up to 3 days.

Sieve what is left in the bowl, pressing down on the residue to extract all the oil and discarding the residue in the sieve. Use this pressed oil only for marinating meats or poultry.

WATER-RENDERED FATS

When animal fats are rendered by frying or baking, they can reach temperatures of up to 500 degrees, at which point they become oxidized, totally indigestible, a plumber's nightmare (for both you and the sink), and deadly.

If they are rendered in simmering water, however, they do not get as hot, do not oxidize, and are light, fresh, full of wonderful flavor, and healthy.

MAKES APPROXIMATELY 2 CUPS

2 cups	poultry or ham fat
8 cups	water

Put the fat in the water, bring to a boil, turn down the heat, and simmer for 1 hour. Strain, refrigerate, and when the fat is congealed, lift it off the water and store it in a sealed container. The water can be used for soups or stocks.

SALMON AND SMOKED SALMON FAT

I know this is a bit esoteric but it is not a completely new idea. Many chefs know about using the skin of smoked salmon one way or another, since by weight it is a lot of money to throw away. Some grill or deep-fry it. In maki hand rolls it is delicious. I water-render the fat from the skin of smoked salmon with or without the skin of fresh salmon. The resulting salmon fat or oil is incredible when drizzled over steamed Chinese dumplings, linguine tossed with parsley and garlic, or Belgian endive salad.

Just put two skins in 5 quarts of cold water, bring to a boil, and simmer for twenty minutes. Strain, refrigerate while the water and fat separate, lift off the fat (save the water for cooking pasta), and store in the refrigerator for up to a week.

CLEANING FAT OFF SAUCES

The fastest, most thorough, and easiest way to remove fat and scum from a sauce is to put the saucepan half on/half off the burner, at medium to low heat, and let the sauce simmer on one side of the pan only. This pushes all the fats to the edge that is off the heat, so that you can spoon them off as the sauce reduces.

CLEANING FAT OUT OF THE COOKING PAN

So that the food you cook supports your life rather than shortening it, always wipe all the cooked fats out of the pan before deglazing the pan with water, stock, or wine to make a sauce.

INGREDIENTS

BEEF PRIME RIB

The success of roast beef depends on having the best quality beef, with very good marbling and about twenty-one days' dry-aging, and using a large rib roast from the loin end.

The two controversies about roasting (baking) beef are whether to salt the meat first, and at what temperature to cook it. It is said that if you salt the beef before putting it in the oven, all the juices will come out. This may be true for a thin slice of beef, but I have never seen it happen with a large cut, and if you do not salt the meat first, or at all, it has little taste. Some say to salt the meat halfway through the cooking process, advice I find difficult and dangerous when it is in the oven and hot. I believe in salting before cooking, which produces the best flavor and a salty crust. The other issue is whether you should start with a hot oven and then turn down the temperature, or use a low temperature throughout. The low-temperature method produces very tender but tasteless meat, so I believe in searing the beef and then turning down the temperature. That way, you get wonderfully crisp fat and "outside" pieces, as well as a range of meat cooked well done to rare.

SERVES 8 TO 10

1	beef rib roast with 5 ribs (about 12 pounds)
½ cup	vodka
3 tablespoons	salt
1 tablespoon	freshly ground pepper
12	bay leaves
4 slices	stale bread

Rub the rib roast all over with the vodka, a process which begins to break down the fat and draws in the seasonings, making the meat very flavorful. Then rub in the salt and pepper. Cut twelve small pockets evenly spaced in the fat, and slip in the bay leaves.

Let the beef sit at room temperature for 2 hours.

Preheat the oven to 425 degrees.

Put the beef in a roasting pan and then in the oven. Bake for 30 minutes, then turn the heat down to 325 degrees and cook for 12 to 15 minutes per pound of beef for rare to medium rare. At this point, the juices will run slightly pink when you stick a skewer or fork into the beef, and the meat will register 125 to 130 degrees on a meat thermometer.

When the beef is cooked, it is very important that it sit in a warm place (on the door of the turned-off oven or in the oven with the door open) for 30 minutes. This allows the meat to soften and reabsorb all its juices.

Place the bread slices under the roast before carving and serve the juice-soaked bread with the beef.

BREAD AND TOAST

One of the most difficult things in cooking is to get toast just right. Not so much breakfast toast, which you can watch while it toasts in an automatic toaster, but the toasts that you make to put other food on, like our canapé toasts, or *croutons* in French, and the base for bruschetta in Italy.

The problem lies in how not to ruin your guest's expensive tie or Armani dress. The toast must be firm enough to hold the food without drooping, but not so dry and brittle that when you bite into it, the toast shatters all over your hand, your clothes, and the floor.

Cook the toasts with or without olive oil or butter until the outside of the slice is firm but the inside is still soft, remembering that after you take the slices out of the oven or from under the broiler they will continue cooking. If the air is humid, you have another problem: keep them in an airtight container or they will droop.

BREADCRUMBS

I cannot think of a single decent-tasting use for breadcrumbs that are made with the crusts left on. Not one, since when they are left on and cooked (again), the resulting flavor is so strong that they overpower anything, even mustard.

2 cups	crustless white bread cubes (1 inch)

Put the bread cubes in a food processor or blender to make the crumbs. Leave out on a tray to become stale if that is what the recipe calls for. Otherwise transfer to a sealed jar and freeze for up to a month.

CHILIES

Wash your hands carefully and thoroughly after working with chilies—their strong oils will be highly irritating if they come in contact with the eyes or sensitive skin.

Ancho Chili Puree

Ancho chilies are dried, ripened poblano chilies, the ones that are closest in shape to a bell pepper, and a purple-green color. They are mild, with a full and complex range of flavors, allowing you to enjoy the taste of chili without the pain that a lot of them bring on.

This puree has an almost infinite range of possibilities as a base for flavoring sauces. Add it to sour cream, sour cream and mayonnaise, butter sauces, vinaigrettes, compound butters, the hollandaise family, fish *veloutés*—well, the list is almost endless. I have even sneaked a teaspoon of this puree into lime juice to pour over mangoes, white peaches, and the new variety of perfumed white nectarines.

MAKES 1 CUP

10	ancho chilies
1	small red onion, peeled, cored, and coarsely chopped
2 cloves	garlic, peeled
2 tablespoons	freshly squeezed lime juice
1 tablespoon	red wine vinegar
1 tablespoon	salt
½ cup	fresh peanut oil

Put the chilies in a bowl and add enough warm water to barely cover. Weight them down with a plate to submerge, and let sit overnight.

Take the chilies out of the water, saving the water. Remove and discard the stems and the seeds.

Put the cleaned chilies in a food processor with all the other ingredients except the oil. Use a little of the soaking water if necessary to allow the ingredients to move freely around the processor bowl. Puree until very smooth.

Push the puree through a fine sieve into a bowl. Mix the debris in the sieve with the reserved soaking water. Strain and save the water.

Whisk the oil into the puree and add salt to taste. Transfer the puree to a sealed jar and store in the refrigerator for up to 2 weeks. Use the chili water in sauces and soups—it can be refrigerated for up to 2 weeks or frozen for later use.

DRIED BEANS

Once you taste dried beans in Europe, you realize that unless you have a special supplier, we get the old crop sent to us here. Or a mixture of old crop years, which is why when cooking dried beans, some become fully cooked while others need more cooking in the same batch.

I could never get my cooks to take the correct precautionary measures: use enough water to cover the beans by 4 inches at all times, and stir them while cooking every 15 minutes at least.

Use the newest crop of dried beans possible and wash them in cold water, removing any floaters or stones. And by all means, soak the beans to cut down on the cooking time, although this is not imperative. Parboiling them covered in 4 inches of cold water until the water boils is, however, and once you smell that first discarded water you will know why.

Cooking beans in poultry or meat stock will provide the richest taste, but it takes a lot, and water will do in a pinch if you use stock in the second cooking.

MAKES 5 CUPS

2 cups	dried beans, such as small white beans, flageolets, cannellini, or black turtle beans
1 gallon	poultry, ham, or meat stock (you need this much to keep replenishing the liquid)
1 head	fresh garlic, root removed, crushed
1	ham bone or knuckle
1 cup	aromatic vegetable mix (see page 14), wrapped in cheesecloth
1	herb bundle (see page 16)
1 tablespoon	freshly chopped garlic
¼ cup	olive oil
	Salt and freshly ground black pepper

Put the washed beans in a pot at least twice the size of the volume of the beans. Cover with cold water by 4 inches. Bring to a boil over high heat, stirring the beans a couple of times. When the water boils, turn off the heat and let the beans sit uncovered for 15 minutes.

Pour the beans into a colander, run them under cold water to wash them completely, rinse out the pot, and put the beans back in it.

Pour in enough stock to cover the beans by 6 inches, and then add the head of crushed garlic, ham bone, vegetable mix, and herb bundle. Bring to a boil and simmer the beans for 30 to 60 minutes or until tender, skimming any foam or scum that rises to the surface and making sure the beans are covered by 4 inches of liquid at all times.

Drain (save the liquid for soups and sauces), discard all the ingredients except the beans, and toss the beans in the garlic and oil. Season and refrigerate until needed.

EDIBLE FLOWERS

Years ago on *Good Morning America* I was asked to feature "California food," including flowers and goat cheese. I had some nasturtiums and the requested cheese. The moment we were on the air, the hostess said, "I hate goat cheese and I think using flowers is silly." That was the end of my three minutes.

This attitude about edible flowers has not changed much, and I think in America it has to do with a puritanical attitude about frivolity. Flowers are taken seriously in the garden, but treated with suspicion and contempt when on the plate.

But they are not just another pretty face. They are a fast and inexpensive way to dress up a salad or any other dish, and they actually taste very good. To make my case, take violets (not the candied ones, and be sure they are pesticide-free) put them in a salad of sweet and slightly bitter lettuces and greens, dress the salad with fruity olive oil and the acid of vinegar or citrus, then add the bite of salt and the perfume of pepper. Bite down on a flower when you have a mouthful of salad and you get a burst of magical and delicious sweetness that adds to and sets off all the other flavors. Not bad.

EGGS

Eggs when called for in the following recipes are large and cold from the refrigerator, unless otherwise specified. And run, don't walk, to get real farm-fresh or natural eggs if you can.

Coddled Eggs

Coddled eggs are a bit of a pain, but once you have used them in almost any recipe that calls for poached eggs to be heated again in another recipe, you will want to use coddled eggs thereafter.

Put the cold eggs into simmering water with a slotted spoon. Take the pot off the stove, and turn the eggs around every ten seconds or so for the first two minutes so that the yolk will end up in the center (which makes peeling easier).

Cover the pot and let the eggs sit for another six minutes. Take the eggs out and put them in ice water, leaving them there for five minutes until cold. Then peel them, carefully.

French-Style Scrambled Eggs

The French method of scrambling eggs is called *oeufs brouillés* or a *brouillade*. No other way of scrambling eggs achieves as superb a texture and flavor. The eggs are cooked slowly over hot water and incorporated with a good deal of butter and a little fresh cream, giving them an ethereal texture and flavor quite unlike the rubber-mat, dry "egginess" of short-order scrambled eggs.

Black-truffled scrambled eggs, first served to me by Richard Olney (in a house perched in an old, terraced olive grove above the village of Solliès-Toucas, near Toulon), are my all-time favorite version of this dish. With those eggs, we drank a tired old Bordeaux, making a memorable marriage of the wine, the eggs, and the earthy, fallen-leaves perfume of the truffles.

If the truffle is frozen, cut it into thin matchsticks while still unthawed, and put them in a bowl. Add the eggs and leave unbeaten, covered, at room temperature for two hours before proceeding, to absorb the flavor of the truffles. You will need to use a hot-water bath (see page 16).

SERVES 4

1½ ounces	black truffles
8	large eggs
4 tablespoons	unsalted butter, at room temperature
2 tablespoons	cold heavy cream
4 tablespoons	unsalted butter, chilled, cut in 4 pieces
	Salt and freshly ground black pepper

Coat the bottom and sides of a 2-quart saucepan with 2 tablespoons of the room-temperature butter.

Beat the eggs until just well mixed, add the seasonings and the remaining soft butter, and put into the saucepan. Put the saucepan in the hot-water bath and stir the eggs with a wooden spoon for about 8 minutes, making sure to scrape all the surfaces of the pan, especially the corners. Never stop stirring or let the eggs stick to the pan. If the eggs get too hot and start to thicken too quickly, remove the pan from the water for a minute or so.

When the eggs are nearly done, stir in the cream and cook 30 seconds more. Turn off the heat and stir in the chilled butter; this will stop the cooking and enrich the texture and taste of the eggs.

Spoon the eggs onto four hot plates and serve immediately with nonsour country bread or grilled brioche.

VARIATION I have taken those truffled eggs and made a three-layer "napoleon"—using toast, not puff pastry. The center layer is a creamed puree of salt cod (see page 174) or a puree of smoked salmon or sturgeon.

Fried Eggs

No matter what the English say, do not fry eggs over high heat until the edges of the whites curl up. Slow cooking is what makes for tender and subtly flavored eggs.

There was an afternoon one day early on at Chez Panisse in Berkeley when I was hosting the famous French chef Denis (later host of the controversial Craig Claiborne $4,000 dinner for two at Chez Denis in Paris). The TV crew coming to photograph him was late, and I was wondering—what do I serve one of the most famous restaurateurs in the world for lunch? "Fried eggs," he said.

I fried some. "*Non, pas comme ça!*" Not like that, at all. "You must never salt the whites! Only the yellows." And "*doucement, doucement,*" gently, and never covered, "*jamais!*" I could spoon a little of the copious melted butter over the yolks if I wanted, but only after they had started to set, so as not to wash off the salt. Personally, I like to cover the eggs. It's faster and easier.

Ken Hom's Truffled Eggs

If the British prime minister keeps returning to Ken Hom and Daniel Taurine's house in Catus each summer, it must be for the Haut-Brion in the cellar and the truffled eggs.

SERVES 4

4-ounce can	Pebeyre Perigord black truffles, labeled "first choice" with the juice
6	eggs, best quality (organic, natural) at room temperature
4 ounces	cold unsalted butter, cut in 1-ounce pieces, kept cold
	Salt and freshly ground black pepper

Puree the truffles and put them in a saucepan with ¼ cup of the juices from the can.

Put the eggs in simmering water and cook for 4 minutes.

Meanwhile, warm the truffle puree over low heat and whisk in the butter. Season. Do not let the sauce boil.

Serve the eggs in egg cups, then slice off the tops and pass the sauce, spooning it into the eggs after each bite.

FATTENED LIVER (FOIE GRAS)

"Daunting" is not an overstatement when the subject of study is foie gras. I recommend Silvano Serventi's book *La Grande histoire du foie gras* (1993), if only for the photo on page 45 showing six ladies sitting around a pile of truffle baskets, each one holding 50 kilos of truffles.

I also recommend Michael Ginor's book *Foie Gras: A Passion* (1999), especially for the history of eating foie gras, from Egypt to fourth century B.C Greece and Rome (where they seemed to have bathed in it), and right up to our time, with a particularly interesting stopover with the Ashkenazi Jews at the end of the first millennium. And read about Carême, and Jules Gouffé, and my heroes Urbain Dubois and Escoffier, but whatever you do with *foie gras*, cook it simply.

I don't like it hot. I suspect that the popular fashion of hot foie gras exists because so few in the United States know how to cook it to be served cold. Ginor does. So does Mark Franz at Farallon in San Francisco. And Ariane Daguin in New York.

FAVA OR BROAD BEANS

I mention fava beans here to say that I know they appear frequently in this book—I couldn't resist. Please don't commit the English culinary mistake of not peeling the beans after taking them out of the pod or you will hate them. The only time you can eat the outer skin is if the beans are to be eaten within the hour of their being picked and if the beans are no more than half an inch across. Fava beans were one of my projects in the vegetable garden when I was a child—no one else, not even the gardener, would spend hours wiping the black flies off the plants, but as the youngest, I had no choice.

FLOURS, MEALS, AND GRITS

Flour in the recipes means all-purpose unless otherwise specified. When buying cornmeal, make sure not to get the self-rising kind (unless that is what you really want), which is what most of the packages contain these days. Buy polenta instead. And when buying grits, try to get real ones that are stone-ground and from a boutique mill or supplier.

GARLIC

It is said in a lot of cookbooks that the growing green part or sprout of the garlic clove is indigestible and should be removed. I say that when you see it, use that garlic for stocks and braising only, and buy some fresh garlic.

And please stay away from that awful mess of indigestible garlic called "roasted garlic puree," unless it is from the first crop of young garlic in the spring. Then follow the directions opposite.

Fresh Spring Garlic Puree

By the mid 1980s, the roasted garlic that I introduced at Chez Panisse twelve years previously had spread far and wide in the United States. Most of the time, it was not understood, and was made by using any old garlic that was available. Roasting older garlic makes an indigestible puree so potent it might as well be raw, so please use the most glorious garlic of all, that from the first crop in spring. The garlic then is fresh and white with pink and purple streaks through the outer leaves, the stems green and soft, the aroma mild and sweet.

If you want to make a garlic puree with the older, drier fresh garlic (which should be as fresh as possible, firm, and free of mildew), it should be poached, not roasted. Take unpeeled cloves and poach them in chicken stock or salted water until soft, about fifteen minutes. Then put them through a food mill or sieve, making a mild white puree for thickening roasting juices to put over chicken, or adding to cream for a pasta sauce, or making garlic soup.

Both the spring garlic and the poached garlic purees stay fresh in the refrigerator in a sealed jar for a week.

MAKES APPROXIMATELY 1 CUP

8 heads	fresh young spring garlic
¼ cup	olive oil
4 sprigs	fresh thyme
	Salt and freshly ground black pepper

Preheat the oven to 300 degrees.

Rub the garlic heads with the oil. Strew the thyme in a heavy baking dish just large enough to hold the garlic in a single layer. Place the garlic on the thyme and season with salt and pepper. Cover with foil and bake until the garlic cloves are just soft when you squeeze them, 30 to 45 minutes.

Take the garlic out of the baking dish. Serve the heads whole (pour melted butter or olive oil over them, and squeeze the puree from each clove to spread on bread or roast lamb) or put them through a food mill to make a puree. Discard the skins. Cover any unused puree tightly and store in the refrigerator for up to a week.

VARIATION To make a butter sauce for poached fish, add garlic puree and either ancho chili puree (see page 32) or a fresh herb to hot shellfish stock, then whisk in chunks of cold butter.

Raw Garlic Puree

When a recipe calls for marinating meats or poultry in olive oil and garlic, I find this way the easiest and fastest. Also the most flavorful.

10 cloves	fresh garlic, unpeeled
½ cup	olive oil

Put the garlic and olive oil in a blender and puree until smooth. Put through a sieve and discard the garlic skins left in the sieve.

HERBS

Dried Herbs

Those bottles of dried herbs standing in hot, bright places above the stove are really only a memory (and a vague and dusty one at that) of the fresh herb. After all, the essential part of the herb is a volatile oil that is delicate and easily dispersed into the air.

Throw out all your old dried herbs when you read this. Buy just what you need for two months and then after that, throw away what is left. Or better, grow your own, even on a windowsill, and when the cold weather comes on, dry them. Or grow enough so that you can dry some of them when they are flowering. The leaves are at their peak of flavor at this time, and the flowers, with their perfume both sweeter and more delicate than the leaves, add a whole new dimension to a mix of dried herbs.

Fresh Herbs

To keep freshly picked herbs, wrap them in slightly moist towels (paper or kitchen) and refrigerate. Basil should go into a plastic bag, but it is even better if you can use it immediately without ever refrigerating.

HUITLACOCHE (*USTILAGO MAYDIS*)

The Aztec truffle. A fungus that grows on corn (maize) kernels in a free-form dark grey or black mass. Absolutely hauntingly delicious, whether fresh (see it at the Chino Ranch vegetable gardens near Los Angeles) or canned. See the blue corn enchiladas on page 155.

INDIAN SPICE MIX

Since a single "curry powder" is the usual Anglicized and Americanized Indian condiment, I went to an American cookbook, *The Epicurean (1893)* by Charles Ranhofer, to see what that version would be.

I have added a few things and taken a few away, but whatever the mix, the spices must be very fresh.

MAKES 1 CUP

6 tablespoons	coriander seeds
4 tablespoons	cumin seeds
1 tablespoon	black mustard seeds
4	small dried red chilies
½ tablespoon	black peppercorns
2 tablespoons	ground turmeric
2 tablespoons	ground fenugreek
1 tablespoon	ground cardamom
1 teaspoon	ginger powder

Put all the seeds and chilies in a hot pan and stir for 45 seconds. Remove to a plate to cool. Grind and mix with the other ingredients. Put through a sieve and store in a covered jar.

PASTRY

I avoid puff pastry since I have never really liked it much (perhaps in a perfect croissant it's fine) and certainly have never liked making it—I get bored too quickly.

But if you want pie crust or tart pastry with the lightness of puff pastry, put aside your machine and use the old-fashioned method of cutting the butter into the flour, and make sure to use just enough water to barely hold the dough together. Always use cold ingredients, mix the dough quickly by hand and only until it just comes together in a loose ball, let it rest in the refrigerator, and then roll it out, working the pastry as little as possible. And use butter only, no shortening.

This way you will get a short pastry that is affiliated with puff pastry in the sense that the butter and flour layers separate a bit, making the pastry puff up.

PEPPER

Whatever variety you buy, make sure you grind your own, either fresh from a mill each time, or at the beginning of a heavy cooking day, grind a batch in an electric grinder and have it handy in a little ramekin by the stove. When very coarse black pepper is called for, sieve out the "dust" and keep it for general cooking.

Putting aside for the moment the other uses of the word "pepper," as in Sichuan pepper, pink peppercorn, Melegueta pepper, Jamaica pepper (allspice), chili pepper, bell pepper, and so on, let's concentrate on black and white pepper, or *Piper nigrum*.

The most common and often the best-quality black pepper comes from the Malabar coast of India: Tellicherry from the north, Alleppey from the south, and just plain Malabar. At Kalustyan's in Manhattan I have also bought Vietnamese, Brazilian, and Madagascan pepper, as well as a favorite, Lampong from Indonesia, which has a high peperine content and very rich aroma.

And remember to lightly toast the peppercorns before using them, so don't put more than a few days' supply in the peppermill. Toasting will bring out the peperine oil flavor of pepper.

Provençal Pepper Mix

This is so delicious a way to use pepper at home that it hardly matters what kind of pepper you use. The secret ingredient is Jamaica pepper or allspice: the mix should be 6 tablespoons black peppercorns, 4 tablespoons white peppercorns, and 1½ tablespoons allspice berries. All of them dried, of course. Consider keeping this mix in your peppermill at all times.

Yellow or Red Bell Pepper Puree

This puree is not a sauce in itself. But add it to mayonnaise, sour cream, whipped cream, sabayon, olive oil, or butter, or whisk it with stock and butter, and you will have countless versatile sauces for salads, grilled fish, poultry, meat, and soup.

This is a basic method for roasting peppers. For strips or dice of roasted peppers, follow the recipe but instead of pureeing, cut the peppers as needed.

For a really colorful effect and more complexity of taste, make separate but similar sauces out of the red and yellow purees, and use them together on the same dish.

MAKES 1½ CUPS

6	large yellow or red bell peppers
3 tablespoons	olive oil

Preheat the oven to 350 degrees.

Rub the peppers with the oil and put them in a baking pan. Cover with aluminum foil and cook until soft, about 45 minutes. Remove from the oven and let stand, still covered, until cool.

Remove the skin from the peppers and discard the stems and seeds. Puree the peppers in a food processor and pass through a fine sieve or food mill.

POULTRY

If you accept that what we eat is important for our health, would you not agree that it's the same for the animals that we eat? If you do accept this theory, buy poultry that has been fed clean food that is true to them, the kinds of things they would eat in the wild or on the range.

Stay away from poultry fed on fish meal and other unmentionable things. Instead, buy organic, chemical- and hormone-free birds, especially if they have had a chance to run around the field once or twice.

RICE

Northern Italian Rice

Basically there are two techniques for cooking rice with broth added slowly throughout the cooking process to end up with the Italian dish called *risotto*. In one method, the flavoring is added at the beginning of the cooking (for those ingredients that need a lot of cooking to develop their taste); in the other, the flavoring is added at the very end (for those ingredients that are already cooked, or will lose their fresh flavors and real colors with long cooking).

The rice used in this slow stewing process should be chosen for its ability to take up the cooking liquids evenly, with the grains remaining firm and separate. The large, high-gluten grains of Carnaroli and Vialone are what to look for, especially since they are categorized as "superfine" grade quality. My favorite varieties are Carnaroli and Vialone, but if all you can find is superfine Arborio, then by all means use that, although it does not hold together as well as the other two.

You need a 3- to 5-quart pot for cooking rice this way. It must have a heavy bottom so that the heat from the stove is evenly distributed over the bottom surface of the pan, and it should be nonreactive so that acids will not pick up the flavor of the pan. After all the work of making a risotto with a fabulous Barolo, you certainly do not want aluminum in it! My favorite pots are the copper-outside and stainless steel-inside All-Clad (called "Master Chef") and their new "Copper Core" with stainless inside and a heavy copper inner core. And, for less money, the Martha Stewart pots are excellent.

Wild Rice

Not a rice at all, but that does not matter, since no one is going to call it *Zizania palustris* or *aquatica*, which is what it is, an annual aquatic grass that should be harvested in the wild by hand (see Resources, page 280) for best flavor and tender texture.

I could never figure out why the wild rice in most restaurants rarely tasted very exciting, certainly not exciting enough to justify its expense. So before writing this recipe, I looked in my favorite general-purpose cookbook, *The Joy of Cooking*, to see what it said. Once I got past the "Wild Rice Popcorn" to serve with drinks, I looked at the basic wild rice recipe: it was for plain boiled, which completely explains the boring rice. For wild rice to be worth its salt, it has to be toasted in the oven after it is cooked in water.

I don't agree with the pilaf method of cooking it, with measured water (4 cups water to 1 cup of rice), because who knows how much water that rice really wants? And the pilaf method can produce a musty flavor.

Use only the longest-grain, highest-quality rice. The broken-up ends of wild rice are a waste of money. And remember, 1 cup of raw rice becomes 2 to 3 cups cooked.

1 cup	wild rice
4 tablespoons	clarified butter (see page 27), melted
1 teaspoon	salt

Wash the rice in a large bowl with enough water in it to cover the rice by 4 inches. Run the water gently over the rice until the water runs clear, skimming off any debris that floats to the top.

Preheat the oven to 375 degrees.

Put the rice in a gallon of boiling salted water, and cook for 20 minutes or until tender. Drain well.

Transfer the rice to a shallow casserole or roasting pan, add the melted butter, and then mix the butter and rice well with your hands so that all the grains are separated. Put the pan in the oven and bake for 20 to 30 minutes, stirring the rice and turning it over from top to bottom every 5 minutes, until the rice is fluffy and you can smell the nutty aroma of toasted wild rice.

This is delicious when served with kasha (buckwheat groats) cooked as described on page 160.

SALT

Cooking Salt

This means kosher salt, since I like the taste and feel of it. A pinch of fine salt is more than a pinch of kosher, so I have always insisted that my cooks use kosher to avoid the danger of oversalting. In some cases for very short cooking processes, fine sea salt will be called for. Adding expensive *fleur de sel* or sea salt to make salt water is a waste of money.

Added Salt

Many dishes, especially salads, truly benefit from salt added after they are plated. Not because they had insufficient salt in the cooking process, but because the flavor, and often the texture, of added salt gives a whole new dimension to the food. Use high-grade sea salt for this purpose.

Hand-Harvested Sea Salt (*Fleur de Sel*)

Whether from France (specifically Brittany, or the Camargue), Hawaii, or another source, this is the finest sea salt available. Lacking this salt, use any sea salt, and use a salt grinder. When I call for sea salt in the recipe, it is this salt to which I am referring.

Salt on Fruit

You have never known ripe cantaloupe until you have sprinkled a little fine sea salt or *fleur de sel* on it. My mother never tasted either of these, but she was the one who showed me the magic of salt on fruit.

Salt in Desserts

Over a couple of decades ending in the late 1990s, most of the pastry chefs I trained thought I was crazy for insisting over and over again not to forget the salt in the desserts. Then in 2000, an article appeared in the *New York Times* extolling the qualities of salt when used with sugar in desserts, and noting that the great Pierre Hermé "takes his own box of *fleur de sel* to restaurants." An ex-pastry chef called to tell me I could now officially say, "I told you so."

As the article says, "salt does the same thing in pastry that it does in cooking. It enhances flavor." And that means you can use less sugar since sugar enhances flavor only up to a certain point and then kills it.

Orange Sichuan Pepper Salt

Once you start sprinkling this salt on food just before serving, you will become addicted to flavored salts and figure out endless variations by yourself. Any of the citrus family will work, although I have my doubts about grapefruit salt unless you use it on fruits, especially tropical ones or watermelon.

Flavored salts will last for a month in a covered jar without losing too much potency. Proportions are not written in stone, but think two-thirds pepper to one-third citrus peel. By all means add a little bit of cumin, cardamom, or fenugreek.

1	large orange (mandarin, blood, or regular)
½ cup	Sichuan peppercorns
2 cups	kosher salt

Preheat the oven to 200 degrees. Remove the zest from the orange with a vegetable peeler, in strips, being sure not to include the white pith. Lay the zest in a single layer on a plate and place it in the oven until dry, about an hour. The peel must be completely dry. Remove the plate from the oven and let the dried zest cool.

Toast the peppercorns in a hot but not scorching frying pan until fragrant, about 2 minutes. Dump them out immediately onto paper towels and allow them to cool.

Mix the rind, peppercorns, and salt together. Grind in a spice mill or food processor with a very sharp blade until uniformly smooth.

SALTED ANCHOVIES

I have never failed to convert an anchovy hater into a devotee after introducing them to salted anchovies. Banish all those little cans of anchovy fillets and buy a can of salted ones—the can is usually round and looks like a lot more anchovies than you need. It isn't.

Open the can and scrape off the top layer of salt, reserving it to top off the remaining anchovies. Lift out the dozen little fish you are going to use, and brush off the salt. Gently. Take all the other fish out of the can, and put them in a glass mason-type jar or plastic container with a lid. Put all the salt back on top of the fish, cover, and store in the refrigerator (for up to three months) until needed again.

Turn on the cold water faucet, and holding each fish cavity side up and under the water (not too much pressure), slit the cavity open with your thumbnail. Open up the fish along the backbone, which you remove and discard. Wash each fillet (two per fish) under the water, remove and discard the little dorsal fin, and put the fillets on a plate. Repeat until all the fish are cleaned and filleted.

Then, and only then, put the fillets together in a bowl of cold water to soak away some of the saltiness. Leave for ten minutes, then repeat. Drain gently, and lay out on paper towels. Put the fillets in a little bowl with extra virgin olive oil, just enough to cover them by ¼ inch.

Leave the fillets in the oil for a few hours, and then use on salads (like Caesar) or with roasted bell peppers, or blend them into butter with fresh tarragon and put on top of a baked potato. Or just put the fish on garlic bread with lots of black pepper and eat as a snack. You will never go near another canned fillet again.

Salt-Preserved Lemons

As a child I could not get enough lime pickle from India. So when in Morocco I tasted preserved lemons for the first time, I fell in love. They improve almost any salsa, relish, chutney, or mayonnaise. They also flavor simple and compound butters and the sauces you can make out of them. The lemons are particularly good when mixed with mint, basil, or tarragon. And a teaspoon here and there of the liquid they are stored in will correct that "something is lacking" in almost any savory dish.

You can also make this recipe with limes, kumquats (which only take a week to cure), and other sour citrus fruits. Do make sure that the spices you use are freshly bought.

Preserved lemons are best to make in large quantities, so give some away as presents, or store for up to three months in the refrigerator. To use, squeeze the juice from the lemon back into the jar (though I do use the juice for flavoring almost anything savory and even some herb pound cakes) scrape away the flesh, seeds, and pith, and chop the rind.

MAKES 16 PRESERVED LEMONS

16	medium lemons
½ cup	sugar
1½ cups	kosher salt
10	whole allspice berries
1 tablespoon	cumin seeds
2 tablespoons	fennel seeds
1 tablespoon	coriander seeds
1 tablespoon	black mustard seeds
2 tablespoons	black peppercorns
1	small cinnamon stick
5	bay leaves
1 cup	freshly squeezed lime juice
4–6 cups	freshly squeezed lemon juice

Roll each lemon around on the table for a minute to release its juices and then cut an X 1 inch deep in both ends of each lemon.

Mix the sugar and salt together in a bowl. Stuff as much of the mixture as possible into the cuts in the lemon and then roll each lemon in the mixture until well coated. Save any leftover sugar-salt mixture for your next batch of lemons. Place the lemons in a big sterilized mason jar or other glass container, packing them in fairly tightly. Cover and leave at room temperature for 8 hours.

Mix all the spices and bay leaves with the two juices. Pour over the lemons, making sure that the liquid surrounds all the fruit. Weight down with a plate and heavy can so that all the lemons stay submerged. Cover and leave out at room temperature for a week, turning the jar every day to evenly distribute the salt, spices, and juices. Then refrigerate for 3 to 4 weeks, again turning the lemons around in the container once a week.

At this point, strain the liquid, and pour it back over the lemons. Keep them covered and refrigerated, and use as needed for up to 3 months.

SALTED CAPERS

Like anchovies, there is a world of difference between wet-brined capers and the salted ones, the salted ones being vastly superior. But either version should be rinsed in cold water, soaked in three changes of water for twenty minutes each time, and then soaked for a day before using in one part white wine, two parts olive oil, and a sprig of fresh thyme or basil or both. Keep the capers refrigerated, covered in this bath until needed for two weeks.

SUGAR AND HONEY

Sugar when called for in the recipes means granulated unless confectioners' or superfine is specified. I don't know anything about substituting honey for sugar so I don't do it. But I do believe in the health-giving properties (even if only mental) of honey, especially Italian chestnut honey. That, I eat by itself as a dessert; and poured over blue cheese, it sings.

Flavored Sugars

2	fresh vanilla beans
3 pounds	granulated sugar

Pound the beans lightly and put in a jar with a close-fitting top. Add the sugar, making sure the beans are not next to each other.

Every 2 days for a week, take out the beans, stir the sugar, and put the beans back in.

After a week, take the beans out and use them for custards or creams.

The sugar will retain its flavor for 3 months.

VARIATIONS Use rose petals, orange flowers, ginger flowers, gardenias, or scented geraniums with the vanilla—or even herbs, like fresh rosemary.

Sugar Syrups

Use light sugar syrup for fruit or for adding to fruit stews, soups, sauces, and compotes, hot or cold. Medium syrup is for sweetening fruit purees to be frozen as ices, and heavy syrup is for sweetening fruit purees to be used in sauces.

Light Syrup	Medium Syrup	Heavy Syrup
MAKES 1¼ CUPS	MAKES 1½ CUPS	MAKES 1¾ CUPS
½ cup sugar	⅔ cup sugar	1 cup sugar
1 cup water	1 cup water	1 cup water

In each case, put the sugar and water in a pan. Bring the water to a boil, stirring constantly, until all the sugar is dissolved. Simmer 5 minutes, then let the syrup cool. Use as needed.

Caramel

There are two ways to make caramel: melt the sugar on its own and then add hot water, or cook heavy syrup (see above) until it turns to caramel.

The disadvantage of the first method is that to make sauce you have to undergo the sometimes dangerous process of adding liquid to hot sugar. The disadvantage of the second is that if there are grains of sugar on the side of the pan and they fall down into the bubbling sugar, the syrup can crystallize and then you have to start all over again.

This crystallization problem can usually be avoided by making the heavy syrup in one pan and cooking it to caramel in another, and by watering down the sides of the pan with a pastry brush as the syrup is turning into caramel. I like the heavy syrup method.

2 cups   heavy syrup (see above)

Bring the syrup to a boil, immediately lower the heat to a simmer, and cook until the syrup turns golden brown. Remove from the heat and wait 5 minutes. As the caramel cools it will find its final color. If it is not dark enough, cook until it is.

SWEETBREADS

Almost everyone these days cooks sweetbreads for a finished dish from the raw state, a practice that shortchanges their potential flavor and texture and gives them a bad reputation. If you braise them first on a flavorful bed of aromatic vegetable mix (see page 14) and fresh herbs, the sweetbreads take on a more complex flavor as well as a smooth and unctuous texture.

Any sweetbread preparation must begin with soaking and then braising, and sweetbreads taste even more wonderful if cooked the day before serving them.

SERVES 4

4	large whole fresh sweetbreads (2–3 pounds)
2	lemons, cut in half
2 cups	fine aromatic vegetable mix (see page 14)
2	bay leaves
2 sprigs	fresh thyme
4 sprigs	fresh parsley
2 cups	chicken, beef, or veal stock (see pages 215, 233)
½ cup	dry white wine

Soak the sweetbreads in cold salty water for 2 hours, changing the water whenever it becomes bloody. Drain them and put them in a 4-quart pot. Add cold water to cover them by 2 inches, squeeze the lemons into the water and then add the squeezed lemons, and bring to a boil. Turn off the heat, and leave for 15 minutes. Drain the sweetbreads and put them in a colander, cover with ice, and run cold water over them for 5 minutes.

Preheat the oven to 375 degrees.

Put the vegetable mix, bay leaves, and thyme and parsley sprigs in a casserole just large enough to hold the sweetbreads side by side. Cover and cook in the oven for 15 minutes. Put the sweetbreads on top of the vegetable mix in the casserole, pour the stock and wine over the top and season the sweetbreads lightly. Turn the oven down to 325 degrees and bake covered for 45 minutes. Remove the casserole from the oven.

Lift out the sweetbreads, brush off any vegetable mix clinging to them, put them in a bowl, and strain the cooking liquid over them. Let them cool in the liquid.

Sweetbreads in a Sealed Casserole

Braised sweetbreads have many variations, but the one I like the most (and that always makes me think of New Year's Eve) is when they are bathed in fresh truffles. But then almost anything with fresh truffles is wonderful. I have included this old classic since it can be made two days before serving, scaled, kept in the refrigerator, and heated up at the last moment. When the crust seal is broken and all the aromas escape out onto the table, the result is spectacular.

If you do not have truffles, try wild mushrooms such as boletus mushrooms or morels, and if you cannot get those fresh, reconstitute dried ones in stock.

You will need four small (2-cup capacity) ovenproof casseroles with covers. Metal charlotte or soufflé dishes from France are ideal.

SERVES 4

2	large braised sweetbreads (see page 45)
2	medium carrots, peeled
1	large white onion, peeled, finely chopped
2 stalks	celery
2	parsnips, peeled and cored
2 cups	braising liquid
½ cup	Malmsey Madeira
4 sprigs	fresh thyme
4 sprigs	fresh tarragon
2 tablespoons	unsalted butter
2 tablespoons	chopped fresh parsley
1 pound	fresh cèpes, chanterelles, morels, or field mushrooms (if you want to use fresh truffle, 2 ounces should do)
½ cup	all-purpose flour
	Salt and freshly ground black pepper

Cut the carrots in 1/16-inch-thick julienne, then cut crosswise to make a precise 1/16-inch dice. Cut the onion, celery, and parsnips into the same size dice. Mix together and set aside.

Add all but 4 tablespoons of the Madeira to the braising liquid and reduce to 1 cup.

Put the vegetable mixture, thyme, tarragon, and butter in a 2-quart pot with 2 tablespoons of water, cover, and sweat over low heat for 5 minutes. Remove the herbs and spoon the mixture equally into the four casseroles.

Pull the sweetbreads apart into ¼-inch pieces, discarding all the membrane. Season and toss in a bowl with the remaining Madeira and the parsley. Divide the sweetbreads among the casseroles.

Chop the fresh mushrooms (and truffles if you have them) and put them on top of the sweetbreads. If you are using dried mushrooms that you have reconstituted in stock, chop them and add to the casseroles.

Put the flour and 4 to 6 tablespoons water in a small bowl and mix with your fingers into a slightly sticky paste so that it can be rolled out in your hands to form ropes. Press the ropes around the outer rim of the covers and then press the covers down on the casseroles so that they are sealed. If the paste falls down, push it back up to seal the cover and the dish. Up to this point the dishes can be prepared the day before and refrigerated.

Preheat the oven to 400 degrees.

If refrigerated, bring to room temperature before cooking. Bake for 20 minutes. Take the dishes to the table and break open the seals to serve.

TOMATOES

People I respect tell me it is just fine to cook with canned tomatoes. I just can't see it. Others tell me there are very acceptable tomato pastes. That really beats me. If you must have tomato sauce in winter, buy fresh tomatoes at the peak of the season, put them in plastic bags, and freeze them whole.

The benchmark for tomato sauce is the one made from tomatoes growing in and around Naples in that volcanic soil. In the summer, the whole plant is uprooted and hung upside down in the sun for a few days. Then these concentrated tomatoes (already packed with flavor) are cooked for fifteen minutes in olive oil and herbs before being poured, still in big pieces, over the pasta.

For fresh tomatoes, you can't go wrong growing or buying the heirloom varieties—a new development that is so wonderful it can never become a fad. They are simply the best.

Chopped Tomatoes

These chopped tomatoes have their skin, seeds, and excess water removed. When finishing a sauce with tomatoes, one must use these tomatoes to avoid watering down the sauce or filling it with seeds.

Put ripe tomatoes in boiling water for about five seconds. Do *not* overcook or the tomatoes will turn to mush. Plunge them immediately into a bath of ice and water for thirty seconds. Peel off the skin and discard. Cut across the equator of the tomato only, for if you cut through the stem and down you will seal off some of the seed chambers and be unable to remove all the seeds.

Hold the tomato halves cut side down and squeeze out the seeds. Dice the tomatoes and put them in a sieve over a bowl to drain. They are ready to use.

VARIATIONS Grilled tomatoes or ones put in wood or charcoal embers develop a wonderful rustic flavor. And tomatoes smoked lightly in a covered grill make a great, even haunting, sauce.

EQUIPMENT

BLENDER

Great for milkshakes or frozen drinks. Other cocktails are always better shaken by hand. Believe me. *See also* Pureeing.

CHEESECLOTH

Very handy for fine straining, wrapping aromatic vegetable mix (see page 14) so it is easily (and in one move) lifted out of the braising dish. Buy some and keep it handy.

COFFEE FILTERS

Get ones that have no chemical smell, and you will love using them for that last clarifying of a stock or broth, for straining shellfish essences (like the lobster essence on page 188), for filtering out the dregs in the last drops of that expensive wine you cannot bear to pour down the sink, and more.

COOKWARE

Black Iron Pans

These are the black metal pans most commonly known as crêpe pans. They are perfect for any little pancake or crêpe, doing a better job than nonstick technology since they let the surface of the pancake brown a bit without overcooking it.

Copper Pots

Copper is the best conductor of heat for even cooking (no hot spots and burning), and the old tin-lined French copperware is a glory to behold and use. But the tin lining is a real pain.

The Sandwich Concept

The first successful attempt to make pots that were highly conductive (thus avoiding the problem of hot spots and burning in the center of the pot) yet non reactive to food acids and chemicals (as stainless steel is), involved sandwiching three metals: stainless on the inside of the pot, conductive aluminum in the middle, and copper or aluminum on the outside.

Now there are copper cores with stainless on the inside and outside, and these are the ultimate cookware.

Earthenware

No material accepts the heat of the oven and retains heat evenly as well as earthenware. I cannot explain the magic of earthenware, but it does have mysterious qualities. No other material can cook a slow gratin without subjecting it to extreme heat. Just cook a gratin of potatoes and cream in stainless steel and then one in earthenware, and you will see what I mean. The gratin cooked in metal tends to boil over, forming overcooked crusts around the edges.

New earthenware should be rubbed with garlic inside and out (according to the master of earthenware, Richard Olney), then filled with water and put in a 350-degree oven for four hours.

The ultimate cooking vessel is the tagine, and you can never go wrong with it. Just shove anything into a tagine and it will be fine. It has all the properties of earthenware, plus even more mysterious powers that must have something to do with moist vapors and perfumes from the cooking caressing the top of the cover, condensing, and falling back down onto the food in the base of the tagine.

The most perfect and easiest roast chicken (or any poultry) is made in a tagine: season the bird, scatter chopped lemons and olives around, add fresh herbs, a cup of stock or water, and ¼ cup olive oil poured over the chicken, and cover it with the top of the tagine. Put it in a 350-degree oven for forty-five minutes, take it out, uncover the tagine at the table, and you couldn't be happier.

For a tagine-cooked chicken with a crisp skin, all you have to do is take the top off for the last ten minutes of cooking so that the whole chicken surface is exposed to the dry heat.

Food Mill

A food mill with several different blades and cutting attachments is the only machine guaranteed to give you the exact texture you want, whether for pureeing cooked vegetables for soups, fruits for smooth fruit purees, or making rough purees of raw or cooked meats to make it easy to finish them through finer sieves.

Food Processor

This is the only electronic machine for chopping, pureeing, and blending (as in flavored butters) that I find not only acceptable, but indispensable, especially for large-quantity work. The secret to quality control is the pulse action. The little ones are a dream for one or two people, or for spices and herbs.

Iron Skillet

Some things cannot be improved upon, and the American black iron skillet or frying pan is one of them. Before the first use, season it with a half cup vegetable oil, place in the oven, and then never wash it, and you have a perfect pan for deep or shallow frying, for blackening or searing, or for cornbread cooked in bacon fat.

Knives

The only dangerous knife is a dull one, because it is never too dull to cut you badly even if it won't cut the chicken.

Since most people don't have a professional sharpening service on hand, I suggest you use what is known as a steel, a long, rough-surfaced piece of metal with a handle. Apply it along the sharp edge of your knife. The best and easiest ones to use are flat.

Electric knife sharpeners are severe and can ruin the knife if you don't know how to use them, so use a handheld manual sharpener if you don't have a steel.

Live-Fuel Ovens

You have not tasted meats and vegetables until you have tasted them cooked in a live-fuel (wood burning) oven. But installing one is obviously an ambitious task, so I will just mention it here as a goal. In a city kitchen with good vents, you can simulate wood-oven flavors with a small handful of wood chips. Light them and let them smolder in a pan in the oven when roasting meats and poultry.

Mortar and Pestle

Why garlic mayonnaise and pesto taste better (fresher, brighter, clearer) and are more digestible when made with a mortar and pestle, we could debate. But it has a lot to do with the slowness of the process, the absence of the heat produced by the speed and force of an electric machine (which causes oxidization), and the degree of exactness that the slowness of the mortar demands.

Buy marble ones, a small smooth marble one for spices, and a large rough marble one for wet purees and sauces.

Ovens

The most important thing for me is that an oven cook evenly, and is able to hold a temperature as low as 200 degrees without going out (if gas) or surging violently (if electric).

It's nice to have a convection oven for even cooking and creating crisp surfaces on poultry and meats.

Slicing Machines (Countertop)

Slicing machines are very ambitious and expensive, as well as very dangerous, for a home, but for slicing hams like prosciutto, or for any very thin and fine slicing, nothing can compare with their accuracy and ease.

Vegetable Slicers

The French stainless-steel professional mandoline is quite expensive and is good for slicing bulk fruit and for cutting vegetables into various shapes, but for the home, buy one of the Japanese plastic ones with several blades. Whichever slicer you choose, always be incredibly careful not to cut yourself.

Wooden Spoons

I cannot stand the sound of metal spoons against metal pots, so I use wooden ones. There are, of course, very good plastic ones as well.

Drinks

I include a mention of drinks here as a reminder that they are as important as food, and that making them well requires the same level of knowledge and passion.

When I look back at personal favorites, at the momentary passions that have come upon me sometimes by accident, I remember when I first had a gin and tonic. It was on the terrace of the Oliver Messel Suite at the Dorchester Hotel in London, one pink-and-blue evening in 1958. The occasion was a going-away cocktail party for me before I returned to America after sixteen years away. To this day, on a hot evening after a difficult day, a tall Waterford crystal glass filled to the brim with ice, an inch of dry gin, the pulp of half a ripe lime, near-freezing Schweppes tonic water, and a few violet flowers can bring perfect peace, for a while anyway.

In the category of memorable drinks, I would also place the margaritas in Yelapa, a little fishing village near Puerto Vallarta. I had gone there for some serious recuperation after the first 90-hour-a-week year at Chez Panisse. (I was doing all the shopping, and cooking lunch by myself and dinner with only one sous-chef, the famous Willie Bishop.) I would lie in that Yelapa hammock and watch the day boat arrive and leave, an occupation that consumed about six margaritas. They were perfection: freshly squeezed lime juice, ordinary cheap white tequila, sugar syrup, no salt on the glass, served very, very cold.

Walking back up the beach after a swim, back to the hammock, with the salty tropical water still dripping down my face, I'd be handed a fresh cold margarita, and the requisite salt was provided by the minute portion of the aquamarine seawater still on my lips.

I remember other great moments: a huge, cold scotch and soda after dinner instead of brandy; freezing champagne after working in my vegetable garden all day in summer; and, on hot, humid days in Manhattan in the 1950s, stopping in a Schrafft's. In the heat, I could never pass one up, both for the air conditioning (my wrists cooling down against the marble counter) and the famous black-and-whites. In those days, the ice cream was good, the chocolate syrup was real, and the soda had big, lasting bubbles. The bite of the soda water against the sweetness of the chocolate was what battling the heat was all about, and never failed to elicit from me a few contented sighs before I stepped out onto the streets again, able to face anything, wearing the invincible armor of pleasure.

The Bloody Mary

Few classic drinks have fallen from grace as much as the Bloody Mary, and I use it here as a benchmark for true bartending.

The classic recipe is made from cold ingredients, then shaken and strained into a frozen stemmed wine glass, a far superior method than on the rocks, where one has the unpleasant sensation of the melting ice not mixing with the tomato juice, and of the ice hitting the front of one's teeth.

The Bloody Mary hits its apotheosis when made from fresh ripe, pureed, and sieved tomatoes.

Celery salt on the rim of the glass is fairly revolting (would you use garlic salt?), so use instead very finely chopped chives (moisten the rim with lemon juice and then dip it in a plate of the chives).

MAKES 1 COCKTAIL

4 ounces	cold tomato juice
½ teaspoon	cold prepared white horseradish
½ tablespoon	freshly squeezed lemon juice
2 splashes	cold Worcestershire sauce
2 splashes	cold Tabasco sauce
2 ounces	frozen vodka (or gin)
pinch	salt
pinch	freshly ground black pepper

Put a shaker full of ice and an 8-ounce wine glass in the freezer for 30 minutes.

Put all the ingredients in the shaker and shake for minutes. Strain into the cold glass and garnish with either a stalk of celery or a scallion, but certainly with a wedge of lemon stuck on the rim of the glass.

CHAPTER TWO
SNACKS, SANDWICHES, PIZZA, *and* FOOD WITH DRINKS

FOOD WITH DRINKS

OLIVES

I think I am among a small minority of olive lovers when I say that I don't really like strongly flavored cured olives, and that, in fact, I prefer the canned California green and black "Colossal" and "Jumbo" olives, even though I can hear the scoffing of my peers. It is not just a cop-out to like these olives, and not just a refuge from trying to remember the hundreds of varieties and names of olives (although that task has always overwhelmed me)—because I think that these canned olives, and many other mild-flavored olives, have great potential to satisfy.

I won't go so far as to admit that I take strongly flavored Greek and North African olives and soak them in white wine before giving them the mild olive treatment, but here is what I do with the mild ones.

And by the way, olive oil is improved by this treatment, picking up flavor from the olives. So if you use regular olive oil instead of extra virgin, that is fine too.

2 cups	mild olives, green or black (canned ones are acceptable)		4 sprigs	fresh thyme
			2 cloves	garlic, peeled
½ cup	fruity white wine		1	small lemon, zested
1 teaspoon	Pernod or other anise-flavored liqueur		10	black peppercorns (preferably Tellicherry or Madagascar)
1	small orange, juiced and zested		1 cup	extra virgin olive oil
2	dried Jamaican pepper (allspice berries)			

Drain and rinse the olives. Put them in a bowl with the wine, Pernod, and orange juice, and marinate for 4 hours.

Drain the olives and transfer them to a glass jar or ceramic crock. Add the orange zest, allspice, thyme, garlic, lemon zest, peppercorns, and olive oil, making sure that the olives are completely covered with the olive oil, and let them marinate for at least 2 days to pick up flavor and up to a couple of weeks before serving. However, if you are in a rush and have only an hour, this olive bath is still well worth the effort.

FAT-PRESERVED POULTRY GIZZARDS

Please don't be shocked. Chicken, turkey, and duck gizzards that have had the tough outer membrane peeled off and have been cooked very slowly in water-rendered poultry fat (in the same way as the duck legs on page 15), then served while still warm, are incredible rolled in cracked black Tellicherry or Lampong pepper, or in orange Sichuan pepper salt (see page 42).

I put them in the same salt marinade (see page 22) as I do the duck legs, but for only 2 hours.

Serve stuck with toothpicks or oyster forks.

POPPADAMS ("PAPPADS")

I am a bit in love with almost anything Indian. But let's face it, no matter where it's from, any food that takes one minute to cook, costs a few cents, and is ultimately satisfying, is great.

I am a huge fan of potato chips, even the unflavored ones in bags, and poppadams, having that quality of "moreness" in common with potato chips, are a bit dangerous that way. A big bowl of huge delicate poppadams, with their crisp texture and seductive flavors, in the middle of a table at the drinks hour cannot fail to excite and please most guests.

Poppadams are made from lentil (dhal or arhad dhal) flour and are purely vegetarian. Buy a package of the plain, the cumin-flavored, the black pepper–flavored, or others. Then prepare them up to four hours before serving. If the air is humid, make them to order. Just deep-fry them one at a time (in 2 inches of peanut or vegetable oil) for about 30 seconds, until they puff up. Alternately, put them on a griddle (pushing them down with a spatula), or grill them over a fire.

LITTLE PAPPADS

Whereas the large pappads are 6 to 8 inches in diameter, the small ones are only 1 inch across, making them perfect little platforms for holding bite-sized portions of food.

Deep-fry these ten at a time in shallow oil, then drain and hold until needed. Top with any of the following:

+ Anchoiade (see the anchovy toast recipe on page 64)
+ Steelhead salmon roe (see page 58)
+ Egg salad (see page 74)
+ Preserved peppered tuna (see page 173)
+ Pickled herring
+ Spiced crab (see page 105)
+ Chopped vegetables (as for the soup on page 107)

FILLED POLENTA CUPS

These are bite-sized containers, like large straight-sided thimbles, for holding fillings you have made especially for the dish, or just from emptying out the refrigerator. They are filled and then heated, or stuffed when hot with a cold (room temperature) filling that needs no further cooking. The contrast of the hot polenta cups with a slightly chilled roasted eggplant, mint, and lentil filling is very special.

You will need a baking pan 12 by 8 inches and 3 inches deep, and two small circular cookie cutters, ½ inch and 1 inch in diameter.

MAKES ABOUT 20 CUPS

2 tablespoons	butter
1 recipe	polenta (see page 153)

Butter the baking pan with half the butter and place it in the refrigerator to chill for 15 minutes.

Cook the polenta as on page 153 and pour into the chilled pan. Rub the remaining butter over the top of the polenta to prevent a crust from forming. Chill until completely set.

Cut out cylinders of polenta with the larger cutter. With the cylinders still in the pan, cut each cylinder in its center with the smaller cutter, but only three-quarters of the way down. Lift out the cylinders and dig out the center plug with a small knife, leaving the bottom intact to hold the filling, cup-like.

Then fill them and heat in a 375-degree oven until hot, 5 to 10 minutes, or heat them for 5 minutes, fill with a room-temperature filling, then serve.

Fill with any of the following:

+ Anchoiade (see page 64)
+ Parsley puree and warm shrimp sauce (see page 237)
+ Black or white truffle puree
+ Grilled and chopped wild mushrooms
+ Heirloom tomatoes (see page 65)
+ Blood sausage and celery root salad (see page 62)
+ Steelhead salmon roe (see page 58)
+ White beans and sevruga (see page 61)
+ Snails with ham (see page 71)
+ Hot lamb sausages (see page 72) or store-bought merguez
+ Melted blue or Crescenza cheese
+ Fresh salsa (see page 239)
+ Lemon and fig relish (see page 243)
+ Mint, sage, and rosemary pesto (see page 244)
+ Russian dressing (see page 250)
+ Nasturtium sauce (see page 253)

You can also sweeten the polenta cups by filling them with caramel or chocolate sauce.

OYSTER TARTAR

SERVES 4

12	very fresh oysters, shucked	1–2 tablespoons	freshly squeezed lemon juice
1 tablespoon	finely chopped fresh Italian parsley	1	small shallot, peeled, very finely chopped
1 teaspoon	freshly ground coarse black pepper	2	teaspoons very finely chopped fresh chives
½ teaspoon	Champagne vinegar		
1 teaspoon	very light olive oil		

Finely chop the oysters and put them in a bowl over ice. Mix the parsley, pepper, vinegar, and olive oil together. Add half the lemon juice, mix and taste. Add up to all the remaining lemon juice if needed to get the right balance of acidity with the salt of the oysters.

Just before serving, add the shallots and chives, and serve in chilled Chinese spoons either on a tray covered with shaved ice, or on a deep tray decorated with seaweed and shellfish shells covered in gelatin and chilled, so the spoons don't slide around.

VARIATIONS Scallop hash or chopped raw lobster or prawns dressed and served the same way as the chopped oysters.

SEAFOOD SHOOTERS

Frozen vodka is the best way to get a party off the ground quickly, but some may balk at unadulterated raw alcohol even if it is the deliciously smooth buffalo grass (*Zubrovka*) version. On the other hand, few could resist these Bloody Mary (or Virgin Mary) shooters presented in a huge punch bowl filled with crushed ice.

Use chilled, 2-ounce shot glasses, counting on at least two per person, and choose cooked crab, lobster, prawn, mussels, or a combination, or the smallest possible raw oysters, such as Olympias. If using other seafood, you will need ½ teaspoon per shot glass.

MAKES 12 SHOOTERS

1 tablespoon	fresh lemon zest
1 tablespoon	chopped parsley
1 tablespoon	chopped fresh garlic
1½ cups	chilled Bloody Mary (see page 51)
12	fresh iced Olympia oysters, shucked

Mix the lemon zest, parsley, and garlic together.

Put a teaspoon of the Bloody Mary in each of the glasses (so that the seafood will not stick to the bottom of the glass) and then the oysters.

Fill almost to the brim with the rest of the Bloody Mary, and sprinkle with the lemon-parsley mix.

STEELHEAD SALMON ROE

One of the most wonderful women I ever met was a Bay Area Indian who brought me freshly processed steelhead caviar eggs every week during the season. Tasting them was a revelation. Until then, I had never seen commercially sold salmon eggs (even from the great Russian-French caviar houses) that were not glorified fish bait—oily, smelly, and inedible. Now of course there are many sources for delicious salmon eggs. Making them yourself is, however, much cheaper.

We used the superb fresh eggs on cornmeal blini, on oysters, on little toasts floating on top of chilled fresh fava bean or green pea soup, or covering the entire top of baked potatoes drenched with chive flower butter.

Do not shy away from buying these eggs the next time you see a sack of them at a fish counter. You can process them yourself quite easily, remembering that the quality of the final salt is important, since there are only two ingredients here—eggs and salt. Use hand-harvested salt from the Camargue, the island of Ré, the Guérande in Brittany, or from Oahu in Hawaii.

MAKES 2 TO 3 POUNDS

1	steelhead egg sack, weighing 2–3 pounds
1 cup	kosher salt
1 ounce or more	hand-harvested sea salt

Choose a glass or metal bowl large enough to hold the egg sack and several cups of water.

Put the eggs in the bowl and cover with 6 inches of cold water. Add the kosher salt and six ice cubes. Stir around with your hands very gently, and wait for 15 minutes. Then start pulling the membrane off the eggs until about half of it is gone. Work as quickly as you can without damaging any of the eggs.

Put the eggs in a sieve with holes just big enough to let the eggs through, and place the sieve over a bowl. Push the eggs around the sieve with your fingers, pulling membrane away and discarding it, while pushing the eggs gently through the holes. Occasionally dunk the sieve back in a bowl of clean iced water if that helps.

When you have collected all the eggs in the bowl, remove any last bits of membrane, and drain the eggs in a fine sieve for 5 minutes. Put them in a dry bowl, add 1 tablespoon of sea salt, and mix gently with your fingers until all the salt is dissolved. Taste an egg. It should have a slightly salty taste; lightly salted or "malassol" roe is at 2½ percent salt. The commercial roe is around 4 percent, which is perhaps why the eggs are bruised and leak moisture.

So for 2½ pounds of eggs, use 1 ounce of salt.

SMOKED FISH SPREAD

This is an easy and wonderful way of eating smoked fish, and of using the ends and scraps of any whole smoked fish you have bought. The one thing to remember is that you cannot blend smoked fish or puree it in a food processor without it turning into blotting paper. So do please cut the fish by hand before giving it a final mixing in a bowl, and then let it sit for a day (and up to three) to develop the flavors.

Smoked fish demands a lot of freshly ground pepper and some lemon, so serve more of both with the spread, and offer hot grilled garlic bread.

You will need four 10-ounce ramekins.

SERVES 4 TO 6

1 cup	smoked trout, salmon, sturgeon, or other smoked fish
½ cup	unsweetened butter
1 tablespoon	freshly ground coarse white pepper
1 teaspoon	freshly squeezed lemon juice
1 teaspoon	lemon zest
	Salt

Flake the smoked fish with your fingers onto a chopping board, removing all the bones and skin. Then finely chop the fish and put it into a mixing bowl.

Let the butter soften just to the point where it can be easily beaten with a spoon, and add it to the fish. Add the pepper, lemon juice, and zest, and beat until well mixed. Taste to see if it needs any salt, adding a pinch if it needs it.

Put into individual ramekins, cover with plastic wrap and refrigerate for a day. Serve at room temperature.

VARIATIONS Use ½ cup of cooked, pureed, and sieved white beans instead of the butter and mix that spread with ¼ cup of olive oil; or use ½ cup of fresh white breadcrumbs (see page 32) instead of butter with the same ¼ cup of olive oil; and instead of smoked fish, try cooked salmon, shrimp, or crab.

Hot Buttered Crumpets with Pressed Caviar

My Russian uncle used to tell me about his time in the Imperial Navy eating caviar. At the entrance to the officers' mess was a huge basket of bread and a 15-kilo wood cask filled with caviar. He thought he had landed in heaven, and every time he went in or out he would swipe a piece of the bread in the caviar. As in all good things passing, after a few months he couldn't stand the sight of a fish egg. But at the bottom of each barrel was something that revived his flagging appetite: the *payusnaya ikra*, or caviar "pressed" under the weight of the caviar on top of it. The bottom-layer caviar was concentrated in every respect, with more protein, fat, salt, and calories than other caviar, and certainly more intense flavor—so much more that many people came to prefer it to the fresh.

When I was in college, *payusnaya* was the only kind of caviar I could afford, and I developed a real taste for it, finding that its "jammy" texture and concentrated flavors cry out for potatoes, crumpets, or English muffins.

Caviar in small quantities is a nasty tease, so always buy as much as you can afford.

SERVES 4 TO 6

4	crumpets
2 ounces	unsalted butter
½ pound	pressed caviar
	Freshly ground black pepper
8	lemon wedges

Toast the crumpets and butter them generously. Spread the caviar on the crumpets, sprinkle with the pepper, and serve with lemon wedges.

LIDIA'S WHITE BEANS WITH SEVRUGA

One hot summer Sunday afternoon, I walked into Lidia Bastianich's house to find a glass of chilled champagne and a dish of beans and caviar on the kitchen counter. Fortunato, the wonderful chef of her New York restaurant Felidia, was grilling bread, which he handed us as soon as it was ready and on top of which we slathered the beans and caviar.

Lidia is one of the few chefs who know that refrigerating a dish can quite often kill it, causing the disparate but connected perfumes and tastes to turn into one smell, one taste. So she hadn't refrigerated these beans after they were cooked, knowing they would be consumed within an hour or so.

She also knew to take the cooling time into account when figuring the cooking time of the beans.

SERVES 6 TO 8

4 cups	cooked white beans (see page 33), let cool to room temperature	1 tablespoon	freshly squeezed lemon juice
		½ cup	extra virgin olive oil
		4–8 ounces	sevruga caviar
2 tablespoons	finely chopped fresh shallots		Sea salt and freshly
4 tablespoons	coarsely chopped Italian parsley leaves		ground black pepper

Put 1 cup of the beans in a bowl, and mash with a fork. Mix in the other beans, shallots, parsley, lemon, and olive oil, and season generously.

Stir in the caviar and serve on grilled hot toasts. Offer the salt separately.

MAX'S BLOOD SAUSAGE WITH CELERY ROOT IN MUSTARD SAUCE

My dear friends the Harrises, in London, invited me to the wedding of one of their daughters. The wedding dinner was held at Monsieur Max, and one of Max's Renzland's dishes with drinks that evening was this blood sausage dish. It blew my mind.

The secret to blood sausage is cooking it enough—until it is really crisp on the outside.

SERVES 4 TO 6

16 inches	blood sausage	2 tablespoons	freshly squeezed lemon juice
1 tablespoon	olive oil	¼ cup	mayonnaise
1 tablespoon	dried thyme	3 tablespoons	Dijon mustard
1	medium celery root (approximately one pound), peeled, cored, stored in lemon water	1 teaspoon	fresh tarragon leaves chopped
			Salt and freshly ground white pepper

Rub the blood sausage with the oil and thyme, and let it sit for 4 hours.

Cut the celery root by hand or machine to produce ⅛-inch-sided sticks, each about 1 inch long. Boil 4 quarts of salted water. Put the sticks in the boiling water for one minute, drain, and squeeze dry. Put the sticks in a mixing bowl, toss with the lemon juice, and season. Let sit one hour. Drain and reserve the lemon juice. Add the mayonnaise, mustard, and tarragon leaves, and mix with the celery root.

Hold the celery root until ready to use, and then add the salt and pepper and check to see if some or all of the lemon juice should be added back. Wipe the thyme off the sausage, and grill or broil for 10 minutes on each side. Slice ½ inch thick and serve the slices with a teaspoon of the celery root on top of each hot slice of blood sausage.

SNACKS

This section is about foods that you can cook when you have the time and then snack on when you don't. Both the ham and the frozen shrimp (see the cocktail on page 70) are perfect examples of this.

COUNTRY HAM

When one remembers Jim Beard, the image of huge platters of sausages and steaming boiled meats, especially pork, is usually conjured up. In those photographs where he is standing in front of a mound of sausages, looking slightly pink and stuffed himself, there is almost always a ham.

Jim and I talked for hours and hours on the subject of hams and the proper way to cook a Smithfield (they are too expensive to make mistakes). Here's what we decided:

1	Smithfield or country-style ham, dried-cured
4 cups	aromatic vegetable mix (see page 14)
1	large herb bundle (see page 16)
1 cup	Malmsey Madeira

Wash the ham in cold water with a stiff brush to remove the pepper, then put it in a pot large enough to hold it vertically, cover with cold water up to the shank, and soak it overnight.

The next day, throw out that water. Fill the pot with cold water up to the shank of the ham again. Bring the water to a boil, add the vegetable mix and herb bundle, and simmer over low heat until the ham shank, or hock, is flexible to the point of breaking off, 5 to 6 hours depending on the size of the ham.

Let the ham cool in the water. Then take the ham out and remove the skin and trim down the fat until there is half an inch left overall. Put the ham in a baking pan, pour two glasses of Madeira over it, cover with foil, and bake in the oven at 350 degrees for 30 minutes. Take the ham out of the oven and let it cool while still covered. The ham is then ready for carving in the thinnest possible slices, and serving with almost anything. I like it with stuffed dates and Sauternes or figs and Madeira.

FRESH GREEN ALMONDS WITH HAM

I am assuming that you will accept my theory that a ham in the refrigerator makes for perfect snacking—for breakfast, sandwiches, flat omelets at lunch, on little toasts with cheese melted in the oven, for an evening salad, or a late-night snack between English muffins with mango chutney, and so on.

But I don't expect you to have green almonds (see Resources, page 280). If you are anywhere around the Mediterranean in the early summer, however, you can grab a handful from any street stall, nip into any food store for the ham, and have an instant picnic or a snack with drinks.

You can break open the green almonds and get the kernels out very easily, since the almonds are soft. Then dip the kernels in olive oil and salt, or in chili pepper, or just eat them wrapped up in thin slices of ham.

The point of mentioning these almonds, really, is to illustrate an alternative to melon with ham, which I really don't like because of the wetness. Do try figs, fresh or dried. Try those huge and wonderful sugar-cured Australian apricots, as well as Tunisian quince pastes and all the other fruit "leathers."

THE ANCHOVY TOASTS OF AUSTIN DE CROZE (*LOU PAN BAGNA*)

One of the first cookbooks I ever bought was a translated edition of Austin de Croze's *What to Eat and Drink in France* (1931), a book dedicated to presenting France to gastronomic tourists as "a diamond with a thousand facets."

This extraordinary book became the basis for my "Regions of France" festivals at Chez Panisse starting in 1973. For all regions anywhere near Provence we would spread this *anchoiade* on baguettes, bake them on trays of pine needles (making the kitchen smell like a fantasy Provençal farmhouse), and serve them piping hot to everyone as they first sat down.

The puree by itself is *anchoiade*, but spread on toast dipped in olive oil it is *lou pan bagna* or, translated from the Provençal, "bathed bread."

This *anchoiade* bears very little resemblance to any other you will encounter, with its hint of Tunisia and perfumes of Moorish Andalusia. It's better.

SERVES 4 TO 6

12	salted anchovies, prepared as on page 42	1	red bell pepper, cooked as on page 39
4	dried figs, stemmed	1	lemon, zested and juiced
1 tablespoon	Pernod	1 tablespoon	orange flower water
2 tablespoons	green Chartreuse	¾ cup	extra virgin olive oil
2 tablespoons	whole almonds, lightly toasted	1 teaspoon	freshly ground black pepper
1 tablespoon	walnuts, lightly toasted	1	baguette
1	red onion, peeled, cored, chopped	2 teaspoons	sea salt
2 cloves	garlic, peeled	1 teaspoon	red chili flakes
1 tablespoon each	fresh thyme, tarragon, fennel seed		

Soak the figs in the Pernod and Chartreuse for 2 hours.

Put the remaining ingredients in a food processor and grind until the texture of whole grain mustard—smooth but not completely so, not like baby food.

Spread on olive-oiled bread and bake in an oven at 400 degrees for 10 minutes. Sprinkle with the sea salt and with red chili flakes, if you are in the mood, as I usually am.

TRICOLORED HEIRLOOM TOMATO TOASTS

Call this a multicolored bruschetta if you like, but whatever you call it, is there a more perfect snack than this? Does anyone not like it?

This recipe avoids the common pitfalls usually encountered in making this dish, since I include the steps that many a cook leaves out: making sure the bread is toasted enough, rubbing it with garlic, and letting the tomato mix sit long enough for the flavors to come together (but not so long that the garlic becomes stale).

I say "beefsteak" here meaning just the large, meaty tomatoes.

MAKES 12 TOASTS

1	red heirloom beefsteak tomato	1 tablespoon	coarse sea salt
1	yellow heirloom beefsteak tomato	2 teaspoons	freshly ground coarse black pepper
1	green (but ripe) heirloom beefsteak tomato	12	slices (¼ inch thick) firm white bread
1 tablespoon	freshly chopped garlic	¼ cup	olive oil
½ cup	extra virgin olive oil	1	clove garlic, peeled, cut in half
1 tablespoon	freshly squeezed lemon juice		

Preheat the oven to 400 degrees.

Prepare and chop the tomatoes in ⅛-inch dice as on page 47.

Put the tomatoes in a nonreactive bowl with half the salt and all the other ingredients. Let the mixture sit for 30 minutes.

Brush the bread slices with the olive oil, and bake in a 400-degree oven, until firm throughout, about 10 minutes. Take them out and rub them generously with the garlic clove on one side. Sprinkle with the remaining sea salt.

Spoon the tomato mixture over the bread and serve.

VARIATIONS Go wild. Add fresh herbs and lemon zest, bake the bread with cardamom on it, garnish the tomatoes with chopped chive flowers or orange blossoms. Or pour the tomato mixture over the anchovy toasts on page 64. Crescenza cheese (see Resources, page 280) spread on the toasts before adding the tomatoes takes this simple dish to a new, sublime level.

SARDINES ON TOAST

Don't laugh.

I cannot think of a canned product that has more of a cult following than sardines. Arguments rage about how long sardines should be aged in the can (yes, there are vintage sardines) and whether they should be Portuguese, French, Spanish, Chinese, or Southeast Asian. In the Philippines, I had the famous delicacy of freshwater sardines from Lake Bombon, but after I saw the polluted lake I was unfairly prejudiced against the fish.

Let's not get into the whole debate about brislings versus sardines, but do read "Oules of Sardines," an article that Elizabeth David wrote for *The Spectator* in 1962. You can find it in her superb *An Omelette and a Glass of Wine* (1984). Or read Alan Davidson's essay "What Is a Sardine?" published in the *Petits Propos Culinaires, No. 2* (August 1979), published by Prospect Books in London.

A plate of good quality, canned sardines is a fully satisfying dish that takes only 10 minutes to prepare. Eat them with horseradish, hot sauce, Meyer or salt-preserved lemons (see page 43), or mayonnaise, but always with freshly grated onion.

SERVES 4 TO 6

2 cans	sardines in olive oil or water	½ teaspoon	sea salt
1	sweet onion (Walla Walla, Vidalia, Maui, or a fresh red one), peeled	1 teaspoon	coarsely ground fresh black pepper
4 leaves	fresh mint		Hot toasted bread, English muffins, or brioche
2 tablespoons	extra virgin olive oil		

Finely grate the onion and chop the mint, and mix in a bowl with a pinch of salt and pepper. In another bowl mix the olive oil, salt, and pepper. Pour the oil or water off the sardines and put them on a plate. Pour the seasoned olive oil over them, turn them over in it several times, and serve on hot toast with the mint relish on top.

VARIATION A bit over the top but amazing is toasted brioche slathered with ham mousse and then topped with the sardines prepared as above.

DEVILED EGGS WITH PICKAPEPPA MAYONNAISE

I use Pickapeppa mayonnaise here, but you could use any of the mayonnaises mentioned in the Sauces chapter (see pages 234–257). I just happen to love Pickapeppa sauce, and putting some of it in mayonnaise is easy, as would be adding Indian lime pickle, or mango chutney, plus hot sauce for a bit of heat, or even beet horseradish.

For a more surprising visual effect and a more complex dish, instead of halving the eggs, cut off the tops and bottoms, scoop out the yolks without damaging the whites, make the deviled yolk mix, then put it in a pastry bag and fill the eggs by piping the egg mixture back into the hollowed-out whites. Serve them standing up with the mayonnaise spooned over.

A whole platter of these eggs for a buffet will pleasantly surprise everyone.

SERVES 4

4	large eggs
¼ cup	sour cream
½ teaspoon	English powdered mustard
1 teaspoon	Dijon mustard
4 drops	hot sauce
	Salt
½ cup	mayonnaise (see page 247)
4 tablespoons	Pickapeppa sauce
2 tablespoons	chopped chives

Put the eggs in a heavy saucepan that will just hold them in one layer, cover them with cold water by 1 inch, and bring to a boil over high heat. The moment the water boils, remove the pan from the heat, cover it, and let stand 10 minutes. Then immediately cool the eggs under cold running water. If the water is not cold, add some ice.

Peel the eggs, slice them lengthwise, and scoop out the yolk. Put the yolks in a bowl and mix with the sour cream, powdered mustard, Dijon mustard, and hot sauce until smooth. Taste for salt.

Put the mixture back in the egg whites and put the egg halves on plates with the flat side down.

Mix the mayonnaise and the Pickapeppa sauce together, and spoon over the eggs to "nap" them. Garnish the eggs and plates with the chives.

Baked Eggs with Garlic and Parsley Butter

"Shirred" used to be the term used for these dishes, but since I had to look the word up in the dictionary to make sure, I will use "baked" instead. So to "shirr" eggs is to bake them in a buttered dish.

Again, these baked-egg dishes scream out for input and imagination. More important than the actual list of ingredients are the cautions: whether cooked in little ramekins, open gratin dishes, or "en cocotte" (in a little ramekin and usually with cream), remember that the eggs will continue to cook after they are removed from the oven.

So if you take the dishes out of the oven when they are perfectly cooked (jiggling them to see that the yolk is still moving slightly), it is too late. You can cook them in a water bath and then the whites on the edge of the dish will not be as "tough," as if you had not used one. But given the awkwardness and even danger of lifting a pan with boiling water out of the oven, or pulling out an oven rack that has a pan half full of boiling water on it, I might choose not to.

You will need four ramekins 2 to 3 inches high and in circumference.

SERVES 4	
4	large eggs, room temperature
5 tablespoons	butter
1 tablespoon	finely chopped garlic
1 tablespoon	finely chopped parsley
	Salt and freshly ground black pepper

Preheat the oven to 350 degrees.

Lightly butter four ramekins and place them on a baking sheet.

Mix the remaining butter with the garlic and parsley.

Break an egg into each ramekin, season (generously with the pepper), and divide the garlic-butter mix equally amongst the ramekins. Bake in the oven for about 10 minutes, until the whites are set, but the yolk is still soft in its center.

VARIATIONS I love eggs baked in a shallow gratin dish with just olive oil and then sprinkled at the end with a mixture of equal proportions of finely chopped garlic and parsley. Baked in cream with cooked artichokes and ham, with mushrooms, or with a puree of fresh cèpes or reconstituted dried ones, they are also wonderful. The ultimate ramekin egg is in cream with fresh white truffles, and in cream with a little very fresh white truffle oil is not too bad either.

POTATO AND SAGE FLAT OMELET WITH RUSSIAN DRESSING

Flat omelets (Italian *frittata*) are an easy snack since they take only a few minutes and are best eaten at room temperature, making them perfect for taking on picnics or cooking in advance and leaving until needed (as long as they have no shellfish in them).

They don't need saucing at all, just a little olive oil and lemon, but the Russian dressing is pretty spectacular with this omelet. If you don't have the caviar, use the tomato and olive oil sauce on page 237 mixed with six fillets of chopped salted anchovies (see page 42).

SERVES 4

8	small red potatoes
¼ cup	fresh sage leaves, coarsely chopped
¼ cup	olive oil
1 tablespoon	fresh lemon juice
4	large eggs
	Salt and freshly ground white pepper
½ cup	Russian dressing (see page 250)

Peel the potatoes and cut in ⅛-inch slices. Mix the sliced potatoes with half the sage leaves. Heat half the oil in a 10-inch frying pan over medium heat and add the potatoes. Cook while stirring for 2 minutes, season, add the lemon juice, cover, and cook over low heat until just tender, about 10 minutes. Turn off the heat and let the potatoes cool.

Beat the eggs in a bowl, season, and add the potatoes and the remaining sage leaves. Mix well.

Wipe out the pan, add the remaining oil, heat it over medium heat, and add the egg-potato mix. Wait a minute, and then shake the pan gently to loosen the egg from the pan. Keep making sure that the omelet does not stick to the pan, and cook over medium-low heat for about 4 minutes on one side. Put a plate slightly bigger than the pan on top of it, flip the omelet over onto the plate, put the pan back on the fire, and slip the omelet, cooked side up, back into the pan. Continue cooking and sliding the omelet around the pan for another 3 minutes.

Serve at room temperature with the sauce on the side.

Warm Prawn Cocktail

I can't believe I am going to suggest that you keep some prawns or shrimp in the freezer, but worse things can happen than to have this favorite instant-food at hand. All I will say is to be sure to buy them fresh and freeze them yourself, since then you'll know how fresh they were before freezing, and how long they have been in the freezer. And you can freeze them in their shells, which is infinitely preferable to shelled shrimp.

One morning at Ventana in Big Sur, feeling the strain of trying for weeks to wean the Carmel Pebble Beach ladies-who-lunch away from canned chef's salad and over to our regional American menu, I regretted the tequila I had shared with my Mexican cooks the night before. Their *jeffe* Pedro saved the day. "Here *jeffe*," he said, "eat this."

SERVES 4

½ pound	fresh prawns
1 cup	fresh salsa (see page 239)
8 sprigs	Cilantro
	Green chili hot sauce
	Lime wedges

Cook the prawns in 1 cup simmering salted water for 5 minutes in a covered saucepan.

Drain the prawns in a colander and save the liquid. Put some ice on the prawns to cool them down, but do not leave the ice on them for more than 10 minutes. Shell the prawns and grind the shells in a food processor with the saved cooking liquid. Put the ground shells and the liquid in the saucepan and simmer for 10 minutes. Drain and save the liquid, and discard the shells.

Meanwhile, coarsely chop the prawns and add them to the saved liquid.

Put the chopped prawns and their broth in large wine glasses. Add the salsa, and put the cilantro on top and serve with lime wedges and hot sauce on the side.

SNAILS IN A RAMEKIN WITH HAM

I will not go into the last time I decided to eat snails that I had gathered from the wild instead of from a can (in a typically mad twist, Richard Olney gave me an old plastic toilet to store and clean them in), but do read about the hilarious wild snail experience of Clémentine in *Clémentine in the Kitchen* by Samuel Chamberlain, now republished by the Modern Library. It is no exaggeration.

And despite the experiences I had and the one in that book, I still adore snails. Having a can or two around at all times lets you make a perfect last-minute dish. The canned ones are very good if you give them a bath, an essential (but usually ignored) initial step of preparation for good-tasting canned snails. If you like snails, give them this bath and store them in sealed jars in the refrigerator. If you put them in ramekins with finely chopped garlic, chopped parsley, and some olive oil or butter, you are only fifteen minutes away from a delicious snack.

For New Year's in 1984, we grilled snails on skewers, then took them off and put them on fresh artichoke bottoms stewed in butter and placed them on top of grilled fresh cèpes. The sauce was a fresh herb hollandaise accented with red bell pepper puree mounted with butter. That was a bit over the top, and I think my first way of using canned snails (this ramekin recipe) is better, and I have never grown tired of it.

Use ramekins 3 inches in diameter and about 2 inches deep.

The Bath:			¼ cup	ham scraps
3 cups	vegetable stock (see page 143) or water		½ cup	mixed fresh herbs (thyme, tarragon, chives, and parsley)
1	bay leaf			
2	shallots, peeled, chopped			
SERVES 4				
The Dish:			4	fresh white mushrooms, chopped in ⅛-inch dice
24	snails			
1 tablespoon	chopped fresh shallots		4 tablespoons	chopped ham
4 tablespoons	butter		2 tablespoons	melted butter
½ tablespoon	fresh tarragon leaves, chopped		4 rounds	white bread, ½-inch thick, cut from center of slice to fit in ramekin
4 tablespoons	dry white wine			
½ cup	chicken stock (see page 215)			

Simmer the bath ingredients for 30 minutes and strain, saving the liquid. Rinse the snails in cold water and drain. Put the snails in the bath while it is still hot and leave them to soak for 1 hour.

Preheat the oven to 375 degrees.

Put the shallots, butter, and tarragon in a pan, and cover; sweat for 5 minutes. Do not brown. Add the wine, chicken stock, and mushrooms and simmer 5 minutes. Mix in the ham and snails.

Divide the snails and the juices amongst the ramekins. Butter the bread rounds and put them buttered side up on top of the snails. The bread should fit flush with the inside top of the ramekin.

Bake for 15 minutes, or until the bread is golden and the snails hot.

CHILLED OYSTERS WITH GRILLED HOT LAMB SAUSAGES

This recipe is fast and easy because you can buy both ingredients (buy merguez-type or little spicy breakfast sausages if you don't want to make the sausage yourself), and by the time you have opened the oysters, the sausages are done.

This dish comes from the coast of Bordeaux, and the inhabitants there figured out long ago that perfection is to eat a piece of hot, grilled, spicy sausage and then swallow a fresh, very cold, salty oyster. The contrast of the two kinds of heat with the cold oyster is tantalizing.

SERVES 4

1½ pounds	lean lamb meat, shoulder or leg	1 teaspoon	fresh marjoram leaves, finely chopped
½ pound	lean veal meat	½ teaspoon	salt
¾ pound	pork fatback, very cold		Freshly ground black pepper
2	fresh serrano chilies, seeded, finely chopped	48	small, very fresh oysters
¼ teaspoon	cayenne pepper	16	lemon wedges
1½ teaspoons	fresh thyme leaves, finely chopped		

Put the lamb, veal, and pork fatback through the medium-fine blade of a meat grinder. The fat must be cold, so that it will not emulsify in the mixture (making for dry and tough sausage).

Mix the meat, chilies, cayenne, thyme, marjoram, salt, and pepper together by hand, being careful not to overmix the sausage (same problem of dry and tough). Fry a small piece to taste the level of seasoning.

Refrigerate the sausage meat for 4 hours to develop the flavors.

Wash the unopened oysters in cold water and keep them cold.

Start a charcoal fire, or heat the broiler.

Form the meat into 2-ounce patties. Open the oysters, put them on platters of shaved ice, and garnish with lemon wedges.

Grill the patties on both sides and serve with the oysters.

SANDWICHES

Sandwiches are the easiest snack, fast, perfectly comforting, and satisfying. Ever since I was old enough to order champagne, the combination of the club sandwich and a great, slightly old, yeasty champagne has been the perfect palliative for many trying moments.

How many times have I arrived in a hotel after sixteen hours in an airplane, too tired to move or too late to go out for dinner, and loved picking up the phone for twenty-four-hour room service, the apothesis of which is the chicken club or its other version, the BLT.

CHICKEN CLUB SANDWICH

The bread is especially important in this sandwich. Ideal is the round "rustic" loaf now found in many American markets. American packaged sliced bread doesn't work.

The slices should be cut across the loaf, parallel to the bottom, ¼ inch thick, so that two round slices, cut in half, serve as one large sandwich.

SERVES 2

6	thin slices bacon or pancetta		Salt and freshly ground black pepper
4	large slices bread (see headnote)	4 pieces	green leaf or curly leaf red lettuce, washed, dried
2 tablespoons	butter	6 slices	ripe tomato, ¼ inch thick
¼ cup	mayonnaise (see page 247)		
1 whole	chicken breast, poached, skinned, shredded by hand		

Lay out the bacon or pancetta in flat strips on a rack and broil or bake in the oven until crisp (or use the microwave).

Grill, broil, or toast the bread until just golden. Immediately butter the bread, and then spread the slices with the mayonnaise. Put the chicken on the mayonnaise and season with salt and pepper. Place the lettuce on top of the chicken, then the tomato slices (season the tomato), the bacon, and then the remaining bread. Cut each sandwich in half and serve with potato chips.

VARIATIONS The sandwich will not tolerate too many frills, but avocado and bacon or pancetta were made for each other; some mild Chinese black bean mayonnaise drifts along easily with champagne or beer; some fresh-roasted pasilla chilies will drive away heavy-morning or late-night blues; and some mushroom hash butter used on the toast comes close to wonderfully excessive. Whatever or wherever, the BLT and the club are the traveler's and the night owl's ideal companions.

OPEN-FACED SANDWICHES

Almost anything tastes wonderful when put on grilled rustic bread or brioche:

+ Sliced artichokes steamed in olive oil with spring garlic, then chopped up with salted anchovies (see page 42)
+ Crabmeat tossed in rémoulade sauce (see page 251), put on hot brioche, and served with deep-fried onion rings
+ Smoked trout with curried mint rémoulade or lemon and fig relish (see page 243)
+ Lobster salad with green goddess sauce (see page 249)
+ Lobster meat with shredded limestone lettuce and Russian dressing (see page 250)
+ Grilled prawns chopped up with roasted Walla Walla sweet onion and garlic mayonnaise (see page 248)
+ Sliced roast beef with Russian dressing (the real one with caviar as on page 250)
+ Sliced roast beef with hot onion rings and smoked chili-garlic mayonnaise (see page 248)
+ Roast chicken with watercress and walnut oil salad
+ Sichuan spiced duck (see page 204) with lemon and fig relish (see page 243)
+ Country ham mousse topped with baked, melting, week-old goat cheese

But I cannot live without an egg salad sandwich.

OPEN-FACED EGG SALAD SANDWICH

SERVES 4

6	hard-cooked eggs (see page 67)
1 cup	mayonnaise (see page 247)
1 tablespoon	tarragon leaves, finely chopped
1 teaspoon	hot sauce
	Salt
4 slices	rustic bread, sliced ½ inch thick, crusts removed
	Herb flowers

Shell the eggs, and chop them very coarsely (½-inch pieces). Mix with all the other ingredients except the flowers and bread, and taste for seasoning.

Toast the bread and pile on the egg salad. Garnish with herb flowers.

VARIATION Top the sandwich with big chunks of cooked lobster tossed in a little green goddess mayonnaise (see page 249).

Open-Faced Shad Roe Toast with Chipotle Chili–Bacon Mayonnaise

Planked shad (fillets nailed onto planks that are propped up near open fires) is one of the great fish dishes of the world. But does anyone outside of expensive New York fish stores sell the fillets without the billions of bones? Unless I am at a Connecticut shad festival, I settle for the roe.

I like to cook them this way and finish them on a wood-fired grill (or under the broiler).

SERVES 4

2 pairs	fresh shad roe (4 pieces)	8 sprigs	fresh thyme
½ cup	mayonnaise (see page 247)	½ cup	clarified butter
1 tablespoon	fresh lime juice		(see page 27)
1 teaspoon	chipotle chili puree	2 tablespoons	chopped fresh parsley
8 strips	bacon	1 tablespoon	fresh lemon zest
8	bay leaves		

Mix the mayonnaise, lime juice, and chipotle puree.

Season the roes and wrap each piece with two strips of bacon. Stick the bay leaves and a sprig of fresh thyme under the bacon on each side of the roe.

In a casserole just large enough to hold the roes side by side, heat the clarified butter and sear the roes on both sides for 1 minute each. Turn down the heat, cover, and cook for 5 minutes. Turning once.

Take the roes out of the pan. Remove the bacon, and broil for 1 minute on each side until crisp. Then chop the bacon and mix it into the mayonnaise.

Grill or broil (high heat) the roes on each side for 2 minutes and serve, sprinkled with the parsley and lemon zest, with the mayonnaise on the side.

OPEN-FACED FOIE GRAS SANDWICH

SERVES 4

	Foie gras in a jar (see page 212)	2 tablespoons	hazelnut oil
4 slices	brioche, ¼-inch thick, crusts removed	pinch	ground cardamom
		2 teaspoons	freshly ground coarse black pepper
1 cup	rocket (arugula) leaves, stemmed, washed, spin-dried	8	nasturtium flowers, stemmed, shredded
1	salt-preserved lemon (see page 43), seeded, chopped		

Scoop out four large spoonfuls of foie gras and put them on a sheet of wax paper. Flatten the foie gras to the size of the brioche slices.

Toast the brioche, and while it is toasting, toss the rocket with the lemon, hazelnut oil, cardamom, and pepper.

Lift the pieces of foie gras onto the hot brioche slices, put some salad on top of each slice, and garnish with the flowers.

TRUFFLE SANDWICH

Ken Hom introduced me to this perfection of truffles, and I would be hard-pressed to think of anything edible as pleasurable as this sandwich, especially when drowned with old, barely cold champagne.

SERVES 4 TO 6

4–6 ounces	fresh black Perigord truffles, brushed to remove sand
1 pound	unsalted butter
1	large loaf 2-day-old rustic bread
	Sea salt
	Freshly ground coarse black pepper

Slice the bread ¼ inch thick. Butter each slice generously on one side. Slice the truffles ¹⁄₁₆ inch thick and lay them on the butter two layers thick. Sprinkle the truffles generously with the salt and pepper. Put a buttered slice of bread, butter side down, on top of the truffles.

Stack the sandwiches and wrap in plastic wrap that has no smell (or use aluminum foil or big zip-lock bags), and then refrigerate for 12 hours.

Preheat the oven to 400 degrees.

Put the sandwiches in one layer on a baking sheet and cook for 6 minutes on each side.

Soft-Shell Crab Po'boy Sandwich

Soft-shell crabs should be cooked very crisp on the outside, with the centers of the crabs remaining moist and full of juices. They can be sautéed or grilled, but for me, deep-frying gives the most even cooking and the crispest results. If deep-frying makes you nervous, shallow-fry them in 2 inches of hot oil in a heavy 6-inch-deep skillet, just large enough to hold them side by side without touching.

Serve with the coleslaw on page 87.

SERVES 4	
8	small, fresh soft-shell crabs
½ cup	flour
2–3 pints	peanut oil
1	long baguette (24 inches)
4 tablespoons	sweet butter
½ cup	rémoulade sauce (see page 251), made with hot mustard
	Salt and freshly ground black pepper

Clean the crabs by lifting up the side flaps and pulling off the feathery gills. Remove the flap underneath. Rinse in cold water, then pat the crabs dry with paper towels.

Heat the oil to 375 degrees.

Season the crabs, dust them very lightly with flour, and immediately but carefully put them into the hot oil, slipping them down away from you into the oil so no hot oil splashes up onto your hands. Fry the crabs for 4 minutes, then turn them over and cook 4 minutes more. Lift them out of the oil, placing them on paper towels or a rack to drain for 10 seconds before serving.

While the crabs are frying, cut the bread in half lengthwise without severing the two halves. Put the bread under the broiler until toasted and hot, then butter the bread. Cut across into four 6-inch lengths.

Put 2 crabs on each piece of bread and slather with the rémoulade.

VARIATION Use 24 deep-fried oysters instead of the crabs.

HAMBURGERS

There is a great line in the movie *Red Heat* when the American detective explains to the Russian "the four major food groups: hamburgers, French fries, donuts, and coffee."

He's not too far off, and I love the fact that some of the dishes most often associated with my cooking have been, like hamburgers, the simplest. I also love the fact that the reason for our success with things like hamburgers is that we followed some simple but essentially important rules: grind the meat yourself with its seasonings of salt and pepper; use the best quality chuck and top round; remember that if you are using a charcoal grill, the beef should have 22 percent fat, if using a flat-top griddle or frying pan, only 18 percent; do not overwork the patties; season them again just before cooking; and serve them on dense, hot buttered buns, English muffins, or baguette bread. The bread must be buttered and toasted for that final sensual "push." I love bacon or pancetta on top of burgers, and also:

- whole poached garlic cloves with basil mayonnaise
- coarsely ground black Sumatran pepper with sour cream
- avocado slices marinated in salt and lime juice served with chipotle mayonnaise
- mushroom hash (see page 17) with garlic mayonnaise (see page 248)
- chopped salt-preserved lemons (see page 43) mixed with chopped fresh mint
- fresh salsa (see page 239)
- fresh salsa, bacon, and avocado
- flavored butters, like Montpelier (see page 246)
- mayonnaise flavored with chopped capers and salted anchovies (see page 42)
- fresh sage mayonnaise
- BLT on top
- fresh horseradish cream sauce

But my favorite is the hamburger made with black truffles.

BLACK-TRUFFLED HAMBURGER

The most ethereal hamburger, my Christmas Eve or New Year's Day lunch, is one studded with fresh Perigord black truffles from the Pebeyre family in Cahors.

The fitting drink with this sandwich, and one without which the burger falls short of its overwhelming effect, is a luscious, old-fashioned, rich and powerful red wine—in a large balloon glass, so the perfumes of the wine and the truffled beef hit one's brain at the same time.

SERVES 4

1	2-ounce fresh black truffle (or if frozen, chop up while still frozen and add to the beef)	¼ cup	mayonnaise (see page 247)
		2 teaspoons	salt
		1 teaspoon	freshly ground black pepper
2 pounds	ground beef chuck, top round or ground sirloin (or a mixture)	4	English muffins (Thomas' type)
		3 tablespoons	butter

Chop the truffle finely and mix three-quarters of it into the beef by hand. Cover loosely and let the truffled meat sit at room temperature for 4 hours, so that the truffle perfume permeates the beef.

Mix the remaining truffle into the mayonnaise. Cover and refrigerate for a few hours.

Season the truffled burger meat and form it into four patties by hand, making neat edges but handling the beef as little as possible so as not to compact and toughen the meat.

Season the burgers, and then fry, griddle, or grill them.

Split the muffins and then toast or grill them and butter each half. Put the burgers on the muffins, spoon 1 tablespoon of the mayonnaise on top of each burger, top with the other muffin half, and serve at once.

PIZZA

The first time I ever saw a small individual pizza was in California in 1974 and its appearance was gratuitous and accidental.

As the chef of Chez Panisse, I was faced with deciding what to serve for the restaurant's third birthday celebration, which was planned as an all-day open house. I was looking through a favorite textbook of those days, *La Bonne cuisine du Comté de Nice* by Jacques Médecin, and on page 76 saw a recipe for something called, aptly enough, "Les Panisses." Excitement caused haste, so I didn't read the recipe carefully, noting only that it was a flat pancake type of thing with something boring on top, which I knew I could improve upon. I wrote the menu

> CHEZ PANISSE
> Menu for 3rd Birthday
> 28 August 1974
> Hors d'oeuvre Variés
> Les Panisses
> Salade Verte
> Glace de Fruits
> Demi carafe de Vin
> $5.00 tout compris

and sent it over to David Goines of St. Hieronymus Press for making into a poster.

Soon the day arrived for me to tell everyone what a "panisse" was, and to order the ingredients. I rushed back to the book and found that the recipe called for chickpea (garbanzo bean) flour, mixed with water and fried in olive oil. I found the flour in an Italian deli in Oakland, and cooked the panisses. They were disgusting. But everyone wanted to know what "panisses" were. "They are basically just like a little pizza," I lied (not knowing what else to say), "don't worry about it." Alice and everyone else was happy with that.

Pizza is what occurred to me because of the round shape of the "panisses," and since we had no room to cook large ones, small individual ones they had to be. As for what to put on them—since money was very scarce in those days—I decided on a simple California goat cheese (then brand-new to the world) and Sonoma beefsteak tomatoes.

A hundred people more than we expected showed up. Facing a crisis brought out my best thinking, and remembering there were still fresh ingredients (clams, prawns, squid, crab, lobster, onions, saffron, garlic, and fennel) left from the previous night's bouillabaisse, I decided to use them all to garnish the pizzas.

What came out of the oven changed slightly every hour all night long, depending on what was left, but it was primarily little bouillabaisse pizzas. They caused a sensation and a lot of press, so individual pizzas hit the U.S. stage, going on to other incarnations at Spago in Los Angeles and Stars in San Francisco.

Here are some favorites that evolved over the years from San Francisco to Singapore, Hong Kong, Seattle, and Manila. I've organized them into the four families of pizza.

Cooked crust topped with cold food:

- Foie gras cooked in a jar (see page 212), topped with herb flower and Italian parsley leaf salad
- Smoked sturgeon topped with chopped deviled eggs (see page 67)
- Egg salad (see page 74) or chopped deviled eggs (see page 67)
- Tricolored heirloom tomatoes (see page 65)
- Steelhead salmon roe (see page 58) and double cream (see page 27)

Cooked crust topped with hot, already-cooked food:

- Roasted and skinned pasilla chilies stuffed with fresh goat cheese, baked, chopped up while still hot, and spread on the pizza
- Rabbit chili and cilantro salad
- Fsh hash

Crust cooked halfway, food added on top, both finished together:

- Fried eggs and white truffles

Uncooked food and crust cooked together:

- Thinly sliced raw tomato, seasoned and covered with fresh basil, Fontina Val d'Aosta cheese, and some grated Parmesan

Pizza Dough

YIELDS 4 PIZZAS

1 package	(¼ ounce) dry yeast
1½ cups	water
½ cup	olive oil
5 cups	bread flour (approximate)
2 teaspoons	salt

Dissolve the yeast in the water. Let sit 10 minutes and stir in the oil. Mix in half the flour and the salt, until smooth. Then while kneading by hand or in a mixer on medium speed with a dough hook attachment, start adding the remaining flour. You may not need it all. As soon as the dough pulls away from the sides of the bowl and is no longer sticky, stop adding flour. Knead until the dough is smooth and elastic, about 15 minutes.

Put the dough in an oiled bowl and let it rise for 1 to 2 hours, or until it is doubled in size.

POTATO, FONTINA CHEESE, AND FRESH SAGE PIZZA

Many pizzas are more exotic or esoteric than this one, but simplicity of flavors should rule, without too many ingredients. This is my everyday (if I were so lucky) favorite.

When the dough is just right, one can savor the deep, simple satisfaction of biting into it and having its hot, yeast flavors float up one's nostrils, the ingredients never overpowering the dough. So this pizza is really the foundation for all good pizza, both the simple and the more architectural versions.

SERVES 4

1 recipe	pizza dough (see page 81)	4 ounces	Fontina cheese, thinly sliced
½ cup	coarse cornmeal	2 tablespoons	freshly grated Parmesan cheese
4 tablespoons	olive oil		Salt and freshly ground white pepper
1 tablespoon	fresh sage leaves, finely chopped		
2	large, yellow, waxy potatoes, peeled, sliced (⅛-inch thick)		

Put a sheet pan or pizza stone in the oven and preheat to 500 degrees.

Divide the dough into four equal pieces. Roll each piece into a 6-inch circle. Stretch each circle another 2 inches by turning and pulling it round and round in your hands. The edge should be slightly thicker than the center.

Dust the bottom of the pizza with the cornmeal, brush the top with olive oil, sprinkle with the sage, and then cover the top of the pieces of dough with one layer of potatoes, leaving a ½-inch-wide margin around the edge. Then cover the potatoes with the slices of Fontina.

Put the pizza on the stone (cornmeal side down) in the oven for 8 minutes, or until the dough is cooked through and the potatoes are tender.

Spit-Roasted Chinatown Suckling Pig Pizza

This pizza has a fully cooked crust with the already-cooked pig added for the last three minutes of cooking, just to heat it up. Or top the hot cooked crust with the already hot pork.

In Manila, this pizza was easy since a perfect boned and cooked 5-pound pig was just a telephone call away. No longer in Manila, I buy the delicious roasted pork sold in Chinatown delis.

SERVES 4

2 pounds	suckling pig or boneless roasted Chinese pork, chopped	1 tablespoon	freshly squeezed lime juice
		1 tablespoon	light sesame oil
1 recipe	pizza dough (see page 81)	¼ cup	orange Sichuan pepper salt (see page 42)
1 cup	coarse cornmeal		
4 tablespoons	olive oil	¼ cup	ketjap dipping sauce (see page 242)
1 bunch	cilantro		

Put a sheet pan or pizza stone in the oven and preheat to 500 degrees.

Divide the dough into four equal pieces. Roll each piece into a 6-inch circle. Stretch each circle another 2 inches by turning and pulling it round and round in your hands. The edge should be slightly thicker than the center.

Dust one side of the pizza with the cornmeal, brush the other with olive oil, and put on the pizza stone (cornmeal side down) in the oven for 8 minutes. Take out and cover with the chopped pork. Put back in the oven for 3 minutes.

Toss the cilantro, the lime juice, and sesame oil together.

Sprinkle the pizza with some of the salt, and put the cilantro salad on top.

Serve with the dipping sauce on the side.

CHAPTER THREE
SALADS

SALAD OF MIXED GREENS

COLESLAW

GREEN ZEBRA HEIRLOOM TOMATO SALAD

MUSHROOM SALAD

ST. JOHN'S PARSLEY AND ONION SALAD

ENGLISH AUTUMN SALAD

WARM SPINACH SALAD WITH CREAMED SALT COD TOASTS

AVOCADO AND ROCKET SALAD

SWEET PEAR AND GORGONZOLA SALAD WITH ROCKET, WATERCRESS,
WALNUTS, AND ORANGE-FLOWER HONEY

RADICCHIO AND LOBSTER SALAD

GRILLED SALT COD AND AVOCADO SALAD WITH HOT PEPPERS

SPIT-ROASTED CHICKEN COBB SALAD

CHILLED POACHED SALMON WITH WHITE BEANS AND RUSSIAN
(BLACK CAVIAR) DRESSING

SALAD OF MIXED GREENS

Now that mesclun (for more on this "mix," see page 17) is everywhere, and often has kale and little cabbage leaves or raw chard in it—I don't want to stand there for hours in the supermarket picking out the cattle food even if they would let me—I go more for mixed greens that I choose and mix myself.

I have developed many variants of the garden salad over the years. This version is the basic one, using whatever greens, flowers, and herbs you have in your garden or find in a market.

SERVES 4

1	small head curly endive	¼ cup	walnut or hazelnut oil
4	small red leaf lettuces	¼ cup	extra virgin olive oil
4	small green leaf lettuces	2 tablespoons	fresh chervil leaves
1 bunch	watercress	1 tablespoon	fresh tarragon leaves
2 tablespoons	freshly squeezed lemon juice	16	fresh rose petals
¼ teaspoon	sea salt	16	nasturtium flowers
2 pinches	freshly ground black pepper	1 tablespoon	calendula petals
		1 tablespoon	fresh sage flowers

Pick over the greens, removing any stems and blackened leaves. Use only the inside tender leaves of the endive. Wash and spin-dry the leaves. Put in a plastic bag and keep cold in the refrigerator.

Mix the lemon juice with salt and pepper in a bowl large enough to hold all the greens. Whisk in the oils.

Put the greens and herbs in the bowl. Toss together thoroughly but gently, and serve the salad on cold plates, scattering the flower petals over the salads.

VARIATIONS Use limestone lettuces whole with a dressing of one part fresh lemon juice to three parts hazelnut oil, with lemon zest sprinkled on top; or cut butter lettuce in quarters (stem removed) and dress gently in a bowl with blue cheese thinned with milk, lots of black pepper, orange zest, and chopped fresh tarragon leaves. Serve with toasts spread with finely chopped toasted walnuts mixed into one-third their volume of butter. Or take leftover cooked vegetables, chop and mix with one-third their volume of butter, and spread the vegetable butter on toasts. Bake, and serve hot with the cold salad.

COLESLAW

Of all the riches and indulgences enjoyed by my Russian uncle and his friends, lobster was the favorite, and since Russians like nothing better than to debate possible alternatives or slightly different treatments of the food they are eating, nothing brought out more heated discussion than lobster—how to cook it and what to drink with it. The decision was that it had to be served with my aunt's coleslaw, potato chips, and pilsner.

The key to the success of this coleslaw, I was gently but very firmly told, is to soak the cabbage in ice water in the refrigerator for four hours. Then the dressed slaw has to sit in the refrigerator for at least a couple of hours to achieve perfectly melded flavors and textures.

SERVES 4 TO 6

1 head	white cabbage	1 tablespoon	finely chopped fresh ginger
4	large ripe tomatoes, peeled and seeded (see page 47)	1 teaspoon	powdered ginger
½ cup	mayonnaise (see page 247)	1½ teaspoons	dry mustard
½ cup	sour cream		Salt and freshly ground black pepper

Discard any of the outer leaves of the cabbage that are wilted or discolored. Cut the cabbage in half from top to bottom and cut out the core. Put each half, cut side down, on a board and cut into ½-inch slices. Put the cabbage in a large bowl, cover with cold water and ice cubes, and refrigerate for 4 hours.

Cut each tomato half into four pieces. Mix the mayonnaise, sour cream, fresh and powdered ginger, and mustard in a bowl. Drain the cabbage very well, put in the bowl with the sauce, and mix thoroughly.

Season with salt and pepper, add the tomatoes, and toss lightly. Refrigerate covered for 2 hours. Toss one more time before serving the coleslaw, very cold.

Green Zebra Heirloom Tomato Salad

Some things that appear in the marketplace quickly become a fad; some of these are enjoyable for a while before fading away, while others end up staying because their value is apparent, clear, and real, and no one wants to live without them. Such is the case with heirloom fruits and vegetables.

I am sure that some odd things will appear, as when the obsession with overpriced "baby vegetables" produced the sorts of things serious gardeners would throw away (like leek thinnings), but these heirloom tomatoes are here to stay.

I have not tasted a yellow one that lives up to any of the green, purple, tie-dyed, rosy, and just plain red ones, but the tiny yellow cherry tomatoes are a miracle all by themselves.

The secret to tomatoes is salting them a few minutes (only) before eating them and, by the way, if you are using regular tomatoes, a sprinkle of sugar with the salt really helps to bring out "real" tomato flavors. And I don't bother to remove the skin of heirlooms.

SERVES 4

4-6	large Green Zebra heirloom tomatoes, depending on size	¼ cup	extra virgin olive oil
24	very small yellow cherry tomatoes, such as the "sweet 100s"	1 bunch	rocket, washed, stemmed, spin-dried
	Sea salt and freshly ground aromatic black pepper	½ cup	fresh basil leaves, washed, patted dry

Using a paring knife, cut down around the stem cores of the green tomatoes and remove them. Slice the tomatoes ¼-inch thick crosswise, and put them in one layer in a flat draining pan, or on a wire rack set over a pan through which the tomato juices can drain but be saved. Sprinkle the tomatoes with a teaspoon of sea salt. Let them sit for 15 minutes.

Put the water from the tomatoes in a mixing bowl large enough to hold the rocket and basil. Put the cherry tomatoes in the bowl, and smash them with a fork or potato masher. Grind a teaspoon of pepper into the bowl, and then pour in the olive oil. Whisk to form an emulsion.

Add the rocket and basil and toss around in the dressing. Serve the slices of Zebra tomato on chilled plates. Put a mound of the rocket and basil on top of the tomato slices, and scatter the remaining cherry tomatoes and dressing around the plates.

MUSHROOM SALAD

I love slicing fresh boletus mushrooms (*Boletus edulis* or cèpes or porcini) tissue thin, covering a large white plate in one layer with the slices, then serving the boletus carpaccio with extra virgin olive oil, sea salt, and lashings of freshly ground white pepper. No lemon or vinegar is needed.

And a drop of champagne vinegar in some mild, yellow extra virgin olive oil is not bad at all when lots of ⅛-inch slices of fresh Caesar's amanita mushrooms are tossed in it.

Alas, most budgets will not allow a dinner party to start off with these amanita, since unlike truffles, a little bit does not go a long way. So we will stick to delicious domestic mushrooms (*Agaricus bisporus*), though if you see the brown variants known as cremini or portobello mushrooms, they are also delicious in this salad.

SERVES 4

1 pound	white button mushrooms, cleaned	1 teaspoon	sea salt
3 tablespoons	freshly squeezed lemon juice	2-3 tablespoons	heavy cream
1 teaspoon	fresh rosemary leaves, finely chopped	2 tablespoons	finely chopped fresh chives
¼ cup	extra virgin olive oil	½ teaspoon	freshly ground white pepper

Slice the mushrooms vertically into ¹⁄₁₆-inch slices.

Put the lemon juice, rosemary, and olive oil in a bowl large enough to hold the mushrooms, and mix together. Add the mushrooms and toss gently, sprinkle with salt, and toss again until the mushrooms are coated with the oil.

Let the mushrooms sit for 5 minutes, then pour the cream over them. Toss again briefly until the cream soaks the mushrooms. Let sit 5 minutes and serve with the chives sprinkled on top and with lots of pepper.

VARIATION For a black truffle salad serving four, use 1 large fresh black Perigord truffle (or more), 2 tablespoons of extra virgin olive oil, ½ teaspoon sea salt, 1 head of curly endive, 1 tablespoon of hazelnut oil, and freshly ground white pepper. Slice the truffle on a truffle slicer, ¹⁄₁₆-inch thick. Put the slices in a salad bowl with the olive oil and salt. Mix gently and let sit while you prepare the endive. Pull off the outer leaves and discard, saving only the heart of the lettuce that is white and yellow. Wash it in iced water and spin dry. Chop the leaves into 1-inch pieces. Add the endive pieces and the hazelnut oil to the bowl with the truffles, and toss everything together. Grind some pepper over and toss again briefly. Serve.

St. John's Parsley and Onion Salad

St. John's in London is one of my favorite restaurants anywhere. It is all about simplicity without pretension, and using fresh ingredients without claiming to have invented the idea. They know these two concepts have been in England for centuries.

I have taken the liberty of adding mint.

SERVES 4			
1	large red onion, peeled	2 tablespoons	freshly squeezed lemon juice
2 cups	flat or Italian parsley leaves, washed, spin-dried	1 tablespoon	freshly grated lemon zest
		¼ cup	extra virgin olive oil
		½ teaspoon	sea salt
¼ cup	large salted capers, prepared as on page 44	2 tablespoons	chopped fresh mint
			Freshly ground black pepper

Drain the capers and put them in a bowl with the lemon juice, zest, and olive oil.

Slice the onions crosswise 1/16-inch thick and put them in a bowl, dividing them into rings. Add the sea salt and mint and toss. Cover and set aside for 10 minutes.

Add the parsley to the onion bowl, and then add everything in the caper bowl to the onion and parsley. Grind lashings of black pepper into the bowl, toss briefly, and serve with big slabs of hot grilled country bread.

ENGLISH AUTUMN SALAD

This salad is one I adapted from Robert May's *The Accomplisht Cook* (1685) and John Evelyn's *Acetaria: A Discourse of Sallets* (1699), both of which I read when growing my vegetable garden in Massachusetts in 1970. When I started as chef of Chez Panisse, I could not wait to start a garden and put these books to use in making these wonderful compound salads, as modern today as they were three hundred years ago.

Evelyn was especially inspirational, using flowers, flower buds, and all kinds of citrus in salad dressing and garnishing. I have omitted samphire (though in my college days, I used to collect it in Maine and cook with it), broom buds, pickled oysters, and "blue-fits" (whatever they are), as well as the roast capon. But by all means add sliced-up capon or any other chopped roast meat.

This is not a small salad and easily serves eight people. All the lettuces are washed in cold water and as Evelyn directs, "spin-dried" in a towel.

SERVES 8 TO 10

Leaves:

1 bunch	watercress, stemmed	1	small curly endive, stemmed, outer green tips removed
1 bunch	sorrel, stemmed, cut in coarse shreds		
1 small bunch	dandelion greens, bottom stems removed	1	small escarole, stemmed, outer green tips removed
1	small red leaf lettuce, stemmed		

Garnish:

6 leaves	fresh mint, coarsely chopped	2	ripe figs, stemmed, coarsely chopped
3	fresh sage leaves, coarsely chopped	3 tablespoons	freshly squeezed lemon juice (or unripe grape juice, called verjuice)
2 tablespoons	capers, drained, rinsed, soaked in white wine for 2 hours, chopped (see page 44)	3 tablespoons	extra virgin olive oil
		¼ cup	walnut oil
4	jumbo black California marinated olives (see page 54), chopped	1	small radicchio, stemmed, cut in fine shreds
		1 tablespoon	orange zest
		¾ teaspoon	sea salt
2 tablespoons	toasted walnuts, coarsely chopped	1¼ teaspoons	freshly ground black pepper

Put all the leaves in a large chilled bowl.

Put the mint, sage, capers, olives, walnuts, and figs in a bowl. Add the lemon juice, and then ½ teaspoon of the salt and 1 teaspoon of the black pepper. Mix until the salt is dissolved. Beat in the olive and walnut oils with a fork.

Pour this sauce over the greens and toss together well. Sprinkle the radicchio and orange zest over the top of the salad, and add a little more salt and pepper to the top.

Warm Spinach Salad with Creamed Salt Cod Toasts

A warm or "wilted" spinach salad is the perfect way to learn the principles of wilted or warm, leafy greens salads: season and acidify the greens and herbs and any garnish (like vegetables or meats) first, then pour over the hot oil or fat. Rendered bacon fat is traditional, but rendered duck or poultry fat, or country ham fat, or mixtures of oils like nut oils and olive are also wonderful.

The choice of acid is between vinegar and citrus juices, and I particularly like sherry vinegar for spinach.

Remember when washing spinach (and all salad greens) to lift it out of the washing water into its second washing or drying spinner, not to pour it out, in which case the sand falls back onto the spinach.

SERVES 4

2 bunches	spinach, stemmed, washed, dried, at room temperature	2 tablespoons	walnut oil
1 cup	creamed salt cod (see page 174)	8	nasturtium flowers, stemmed, torn into pieces
1	baguette loaf of bread		Sea salt
¼ cup	extra virgin olive oil		Freshly ground pepper
1 tablespoon	sherry vinegar		
1 tablespoon	fresh marjoram leaves, finely chopped		

Preheat the oven to 400 degrees.

Cut 8 slices from a baguette diagonally across the loaf, ½-inch thick. Brush 2 tablespoons of the olive oil on the bread slices, then put them on a baking tray and into the oven for 5 minutes. Remove and cool.

Spread the creamed cod thickly on the toasts and put back in the oven for 5 minutes.

Put the spinach in a bowl; add the sherry vinegar, marjoram, ½ teaspoon of salt and lashings of black pepper. Toss together well.

Put the remaining olive oil and the walnut oil in a small saucepan and heat almost to the smoking point. Pour the hot oils over and around the salad. Mix the spinach well and very quickly. Serve immediately with 2 toasts on the side of each plate, and the nasturtium flowers on top.

AVOCADO AND ROCKET SALAD

Rocket or arugula (*Eruca sativa*; also called *rucola* in Italian, and *roquette* in French) is one of my favorite things. Its perfect liaisons are avocado, and nut oils, like hazelnut and walnut. Rocket and avocado is one of those flavor combinations made in heaven, like rosemary and lamb, savory and favas, and vanilla and cream.

I see no reason why in America we should not call rocket by its venerable old English name, even if in danger of appearing guilty of inverse affectation.

SERVES 4

2	ripe avocados	½ cup	chopped tomato
2 tablespoons	freshly squeezed lime juice		(see page 47)
¼ cup	walnut oil	pinch	salt
1 tablespoon	extra virgin olive oil	pinch	freshly ground
1 cup	fresh chervil leaves		black pepper
½ cup	mayonnaise (see page 247)		
1	large bunch young rocket, stemmed, washed, dried		

Put the lime juice, salt, and pepper in a salad bowl, and mix together. Once the salt has dissolved, whisk in the two oils.

Chop the chervil leaves very finely and mix them into the mayonnaise.

When ready to serve the salads, cut the avocados in half lengthwise, remove the pits, and scoop out the flesh in one piece with a large spoon. Put the avocado halves cut face down on a board, and slice them crosswise into ⅛-inch-thick slices. Pick each half up with a knife or flat spatula, and lift it onto a chilled plate. Press down with your hand to fan out each half.

Put the rocket in the bowl with the lime dressing, and toss until the rocket is well coated. Then put the rocket on the inside curve of the fanned-out avocado. Put the tomato in the same salad bowl, and toss it in whatever lime juice and oil is left. Put the tomato on top of the rocket.

Drizzle the chervil mayonnaise over the salads.

VARIATIONS Instead of using chervil, flavor the mayonnaise with 1 tablespoon chopped fresh galingale (or young pink ginger) and ½ tablespoon chipotle chili puree (canned is fine). And if you can find Rangpur limes, use the juice and grated zest from them.

Sweet Pear and Gorgonzola Salad with Rocket, Watercress, Walnuts, and Orange-Flower Honey

This salad first appeared in Robin Leach's *Lifestyles of the Rich and Famous* (1986) cookbook and became an instant hit in my restaurants because the intense flavor of the pears is concentrated by long and slow heating.

If you can find Zante or Champagne grapes, they are the perfect garnish for this dish, but Concords would not be bad either.

SERVES 4

4	ripe Comice pears, prepared as for oven-roasted fruits on page 138	½ cup	walnuts, toasted, coarsely chopped
1 tablespoon	freshly squeezed lemon juice	2 tablespoons	orange flower honey
¼ cup	walnut oil	½ cup	edible flowers, such as sage, rocket blossoms, rose petals or nasturtiums
1 bunch	watercress, washed, spin-dried, stemmed		
1 bunch	rocket, washed, spin-dried, stemmed	pinch	salt
¼ cup	fresh basil leaves	pinch	freshly ground black pepper
¼ pound	Gorgonzola, rind removed, crumbled		

When the pears are cool enough to handle, remove the cores and slice them crosswise in ⅛-inch sections.

Put the lemon juice in a salad bowl with salt and pepper and mix to dissolve the salt, then whisk in the oil. Arrange the slices of pears one pear per plate, in one layer in the center of the plate, leaving a 3-inch gap in the center for the watercress and rocket. Scatter the cheese and then the walnuts over the pears, and then drizzle the honey on top of the walnuts and cheese.

Put the watercress, rocket, and basil in the salad bowl and toss together. Then place the salad in the center of the pears.

Garnish with the flowers.

VARIATION I like to make this salad with ripe white peaches and rose peppercorns sprinkled over the peaches and cheese.

RADICCHIO AND LOBSTER SALAD

There is something irresistible about the radicchio and endive families, especially when paired with lobster. My favorites are the three from Treviso (excluding the fourth, the rounded one with compact leaves called Chioggia, which one sees most often)—the incredibly beautiful lettuce-shaped one that is creamy light green with purple shot through it (Castelfranco), the slightly blanched one with small leaves called *Treviso tardivo*, and the full Belgian endive–shaped one with big long leaves called *radicchio di Treviso rosso precoce*—and red or white Belgian endive (*Cichorium intybus*).

Add hazelnut oil, tarragon, and a whisper of garlic, and you have an instant and outstanding Saturday lunch.

Please remember to cut the radicchio and endive at the last minute so they will not brown.

The lobster essence and the steelhead eggs push the dish way up the satisfaction scale, but don't dismiss the salad if you do not have them.

SERVES 4

2	radicchios of Treviso, either the late-season one or the long-leafed one, or regular radicchio	1 tablespoon	lobster essence (see page 188)
		1 tablespoon	freshly squeezed lemon juice
		½ teaspoon	finely chopped garlic
2	Belgian endives	20 leaves	fresh tarragon
1 cup	cooked Maine lobster meat (method II, page 175)	1 tablespoon	extra virgin olive oil
		3 tablespoons	hazelnut oil
4 ounces	fresh steelhead eggs (see page 58)		Salt and freshly ground black pepper

Mix the lobster essence, lemon juice, garlic, tarragon, and salt and pepper to taste in a bowl. Whisk in the oils.

Cut the bottom cores out of the Treviso radicchios and endives. Trim away any brown spots, and pull the Treviso and endive leaves apart. Cut the leaves of the endive one-third lengthwise into long thin strips and leave the Treviso leaves whole.

Put the Treviso leaves in a salad bowl and pour one-third of the dressing over them. Toss gently, then arrange them in a circle like spokes of a wheel, curved side down, on four chilled plates. Put the endive strips in the bowl and pour another third of the dressing over them. Toss gently, and put the endive in the center of the circle of Treviso leaves.

Put the lobster meat in the bowl and dress with the remaining sauce. Put the lobster on top of the endive, and spoon the steelhead eggs onto the Treviso leaves.

CHILLED POACHED SALMON WITH WHITE BEANS AND RUSSIAN (BLACK CAVIAR) DRESSING

The best poached salmon—hot or cold—will be from a fish poached whole, but that is a lot of fish and expense if not for a lot of people. So if you are cooking for four, buy a whole piece of filet and cook it very slowly, so that it does not dry out and get that white "cardboard" effect on the outer layer of flesh.

For poached salmon (or any other fish) to be served at room temperature or slightly chilled, it is best to leave it in the poaching liquid to cool down, since it stays more moist that way and picks up added flavor. This makes the timing more difficult, however, so take into account the decreased cooking time involved if you are using this method.

Save the strained poaching liquid for soups, or reduce with white wine for fish essence (see page 188). By all means, feel free to add some cooked artichoke bottoms (sliced and marinated in lemon juice, olive oil, and black pepper) to the white beans. Or celery root done the same way. And don't forget to get some cheesecloth before starting this dish.

SERVES 4

2 pounds	salmon fillet, skin left on	1 tablespoon	freshly grated lime zest
1 quart	vegetable stock (see page 143)	2 cups	cooked white beans (see page 33)
4 sprigs	fresh tarragon, stemmed, stems and leaves saved separately, leaves chopped	1 tablespoon	finely chopped fresh garlic
		1 teaspoon	powdered cardamom
3	bay leaves	2 tablespoon	finely chopped shallots
¼ cup	extra virgin olive oil	¾ cup	Russian dressing (see page 250)
1 tablespoon	freshly squeezed lime juice		Salt and freshly ground black pepper

Wrap the salmon fillet in cheesecloth, tying the ends and leaving 4-inch pieces on each end as "handles." Put the salmon in a pan just large enough to hold the fillet, and add the stock. It should cover the fish by 1 inch. If it does not, add water. Add the tarragon stems and bay leaves. If the stock is not salted, add 1 tablespoon salt.

Bring to a bare simmer over high heat, then turn off the heat. Let the fish sit 5 to 10 minutes depending on the thickness of the fillet. By all means, lift it out to check for doneness. If the fish is raw in the center put it back. If just barely translucent in the center, it is done. Let the stock cool and put the fish back in the cooled stock. Then unwrap the salmon and remove the cheesecloth. Remove the skin, and divide the salmon into portions. Mix the olive oil with the lime juice, the chopped tarragon leaves, and a pinch of salt. Brush the mixture over the salmon and set aside.

When ready to serve the salmon, mix the white beans, garlic, cardamom, lime zest, and shallots together. Salt and pepper generously.

Put the beans in the center of the plates, the salmon pieces on top of the beans, and a dollop of the caviar-infused Russian dressing (see page 250) on top of each piece of fish, passing the rest of the sauce.

VARIATION Mix four slices of chopped cooked hot bacon or pancetta and a tablespoon of shredded rose petals into the white beans, or put the salmon in the center of some cooked vegetables (green beans, asparagus, favas, carrots, and so on) marinated in lemon juice, basil, and sesame oil. Then sprinkle chopped hot bacon or pancetta on top along with the shredded roses or other flowers.

GRILLED SALT COD AND AVOCADO SALAD WITH HOT PEPPERS

The flavor of the chilies is more important here than their heat, so I have chosen poblano chilies, seared over the fire to remove the skin and cooked a bit to bring out the flavors. If you cannot find poblanos, use Anaheims, either red or green.

Make your own salted cod, especially since a lightly salted piece of fish is more suitable for this dish. If you buy it, get the kind that comes in boxes because it is fleshier and less dry than a whole fish and prepare it as on page 174.

This recipe is for a main course for lunch or a summer supper. Use a smaller piece of fish if serving it as a first course.

SERVES 4

4 pieces	fresh cod, each 4 ounces (about 2 inches thick)	½ tablespoon	chipotle chili puree (canned is fine)
4 cups	wet brine (see page 22)	2	ripe avocados
½ cup	extra virgin olive oil	1 tablespoon	freshly squeezed lime juice
2 sprigs	fresh thyme, stemmed, leaves coarsely chopped	1 cup	warm shrimp sauce (see page 237)
3	fresh poblano chilies		Salt and freshly ground black pepper
½ cup	sour cream		
10 leaves	fresh mint, finely chopped		

Put the pieces of cod in a 4-to 6- inch-deep dish just large enough to hold them. Pour the cold brine over them, cover with cling-wrap, and refrigerate for 8 to 10 hours. Then wipe the fish pieces dry, rinse and dry the dish, and put the fish back in it along with the olive oil and thyme. Rub this mixture all over the fish and let sit for an hour.

Meanwhile, roast the chilies over a flame until the skins are blistered all over. Put them in a dish, cover, and let sit for 15 minutes. Then take out the stems and seeds, and scrape off the blistered skin. Chop the chilies coarsely.

Put the sour cream in a bowl with the mint and the chipotle puree, mix well, and taste for salt.

Halve the avocados, scoop out the flesh in one piece with a spoon, and slice them across in ⅛-inch pieces. Fan the halves out lengthwise on chilled plates, and slice down their centers again lengthwise, pushing each piece apart to leave a space in the middle for the fish.

Wipe the thyme off the fish, salt and pepper the pieces, and grill or broil 5 to 10 minutes, or until the flesh just starts to lose its translucency in the center. Put the fish in the center space of the avocados, spoon some of the shrimp vinaigrette over the fish and avocado, and put a dollop of the chipotle cream on top of each piece of fish.

SPIT-ROASTED CHICKEN COBB SALAD

Which of the world's hundreds of chicken salads to choose? Obviously the easiest and most delicious one. I love the simple "Club Salad" of Jim Beard, who credits the women's committee of the Baltimore Museum for taking a chicken B.L.T. club sandwich, removing the toast, and turning it into a salad.

I love chicken and lobster together, making a salad with sliced celery, cooked thin green beans, cooked celery root, and watercress dressed in walnut oil, lemon juice, and chopped shallots, with lobster mayonnaise on top of the chicken and lobster. I believe the best chicken salads come from large rotisserie-roasted birds. I pull one apart, marinate it with chopped fresh thyme and a little olive oil, and put it on a bed of curly endive dressed with lemon and walnut oil. On top of the chicken, first throw some chopped jicama and water chestnuts (with basil, olive oil, salt, and pepper), then green goddess sauce (see page 249), and then a cilantro salad dressed with lemon juice and sesame oil.

But my favorite is this spit-roasted chicken Cobb salad with pancetta and avocado. If you have a store with spit-roasted chicken that you trust, use them for this recipe if you don't want to roast the chicken yourself.

SERVES 4 TO 6

1	spit-roasted chicken		4	hard-boiled eggs (see page 67), shelled, quartered
1 tablespoon	fresh thyme leaves, finely chopped		2	ripe avocados, peeled, pitted, chopped into ½-inch cubes
1 tablespoon	freshly squeezed lemon juice			
2 tablespoons	olive oil		½ cup	blue cheese, rindless, crumbled
8 strips	pancetta or apple-wood smoked bacon		¾ cup	mixed chopped fresh herbs (basil, chives, Italian parsley, tarragon, chervil, marjoram)
2 tablespoons	white wine vinegar			
6 tablespoons	extra virgin olive oil			
½ cup	chopped tomato (see page 47)			Salt and freshly ground black pepper
1	small head romaine lettuce, cored, stemmed, roughly chopped (¾ inch pieces)			

Take the meat off the chicken and pull it apart by hand into bite-sized pieces. Chop the skin and mix it with the meat. Add the thyme and lemon juice, salt and pepper, mix well, and whisk in the oil. Add the chicken and toss it in the olive oil–lemon dressing. The seasoned chicken will hold for a day in the refrigerator, but when serving, make sure it is room temperature.

Broil the pancetta or bacon, drain, and chop coarsely.

Put the vinegar with salt and pepper in a chilled salad bowl, and whisk in the olive oil. Put the tomatoes in a little bowl, add a tablespoon of the dressing, season, and mix.

Put the romaine in the salad bowl, and place the pancetta, eggs, avocado, blue cheese, and fresh herbs in alternate piles on top of the lettuce just inside the edge of the bowl, two piles of each. Then place the tomatoes in the center of the lettuce.

At the table, toss the whole thing together for 2 minutes and provide a pepper grinder.

CHAPTER FOUR

SOUPS

GRILLED FISH GAZPACHO

CHILLED FRESH PEA AND FAVA BEAN SOUP WITH ROSE PETAL CREAM

CHILLED MUSHROOM SOUP WITH SPICED CRAB

CHILLED MELON AND WHITE NECTARINE SOUP
WITH RED CHILI RICOTTA

FAST AND EASY LIGHTLY CREAMED LEFTOVER VEGETABLE SOUP

TWENTY-MINUTE SPRING GREENS AND HERB SOUP
WITH ASPARAGUS

EASY FISH SOUP

FISH SOUP

OYSTER SOUP WITH CAVIAR

RICH MUSSEL BISQUE WITH SHRIMPMEAT GARLIC TOASTS
AND NASTURTIUMS

CREAM OF BOLETUS SOUP

PARSNIP SOUP WITH WHITE TRUFFLES

ROASTED EGGPLANT AND LENTIL SOUP WITH CUMIN,
LIME, MINT, AND BASIL

COLD SOUPS

GRILLED FISH GAZPACHO

In the first version of this dish, I used grilled Caribbean or Pacific "painted" spiny lobster meat in the centers of the big, flat oval dishes on which I presented the soup. Later, in the south of France, I used Mediterranean slipper lobster, then in Sydney and Singapore we used bay lobster or "Balmain bugs." But whatever the lobster, there were always three American caviars for garnish: golden whitefish from the Great Lakes, paddlefish from Louisiana, and steelhead from the Northwest.

Nowadays I eat the lobsters by themselves, the caviar by itself, and serve this wonderful summer soup with ancho chili–grilled fish salad instead of the lobster. It is delicious, fast, as impressive as the lobster version, and a great deal cheaper.

Since the success of this dish depends on the flavor of the tomatoes, my favorite way to do it is to use three different colors (and flavors) of heirloom varieties—red, green, and yellow—and to garnish the soup with tiny cherry tomatoes, also of different colors. Sometimes, I roll these little tomatoes in orange Sichuan pepper salt (see page 42) before putting them on the plate, and sometimes I just sprinkle that salt all over each of the dishes at the table.

SERVES 4

8 ounces	fresh fish fillet (cod, snapper, halibut, striped bass)	1	red bell pepper
1 stem	fresh basil, coarsely chopped	1	yellow bell pepper
½ cup	extra virgin olive oil	1	English cucumber
2 tablespoons	ancho chili puree (see page 32)	3 tablespoons	freshly squeezed lemon juice
½ cup	sour cream	1 tablespoon	sesame oil
6	large ripe tomatoes (2 red, 2 yellow, 2 green like Zebra)	12	fresh chive stems, cut into 1-inch lengths
			Salt and freshly ground black pepper

Mix the basil and the oil in a bowl, and spread the mixture on both sides of the fish fillet. Cover and let the fish marinate for an hour in the refrigerator.

Mix the ancho chili puree and sour cream together in a bowl, cover, and refrigerate.

Peel, seed (see page 47), and puree the three types of tomatoes one at a time through a food mill. Refrigerate the three purees separately.

Wipe the marinade off the fish, season, and grill or broil until just cooked, 5 to 10 minutes. Flake the fish (½-inch pieces) into the bowl with the sour cream, removing any bones. Season and mix well, but without breaking up the fish too much.

Stem and seed the bell peppers and cut into ⅛-inch dice. Peel and seed the cucumber and cut into ⅛-inch dice. Combine the peppers and cucumber in a bowl. Add the lemon juice, sesame oil, and a pinch each of salt and pepper. Mix and refrigerate (not for more than 10 minutes).

Mix each of the tomato purees with a small pinch each of salt and pepper, and whisk 2 tablespoons of the remaining olive oil into each puree.

Pour the purees onto chilled large rimmed shallow plates, making whatever pattern you like. Put the fish salad in the center of the plates, and scatter the pepper and cucumber mixture around the plates.

Sprinkle the chives on top of the fish. Serve immediately.

VARIATIONS Instead of the fish fillet, use spiced crab (see page 105). Or grill any fish and mix it with one of the flavored mayonnaises on page 247.

CHILLED FRESH PEA AND FAVA BEAN SOUP WITH ROSE PETAL CREAM

The secrets of this very simple soup and its big impact are: use very fresh, first-crop tender young peas and fava beans; cook them in the moisture of the lettuce; cook quickly; and then chill the puree immediately in a bowl already sitting in an ice bath. This instant chilling holds the fresh flavor and color of the peas and beans.

Do not make this soup more than four hours in advance or the fresh flavors will be compromised.

SERVES 4

1	Bibb lettuce, cored, leaves separated	1	sprig winter savory
1	medium white onion, peeled, finely chopped	4	sprigs fresh chervil
2 cups	fresh garden peas (1½ pounds of pods)	4	fresh mint leaves
		½ cup	heavy cream
1 cup	fresh fava beans, podded and peeled twice		Salt and freshly ground white pepper
2	sprigs Italian parsley	2	large deep pink roses, petals only

Put the lettuce and onion in a stainless-steel heavy-bottomed pot that has a cover. Add a pinch of salt and ½ cup water, then cover and "sweat" over very low heat until the lettuce and onion are just tender (5 minutes).

Prepare an ice bath and put a metal bowl in it.

Add the peas, fava beans, herbs, and 3 cups of boiling water to the pot, and simmer another 5 to 10 minutes, or until the peas are tender. Immediately pour the cooked vegetable mixture into the bowl in the ice bath. Stir until cold, and then puree. Season, strain, and keep cold over the ice bath.

Put three-quarters of the rose petals in a food processor and puree until fairly smooth. Add the cream and a pinch of salt, and process for a few seconds until the cream has some body. Cut the rest of the petals into fine strips.

Serve the soup in chilled open bowls with a dollop of the rose cream in the center. Scatter the "chiffonade" of petals over the soup.

VARIATION If you balk at roses, make one puree of ½ cup cooked fresh corn, and one of ½ cup chopped tomatoes cooked for 2 minutes. Whisk heavy cream into both until each puree has enough body to stay on top of the soup. Then you have three colors, light green, yellow, and red, and three flavors that all complement each other.

Chilled Mushroom Soup with Spiced Crab

Any edible mushrooms I have ever tasted make a soup far greater than the effort it takes to make it. I would probably not tell you to make Caesar's Amanita mushrooms into a soup, but if I lived outside Florence all one winter I would, and garnish it with one of those sausages made out of a cock's head and neck. Here we won't. Another garnish that would tempt me is black trumpet mushrooms that I would sweat in olive oil and garlic and then mix with artichoke mascarpone (a puree of artichoke leaves, sieved and mixed into mascarpone with some chopped Italian parsley leaves).

I have made this soup as a jellied consommé and piled pickled crayfish tails on top. And I have served it hot, mixed with parsnip puree, with a little corn pudding soufflé in the center, topped with ancho chili and basil creams.

But I love it cold with curried crabmeat or prawns.

SERVES 4

1 pound	white button mushrooms	½ cup	sour cream
1 tablespoon	butter	4–6 ounces	fresh crabmeat, picked over
1	small leek, trimmed of root		for shell fragments
	and end of greens,	2 cups	chicken stock (see page 215)
	chopped, washed	½ cup	heavy cream
½ cup	chopped celery, washed		Herb flowers, such as
2	cloves garlic, peeled,		chives, sage, and hyssop
	chopped		Salt and freshly ground
1	sprig fresh thyme		black pepper
2 tablespoons	chopped fresh parsley		
2 tablespoons	Indian spice mix		
	(see page 38)		

Melt the butter in a pot. Add the leek, celery, garlic, thyme, and parsley. Cover and sweat over low heat for 5 minutes.

While this is cooking, add the Indian spice mix to the sour cream and mix well. Cover and keep chilled, stirring a couple of times to thoroughly dissolve the Indian spice mix in the cream. It should sit at least 30 minutes. Then gently mix the crabmeat into the spice cream.

Uncover the pot with the vegetables. Stir in the mushrooms and a pinch of salt. Cover and sweat another 10 minutes. Add the chicken stock, bring to a simmer, and cook for 5 minutes more.

Prepare an ice bath and place a bowl in it.

Puree the mushrooms and vegetables, and put them through a coarse sieve into the bowl in the ice bath. Stir the soup until it is cold, and then add the heavy cream. Season and keep chilled (but not too cold) until ready to serve.

Serve in chilled open soup bowls or plates, with a dollop of the curried crabmeat in the center. Scatter the herb flowers over the crab.

VARIATION Fast mushroom soup: Make some mushroom hash as on page 17, then mix it with half its volume of cream, heat but do not boil, and season. Serve with a piece of garlic toast on top.

CHILLED MELON AND WHITE NECTARINE SOUP WITH RED CHILI RICOTTA

When it is so hot that no food really appeals, fruit soups will always awaken a flagging appetite—especially if there are a few bottles of Muscat or Alsatian Riesling in an ice bucket nearby.

SERVES 4

1	ripe honeydew melon, rind and white cut off, cubed (about 2 cups)	¼ teaspoon	cardamom powder
		1 cup	Riesling
6	large ripe white nectarines or peaches	1 teaspoon	freshly squeezed lemon juice
1	cup ricotta cheese	¼ teaspoon	salt
1-2 tablespoons	milk		Edible flowers, like nasturtiums
1 teaspoon	red chili flakes		

Mix the ricotta, 1 tablespoon of the milk, the chili, cardamom, and a little salt to taste. Let the mixture sit for an hour. If the ricotta is too stiff (it should be like ice cream just beginning to soften) then mix in some more milk.

Bring a pot of water to the boil and prepare an ice bath.

Put the nectarines or peaches in the boiling water for 10 seconds, then lift them out with a slotted spoon and put them in the ice bath.

The moment the fruit is cool enough to handle, peel, pit, and chop it. Reserve the ice bath. Put the nectarine pieces in a nonreactive steel saucepan and add ¼ cup water, half the wine, and the lemon juice. Add the melon, cover, and bring to the boil. Cook 10 to 15 minutes, or until the nectarines are tender enough to be pureed. While the fruit is cooking, place a bowl in the ice bath and add more ice if necessary. Immediately, put the fruit in the iced bowl, stirring the mixture constantly until it is cold. Puree the fruit mixture and keep chilled.

Taste the fruit puree for salt, add the remaining wine, and serve it in chilled, shallow soup plates with a dollop of the spiced ricotta in the center and the flowers sprinkled on top.

VARIATIONS I like the combinations of watermelon and raspberry (heat together 5 minutes, sieve, chill, and serve with basil cream); also plum and raspberry; or strawberry with red currants. And if you ever see cloudberries, or brook cloudberries, run, don't walk, to the cash register with all of them. They are the noblest of all berries, and are found in British Columbia and northern Europe. And for a greater visual impact with this soup, use two or three kinds of melons, pureed separately and put separately on the plate to produce two or three colors.

HOT SOUPS

FAST AND EASY LIGHTLY CREAMED LEFTOVER VEGETABLE SOUP

I am almost embarrassed to give this recipe (but only almost) because it is so simple. I am not embarrassed, however, at how delicious it is.

It is a recipe that changes depending or what leftover vegetables you have, but not in the way it is made. The procedure is so basic that my cooks rarely got it right, most of them having no confidence that a lack of complex procedures could achieve great effects. The concept is this: take all your leftover cooked vegetables, chop them finely, add equal amounts of stock and light cream, bring the mixture almost but not quite to a boil, season, and serve.

All vegetables go together, but bear in mind that anything from the cabbage family will dominate, as will mushrooms.

SERVES 4 TO 6

2 cups	cooked leftover vegetables
2 cups	chicken stock (see page 215)
2 cups	half-and-half
	Salt and freshly ground white pepper

Using a food processor, chop the vegetables into ⅛-inch cubes.

Put them in a saucepan, add the stock and cream, and heat, but not to a boil. Season and serve immediately.

VARIATIONS Use just stock (no cream), with a dollop of one of the simple or compound butters in the Sauces and Relishes chapter (see page 245). Throw chopped herbs on top; I also love to take a piece of stale baguette, cut it lengthwise ⅛-inch thick, toast it, and spread with Crescenza cheese, or top it with chopped yellow and red tomatoes and basil and float it in the soup.

Twenty-Minute Spring Greens and Herb Soup with Asparagus

Until the advent of year-round fresh produce, every Western country had a version of this early spring soup, created in celebration of the first life-giving young shoots appearing in the fields after a long bleak winter. For a population starved of fresh vegetables, these soups were something of a spring tonic, fast, easy, and very healthy. Called "green" soup, or "garden" soup, it uses whatever greens and herbs are in the garden: lettuces, endives, sorrel, herbs (including parsley and lovage), vegetable tops, and watercress. Water as the base will give a purer, truer taste of the greens themselves. A light chicken stock will make it richer, but I prefer water.

Serve it either hot or cold. If cold I put the soup into a bowl, sitting it in an ice bath immediately after it is pureed so the flavors and colors are set.

SERVES 4 TO 6

1 cup	loosely packed sorrel leaves, stemmed	1	large potato, peeled, diced
½ cup	loosely packed watercress leaves	4 cups	water or chicken stock (see page 215)
6 cups	loosely packed tender mixed lettuce leaves, coarsely chopped	¼ cup	half-and-half
1½ teaspoons	fresh tarragon leaves	2	hard-boiled eggs (see page 67), shelled, whites and yolks sieved separately
2 tablespoons	fresh basil leaves		Salt and freshly ground black pepper
1 tablespoon	fresh chervil leaves		
8 stems	thick asparagus, peeled (see page 119), cut into 1-inch pieces		

Put the potato and water or chicken stock in a saucepan. Add 1½ teaspoons of salt and bring to a boil. Simmer until the potato is tender, about 10 minutes.

When the potato is cooked, add the sorrel, watercress, lettuce, tarragon, basil, and chervil. Bring back to a boil over high heat, until the greens are wilted, stirring to make sure the leaves cook evenly. Puree the soup, leaving some texture to the leaves. Stir in the cream and season the soup.

Cook the asparagus in salted water for 5 to 8 minutes, or until tender. Drain them on a paper towel for 1 minute.

Divide the asparagus among the centers of hot shallow soup plates. Fill the bowls with soup, and then sprinkle the egg yolks and whites over the surface of the soup.

VARIATIONS Add a tablespoon of butter to the center of each soup plate before pouring in the soup, and shave a few black truffles over it, or add some of the first-crop morels, stewed in butter and chopped.

Easy Fish Soup

This soup is an adaptation from old Floridian cookery, specifically Tarpon Springs, with its Greek influence evident in the lemon-egg-garlic enriching and thickening treatment at the end.

Sea bass, monkfish, ling cod, or halibut would be almost as good as the red snapper.

SERVES 4

2 pounds	red snapper fillets, skinned, cut into 1-inch cubes	1 teaspoon	fresh thyme leaves, chopped
1	large red onion, peeled, finely chopped	¼ cup	olive oil
2 stalks	celery, finely chopped	3 cups	fish stock (see page 187)
2	bay leaves	3	egg yolks
1 teaspoon	fresh oregano or marjoram leaves, chopped	1	lemon, juiced
3	sprigs parsley, stemmed, chopped	2	cloves garlic, peeled, very finely chopped
			Salt and freshly ground black pepper

Mix the fish, onion, celery, bay leaves, and herbs together and let marinate for 1 hour. Then separate the vegetables from the fish and put them in a pot. Add the oil, ¼ cup of the fish stock, the bay leaves, and the herbs from the marinade. Cover and sweat over low heat for 15 minutes.

Add the fish and a pinch of salt and continue sweating another 5 minutes, then add the remaining fish stock. Over high heat, bring the stock almost to a boil and turn off the heat. Skim off any scum from the surface of the soup. If the fish is not already cooked (tender and opaque all the way through), leave it in the pot a couple of minutes. When done, remove the fish and keep it warm, leaving the broth in the pot.

Beat the egg yolks, lemon juice, and garlic together. Bring the broth back to a boil, turn off the heat, wait a minute, stir ½ cup of the broth into the egg mixture, then stir it all into the soup. Stir until the soup thickens a bit. Check the seasoning and return the fish to the soup. Serve immediately in a tureen and pass lots of garlic bread rubbed with red pepper flakes.

FISH SOUP

In her great *French Provincial Cooking* (1960), Elizabeth David stated that she didn't think it possible to make fish soup "without all those odd little Mediterranean fish, which are too bony to be used for anything except 'la soupe.'" But she changed her mind after tasting my London version a couple of times, deciding that a more than passable facsimile could be made outside of France, as long as there were enough varieties of cheap fish in the soup. "Bony" is the clue here: we are talking the uglier the fish, the better, especially the kind that hide out around or under rocks.

The soup takes two days, and costs a fortune if you include shellfish, but the reward comes when the tureen is brought to the table, and one sees a faded but deep coral-pink liquid, the hue of worn Mexican tiles, and smells the rich aroma of the ocean when the top is lifted off. The taste is as broad a spectrum of flavors and essences as anything I know. If you have ever loved the sea and fish and shellfish, you'll find their entire mystery in that bowl of simple liquid.

If you forgo the shellfish and use only fish carcasses (of non-oily white-fleshed fish: cod, bass, rockfish, conger eel, and flatfish), the results, though not sublime, are still really delicious.

The soup is not clear because it has "body" from pureeing the carcasses after they are cooked.

You will need a food mill.

SERVES 6 TO 8

6 pounds	fish carcasses and heads		1 piece	orange zest, 3 inches by 1 inch
½ cup	olive oil		2 quarts	rich fish stock (see page 187)
2	large onions, peeled, thinly sliced		½ teaspoon	saffron threads
4	large ripe tomatoes, chopped		1 cup	dry white wine
10	cloves fresh garlic		1 cup	red pepper–garlic mayonnaise (see page 248)
3	sprigs fennel tops		8	toasts, ¼-inch thick, 3 inches in diameter
1	large herb bundle (see page 16) of thyme, bay leaves, leek tops, parsley			Salt and freshly ground black pepper

Remove all innards and gills from the fish heads and carcasses.

Put ¼ cup of the olive oil, the onions, tomatoes, garlic, fennel, herb bundle, orange zest, and ½ cup of the fish stock in a 5-quart pot. Cook over low heat for 5 minutes. Add the fish carcasses and heads and the remaining stock. Bring to a boil and skim off any scum from the surface of the stock. Simmer for 20 minutes. Warm the saffron in the white wine. Add the saffron-infused wine to the stock and simmer 25 minutes more.

Take the stock off the heat and put the fish and broth through a food mill fitted with a medium-hole disk or press it through a coarse sieve. Clean the pot and return the broth to it. Correct the seasoning if necessary and serve very hot in large soup plates. Spoon the garlic mayonnaise (*rouille*) onto the toasts and float them on the soup.

VARIATIONS Double fish soup: If you want truly amazing essence-of-fish soup, repeat this process all over again, using this soup as the fish stock to pour over a new batch of fish bones.

If you want a clear double fish soup, served either hot, or cold as a jellied soup, then do not puree the mass of fish (and shellfish), but rather decant the stock each time from the debris of the cooked fish. If you are near a place where Dungeness or blue crabs are cheap, then use one-third fish and two-thirds crab, the first time fish only, and then the crab just long enough the second time to cook it. That way you get to have hot or cold cracked crab as well as the soup, which I would garnish with tortillas cut in strips and lightly toasted, and a teaspoon of finely chopped serrano chilies.

Or turn this into a "minestrone," as at Prunier in Paris, by adding cooked white beans (see page 33), green tagliarini, mussels, and vegetables; or stuff cooked large pasta tubes or squash blossoms with shellfish or mushroom hash (see page 17), and put them in the soup.

OYSTER SOUP WITH CAVIAR

A great soup from unsung American (New York) hero Michael Field takes only fifteen minutes to make once you have the freshly shucked fresh oysters.

SERVES 4 TO 6	
20	fresh oysters, shucked, kept in their "liquor"
2 tablespoons	unsalted butter
2 cups	half-and-half
4–6 tablespoons	fresh osetra or sevruga caviar
	Salt and freshly ground white pepper

Put the oysters and their liquor, butter, and half-and-half in a nonreactive sauté pan. Bring rapidly up to a near boil and immediately turn off the heat. As soon as the oysters plump up (about 30 seconds), puree the oysters and cream. Taste for salt, reheat, and pour into warmed bowls. Put a spoonful of caviar in the center of each portion of soup.

RICH MUSSEL BISQUE WITH SHRIMPMEAT
GARLIC TOASTS AND NASTURTIUMS

Billi-Bi is a mussel soup made famous by Maxim's in Paris, and I can never think of mussel soup without thinking of some very louche lunches there, when I always ordered this soup.

As with the Billi-Bi, in my restaurant we didn't put the mussels in the soup, if only for profit reasons (getting money for the mussels twice). They were used at lunch in a creamed gratin (no cheese) or served as a snack sizzling in garlic oil. Sometimes we made a sandwich out of them with hot nan from our tandoor oven, stuffing the nan with the mussels and a cream flavored with salt-preserved lemons (see page 43) and mint. You could put them on English muffins, with the lemons and mint cream on top, and serve with the soup.

You can chop the mussels up and put them in the soup or, for a richer and thicker bisque, puree half of them and whisk into the finished soup with the other half either put into the soup whole or pureed and put on the toasts instead of prawn meat. The nasturtiums, apart from looking wonderful, add a peppery flavor. Use them only when you can pick them yourself from your garden or can buy them guaranteed pesticide-free.

SERVES 4 TO 6

Soup:			
2 pounds	mussels, washed, "bearded"	½ cup	fresh white breadcrumbs from 2-day-old bread (or bread dried in oven)
4 tablespoons	butter	2 cups	heavy cream
6	shallots, peeled, finely chopped	½ teaspoon	saffron powder mixed with the remaining 2 table-spoons butter
1	sprig fresh thyme		Salt and freshly ground white pepper
1	bay leaf		
½ cup	dry white wine (Sauvignon Blanc, for example)		
4 cups	fish stock, or a mixture of fish and clam (see page 187)		

Garnish:	
8	large cooked fresh prawns
2 tablespoons	sour cream
⅛ teaspoon	cardamom
1 teaspoon	fresh tarragon, finely chopped
1 teaspoon	freshly squeezed lemon juice
4 slices	white bread, cut ½-inch thick, cut into 4-inch rounds, dried out in oven
6	nasturtium flowers, stemmed, shredded

Put 2 tablespoons of the butter in a pot with the shallots, thyme, and bay leaf. Add a tablespoon of water, cover, and sweat for 10 minutes over very low heat until the shallots are tender and translucent.

Add the mussels and white wine, turn up the heat to high, cover, and cook 3 minutes, shaking the pot often. Add the stock and cook another 3 minutes or until all the mussels have just opened. Take them out and drain, saving any juices (to be added back to the pot). Decant the liquid out of the pot with a ladle into a bowl, so that any sand stays in the bottom of the cooking pot. Throw away the residue and rinse out the pot.

Put the saved liquid back in the pot with the breadcrumbs and simmer over medium heat for 5 minutes. Put through a sieve, add the cream, and put in a pot to be heated when needed. Up to this point the soup can be prepared several hours ahead and refrigerated.

Finely chop the prawns and mix with the sour cream, cardamom, tarragon, and lemon juice. This is best prepared at least 1 hour ahead.

To serve, bring the soup to a simmer, turn off the heat, whisk in the saffron butter, and season. Ladle the hot soup into warmed, flat, open soup plates.

Spread the prawn meat on the toasts and float one toast in each bowl of soup. Sprinkle the shredded flowers over the toasts.

CREAM OF BOLETUS SOUP

This is not as spiritually extravagant as the puree of fresh black truffle soup at L'Arpege, Alain Passard's great Parisian restaurant—but then what could be? However, it's close.

It is from my beloved Edouard de Pomiane, in this case his *Le Carnet d'Anna* from 1938.

SERVES 6

4 ounces	dried boletus, cèpes, or porcini
6 cups	chicken stock (see page 215)
1 cup	heavy cream
¼ cup	freshly grated Parmesan cheese
	Salt and freshly ground white pepper

Put the dried mushrooms in a pot with the stock. Bring to a boil, lower the heat, and simmer for 30 minutes, or until the mushrooms are very tender.

Strain and reserve the liquid. Rinse out the pot in case there is any sand in the bottom. Cut the bottom of the stems off the mushrooms in case they are sandy.

Use a ladle to decant the mushroom stock into another container, leaving the sand behind in the bottom of the first container.

Puree the mushrooms in a food processor with the decanted stock until completely smooth, and put the puree back in the pot. Add the cream and simmer for 2 minutes. Season with salt and pepper and serve, passing the Parmesan separately.

PARSNIP SOUP WITH WHITE TRUFFLES

My beloved parsnip, with its semisweet flavor that seems to confuse most palates, is not loved by all. The ancient Romans liked them a lot, and then no one else, until the English. The Romans would have served this soup with a huge hunk of foie gras (from geese fed on figs) in the center.

Parsnips are great peeled and roasted with cumin and lots of black pepper as an accompaniment to any kind of fresh pork. Covered with lime juice and chilies and then baked, they are perfect with roast pig, or any of the tropical "oily" fish.

And they make a great soup, especially a cold one. Peel the parsnips very lightly, since the flesh between the skin and the center "root" is the part that we want to use. Make sure the parsnips are quite fresh, not huge, old, and woody.

SERVES 4

8	medium parsnips	3 cups	water (let tap water stand 2 hours before using to release the chlorine) or vegetable stock (see page 143)
1 tablespoon	butter		
1	large white onion, peeled, coarsely chopped		
1	medium potato, peeled, chopped into ½-inch cubes	½ ounce	fresh white truffle
			Salt and freshly ground white pepper
1	sprig fresh tarragon		
2	sprigs fresh parsley		

Peel the parsnip, cut off the top and the thin root ends and discard. Using the peeler, cut away and save all the rest of the parsnip except for the core. Put the saved parsnip in a heavy pot that will hold it in one layer. Add the butter, onions, and potato. Add ¼ cup water, a teaspoon of salt, cover, and sweat over medium-low heat for 10 minutes. Add the tarragon and parsley and sweat another 5 minutes, then add the remaining water and simmer until the vegetables are tender, another 5 minutes or so.

Drain and save the liquid. Puree the mixture with some of the liquid, and add the remaining liquid to the puree.

Heat, test for salt, and serve in warmed shallow soup plates. Shave the white truffles over the top of the soup at the table, and then grind white pepper over the truffles.

VARIATIONS Since the fresh truffles will cost about 15 dollars per person, this soup can be served with white truffle, herb, or mushroom oil on top instead. In the restaurants, we finished the soup to order with whipped cream, and then added a large shitake mushroom pot sticker (wonton-wrapper dumplings of shitakes, fresh ginger, garlic, and preserved lemon); the dumpling was then covered with chopped Italian parsley and flowers.

The soup can also be served chilled without the truffles and with the same oils, but if it's cold do not use any butter, though perhaps some cream. Another variation is to use fresh cardoons instead of parsnips (they taste quite a bit like artichokes).

ROASTED EGGPLANT AND LENTIL SOUP WITH CUMIN, LIME, MINT, AND BASIL

If lentils were not the first vegetable man ever ate, they certainly were an early favorite. In 1967, when William Heinemann and Harvard University Press reprinted *Athenaeus: The Deipnosophists* in seven volumes, I plowed through four, and on the inside cover I listed what got my attention: "grilled sturgeon belly, scotch broth, pickled turnip, fresh cheese salad, underground refrigerators, sweet chickpeas, lentil soup with parsnips." Since I love both lentils and parsnips, I tried the soup.

SERVES 4

12	Japanese eggplants, stems cut off	1 pod	ancho chili, stemmed, seeded, broken up in a food processor
½ cup	lentils, washed, soaked for 1 hour	1	medium parsnip, peeled, cored, chopped
½ cup	olive oil		
4 sprigs	fresh mint	4 cups	chicken stock
1 sprig	fresh thyme	½ cup	basil leaves
4	cloves garlic, unpeeled, crushed	½ cup	heavy cream
		1 tablespoon	freshly squeezed lime juice
2 teaspoons	ground cumin	1 tablespoon	red chili flakes

Make four equally-spaced cuts ⅛-inch deep lengthwise around each of the eggplants. Put them in a bowl with the olive oil, mint, thyme, garlic, 1 teaspoon of the cumin, and the ancho chili. Toss together, cover, and let marinate 1 hour.

Take out the eggplants, wipe them clean, saving the marinade, salt them, and cook over a low gas flame for about 8 minutes, turning them constantly. If you don't have a gas stove, skip this step—you will miss a wonderful smoky flavor, but it is worth doing the soup anyway. Even better if you have a wood-burning "pizza" oven.

Preheat the oven to 325 degrees.

Put the eggplants in a pot with the parsnip and all the reserved marinade. Add ½ cup of the stock, cover, and sweat over low heat for 15 minutes. Add the lentils and the rest of the stock, and simmer for 30 minutes, or until the lentils are tender enough to puree.

Puree everything and put through a medium-fine sieve.

Chop the basil leaves and mix them with the cream. Add a little salt and whisk until firm peaks form.

Heat the soup and season with salt, pepper, the remaining teaspoon of cumin, and the lime juice. Serve in warm open soup plates with a dollop of the basil cream in the center and the chili flakes on top of the cream.

VARIATION Use mascarpone instead of the cream, and use fresh mint and basil with a touch of ancho chili puree (see page 32) instead of the flakes.

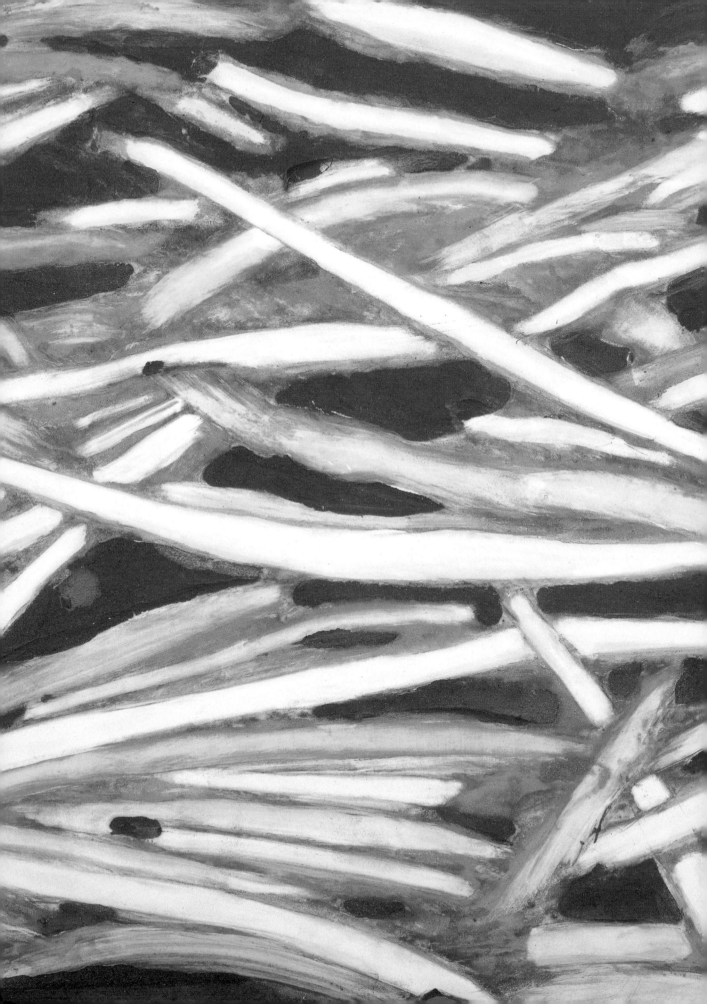

CHAPTER FIVE
VEGETABLES

WARM MIXED VEGETABLE STEW

ASPARAGUS GRATIN

ASPARAGUS WITH CODDLED EGG AND MUSTARD

ARTICHOKE BOTTOMS STUFFED WITH FAVA BEAN PUREE

OVEN-COOKED TOMATOES

FRIED GREEN TOMATOES WITH A SWEET CORN TIMBALE

CHARLES GAINES'S GRILLED CORN

SQUASH BLOSSOMS STUFFED WITH MOREL MUSHROOMS AND FRESH CORN

LENTIL PILAF

SPICED EGGPLANT AND LENTILS

WINTER SQUASH IN WHITE TRUFFLE OIL

SAVOY CABBAGE WITH WHITE BEANS AND MUSHROOM BUTTER

THE BLACK BEAN CAKE

MY BAKED BEANS

GRILLED LEEKS CATALAN STYLE (*ESCALAVADA*)

COWBOY-STYLE FIRE-ROASTED ONIONS

FRESH MOREL MUSHROOM STEW WITH FAVA BEANS AND PEAS

BAKED POTATO WITH SMOKY EGGPLANT-LENTIL PUREE AND INDIAN SPICED BUTTER

OVEN-ROASTED ROOT VEGETABLES

OVEN-DRIED FRUIT FOR ROASTED MEATS, GAME, AND POULTRY

GRILLED MUSHROOM CAPS

CAULIFLOWER WITH WHITE TRUFFLE SAUCE

STEAMED BLACK PERIGORD TRUFFLES WITH POTATOES

VEGETABLE STOCK

WARM MIXED VEGETABLE STEW

No better appreciation of vegetables can be found than this ragout from Richard Olney's *Simple French Food* (1974).

The combination here is only one of many, though I never use more than seven vegetables, and never use tomatoes (unless they are cherry tomatoes), because they water down the sauce and dominate the flavors. The addition of chopped garlic and herbs just before you bring the stew to the table causes a burst of rich fragrance, which perfects the dish.

I prefer water to chicken stock for a cooking liquid—the resulting sauce has a much fresher and purer vegetable taste—and I use either butter or olive oil to finish the dish. If the word *ragoût* comes from the French *ragoûter*, meaning to revive the taste, then this is the dish to do it.

SERVES 6 TO 8

16	small pearl onions, peeled	8	large green asparagus, bottom ½ inch of stem cut off, peeled, cut in half across, and halved lengthwise
1	red bell pepper, stemmed, seeded, cut in thin strips lengthwise	24	fresh squash blossoms
1	yellow bell pepper, stemmed, seeded, cut in thin strips lengthwise	1 tablespoon	mixed fresh herbs (thyme, marjoram, tarragon, and parsley), finely chopped
1 large sprig	fresh thyme	2 cloves	garlic, finely chopped
2 sprigs	fresh tarragon	¼ pound	unsalted butter, cut into ½-ounce pieces
24	baby carrots, trimmed and peeled		Salt and freshly ground black pepper
4	small zucchini, halved lengthwise		
4	small yellow zucchini, halved lengthwise		
24	small French green beans		
2 pounds	fava bean pods, beans removed and peeled, pods and peels discarded		

Bring a pot of salted water to the boil and maintain it at a steady boil.

Put the onions, bell peppers, thyme, tarragon, 1 cup of water, and a pinch of salt in a 12-inch sauté pan. Cover and simmer for 5 minutes.

Put the carrots into the boiling water for 1 minute, then lift them out and add them to the onion mixture.

Put the zucchini into the boiling water for 1 minute and then add them to the other vegetables. Toss together. Cook the green beans, fava beans, and asparagus in the boiling water for 1 minute, then add them to the other vegetables. Toss, cover, and cook 2 minutes. Make sure about 1 cup of liquid remains in the vegetable pan.

Uncover the pan. Add the squash blossoms, herbs, garlic, and butter. Turn the heat to high and toss the vegetables together until the butter is melted and the sauce thickens a little. Season and serve immediately.

VARIATION At one of the California Wine Perspective events at the Pierre Hotel in New York in the mid-1980s, we served the ragout, finished with a black truffle and wild mushroom butter, in little hollowed-out polenta cups (see page 56), to great acclaim.

ASPARAGUS GRATIN

My memory of asparagus starts in England, when at the age of eight I was given co-management of our vegetable garden and its asparagus bed. I had my own vegetable project in Australia before that, but no asparagus. When I first saw the English bed, it was full of gloriously luxuriant mature asparagus ferns, and I was very disappointed when I was told they were no good to eat. But a year (and many wheelbarrows of muck from our stables) later, we were inundated with those beautiful edible spears.

My mother would not let us eat asparagus except with Jersey butter, sometimes buttered breadcrumbs, and occasionally hollandaise. I agree with Ogden Nash about the necessity for hollandaise— "a sauce supreme in many ways"—and my personal preference for both flavor and texture, whether green or white, whether from New Jersey or Long Island, is asparagus so thick that the stems must be peeled in order to cook them at the same rate as the tips.

Please boil the asparagus in lots of salted water—all that steaming, standing upright, tips out of the water business generates uneven cooking and is of dubious value. Cut off the bottom (white) half-inch of each stalk that is dried out, and discard.

SERVES 4

20	large thick (¼ inch) green asparagus
2	cups whipped cream hollandaise (see page 254)
1 tablespoon	butter

Peel the asparagus starting at the bottom and peeling upwards—more deeply at the root end (thicker and tougher) and less deeply towards the tip where you can feel the stalk becoming more tender (about one inch below the tips). The asparagus should be the same diameter along the length of its stalk as it is just under the base of the tip.

Preheat the broiler to full heat.

Rinse away any stray peelings, and tie the asparagus with soft white string, wrapping the string around all the spears from the top of the bundle to the bottom. Put in a large pot of boiling salted water (enough to cover them by 6 inches) and simmer for 7 to 10 minutes depending on the thickness of the asparagus, until they are just barely tender when stuck with a paring knife.

Take out the asparagus and drain them on a towel while you cut away the string. When drained, lay the asparagus next to each other with all the tips at one end in lightly-buttered individual gratin dishes, or in one large dish. Spoon the hollandaise over all the asparagus. Put the dish or dishes under the broiler for 2 to 4 minutes until the top of the sauce becomes light golden. Serve immediately.

ASPARAGUS WITH CODDLED EGG AND MUSTARD

In France, there are special asparagus plates that have a "sauce well" at the side, in which one can make one's own sauce from oil, vinegar, blood orange, or lemon juice, salt and pepper, mustard and so on. I have never seen them in the United States, but this recipe gives you the idea. Put the individual ingredients in pots or jugs on the table and then mash up your chosen ingredients on your plate to make a sauce for dipping the asparagus (hot or cold). If you don't have asparagus plates, use large, shallow soup plates.

SERVES 4

20	large asparagus, peeled and cooked as on page 119
4	coddled eggs (see page 34), cooked 2 minutes extra
4 tablespoons	fresh tarragon leaves, chopped
2	blood oranges, zested and juiced
	Extra virgin olive oil
	Dijon mustard
	Salt and freshly ground black pepper

Serve the hot or room-temperature asparagus on plates, each with either a room-temperature or hot coddled egg.

Each person smashes the egg with a fork and mixes it with tarragon, blood orange juice and zest, olive oil, mustard, salt and pepper, to spoon over the asparagus.

Artichoke Bottoms Stuffed
with Fava Bean Puree

Marcel Boulestin started writing his "Finer Cooking" series for *British Vogue* in 1923, and his menus and recipes set a standard that still holds. One of his favorite vegetable dishes, artichoke bottoms stuffed with fava bean puree, is also one of mine. And even though I put a similar dish in my first book, I must include this version here, since it is one of the great, timeless classical garnishes. Few dishes are as sublime. Boulestin's version, called *saintongeoise,* had a little Mornay sauce ("rather light and thin") poured over the artichokes and fava puree, which was then topped with a little "grated cheese before finishing them under the gas grill or in the oven." They are delicious that way too, but I like them plain.

Tasting them for the first time in Provence in the early 1970s, I discovered the natural affinity of winter savory for fava beans, a happy marriage that belongs in the short lexicon of flavors that should never be separated, like strawberries and red currants or, as is more common, fresh rosemary and lamb.

To this list, I would also add artichokes and fava beans, both of which are celebrated by the winter savory. As a recipe, it is easy to see why it never appears in restaurants today: the prodigious amount of favas required to make the puree in any quantity, and the labor it takes to peel them. But the dish can be appreciated in the home, because to make it for four is not all that daunting and well worth the effort. In the nineteenth century, this dish was always served with roasts of chicken and lamb, but now I love it as a first course, eaten all by itself.

And yes, the fava puree does need this much butter and will happily take it.

SERVES 4

4	large artichokes
1	lemon
4 pounds	fresh fava (broad bean) pods
2 sprigs	fresh winter savory or thyme
½ pound	butter
	Salt and freshly ground black pepper

Cut 3 inches off the top off each artichoke and discard. With a stainless-steel paring knife, continue to cut around the artichoke, rotating it in your hand as you cut, until only the very bases of the leaves remain on the bottom of each artichoke. Trim the stem to ⅛ inch. Store each artichoke bottom in cold water into which you have squeezed the lemon and then added the lemon halves.

When all the bottoms are trimmed, put them in a stainless steel pot with the lemon water and lemons, add a tablespoon of salt, and bring to a boil. Simmer for 10 minutes, or until the artichokes are just tender when pricked with a paring knife. Remove the artichokes and put them in a colander stem end up. Cover with ice and let them drain and cool for 10 minutes. When cool, cut out the chokes or center fibers and discard.

Take all the fava beans out of the pods and remove the outer pale green skins from the beans. Put the beans and savory in a sauce pan and cover with water by 1 inch. Add ½ teaspoon salt, bring to a boil over high heat, then simmer for 8 minutes. Drain, reserving the cooking liquid and the beans separately. Put all but 24 of the beans through the medium blade of a food mill, or puree in a food processor, using up to half the cooking liquid to help the process. Press the puree through a fine sieve. Cover and set aside. Keep the 24 beans warm.

Put the artichoke bottoms in a sauté pan just large enough to hold them. Add the remaining bean-cooking liquid and 1 tablespoon of the butter. Cover and simmer over low heat for 5 minutes. While they are cooking, put the bean puree in a double boiler and heat it. When it is hot, add 6 tablespoons of the butter and stir. Season, remove from the heat, and keep warm.

Remove the cover from the artichoke pan. Spoon the bean puree into the artichoke bottoms, put the cover back on, turn off the heat, and let sit for 5 minutes. Then put the filled artichoke bottoms on hot plates. Toss the reserved favas in the remaining tablespoon of butter, season, and spoon the warm beans around the filled artichokes.

VARIATION Serve with cooked and sieved red and yellow bell pepper purees (½ cup each), heated and mounted with butter (1 tablespoon each).

OVEN-COOKED TOMATOES

Like the oven-dried fruit on page 138, this technique concentrates the flavors and sugars of tomatoes by getting rid of a lot of the irrigation water. They will never be as good as the tomatoes grown in the volcanic soils outside of Naples where the whole plant, full of ripe tomatoes, is pulled up and hung upside-down on a south-facing wall for a few days. But these come close.

YIELDS 20 TOMATO HALVES

10	ripe tomatoes (red or yellow), cut in half across the equator	4 tablespoons	kosher salt
		2 tablespoons	freshly ground black pepper
1 cup	olive oil	4 tablespoons	fennel seed, toasted, chopped
2 tablespoons	freshly chopped garlic		
¼ cup	fresh rosemary and thyme leaves, chopped		

Preheat the oven to 150 degrees.

Put all ingredients in a bowl, toss gently, and leave 30 minutes to marinate.

Put a fine-mesh cake rack in a baking tray with a 1-inch lip, and lay the tomatoes out, cut side down, ½ inch apart.

Put in the oven and leave 6 to 8 hours, or overnight. Take out and let cool. Refrigerate or store in olive oil in the refrigerator.

VARIATION If you have a smoker, smoke the tomatoes, puree them in fish or chicken stock (or water), and mount them with butter. You will end up with one of the most haunting sauces ever.

FRIED GREEN TOMATOES
WITH A SWEET CORN TIMBALE

When I was a child in England, trying to ripen tomatoes in our kitchen garden was always a race with the weather, and when my mother gave up on tomatoes, I still insisted on planting them every year. Even when I started the plants in a greenhouse to get a head start on the season, the tomatoes rarely made it to full red ripeness before the sun disappeared into the October fogs. Perhaps it is no coincidence that Jane Grigson's *British Cookery* lists no recipes for tomatoes.

So in England we had to do with green tomatoes. When they first appeared on the table, fried, all the children were shocked (though not so much as when an apple and green tomato pie was put onto the table), but I have adored them ever since. Now I would be tempted to use Green Zebra heirloom tomatoes, even though they are not "green" as in unripe, and would therefore fry them for half the time given here.

You will need four 6-ounce ramekins.

SERVES 4

Timbales:		Tomatoes:	
2 cups	fresh, young corn, kernels cut from the cobs (about 6 cobs)	3-4	large green tomatoes, cored
¼ cup	fresh chervil leaves, chopped	2 cups	all-purpose flour
		½ cup	vegetable oil
1 ½ cups	milk	1 cup	milk
4	egg yolks	½ cup	tomato, lemon, and olive oil sauce (see page 237)
2 tablespoons	butter	½ cup	nasturtium or herb flowers
pinch	salt		Salt and freshly ground black pepper
	Freshly ground white pepper		

Cook the corn in boiling salted water for 5 minutes, drain, and puree, adding 4 tablespoons of the cooking water, until smooth. Mix in the chervil.

Preheat the oven to 375 degrees, and boil 3 quarts of water.

Beat the milk, eggs, salt and pepper until smooth. Add the corn-chervil mix and stir well.

Butter the four ramekins.

Put the corn puree in a nonreactive saucepan and cook over medium heat, stirring constantly until the mixture just begins to thicken. Immediately pour the mixture into the ramekins, and put them in an ovenproof dish or baking pan that is just deeper than the ramekins. Put the pan in the oven, and fill it with boiling water to come three-quarters of the way up the ramekins.

Cook until the corn custard mix is just barely set (20 to 30 minutes) and take them out of the oven and water to cool.

While the timbales are cooking, mix 1 teaspoon salt and 2 teaspoons black pepper into the flour. Cut the tomatoes into 8½-inch slices. After you take out the timbales, dredge the tomato slices in the flour. Heat the oil in a skillet, and fry the tomatoes on each side over medium heat for 3 to 4 minutes per side, or until the tomatoes are tender but still have some firmness. Keep the slices hot until all are fried.

Pour the milk into the skillet and simmer for 5 minutes, scraping all the bits stuck to the pan.

Put two slices on top of each other in the center of each hot plate. Pour the gravy over. Invert the timbales on top of the tomato stack and spoon some of the tomato, lemon, and olive oil sauce on top, passing the rest separately. Garnish with the flowers.

VARIATIONS Add deep-fried okra to the dish, served around the tomatoes. Or use mint-sage-rosemary pesto sauce (see page 244) on top of the timbale.

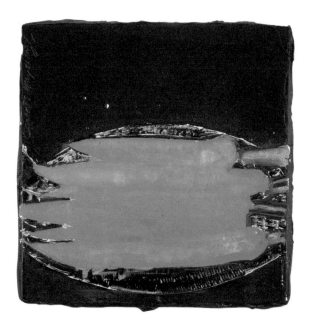

CHARLES GAINES'S GRILLED CORN

Charles Gaines is one of America's best writers on fishing. He and his wife, Patricia, are wonderful cooks. Like Charles, I have never seen the point of grilling corn with the husks on—seems like steaming to me, and I would rather quickly boil them.

One summer night at Charles and Patricia's Nova Scotia property, watching the resident martins catch the bugs that were trying to catch us, we grilled this corn and ate it along with mussels from nearby Prince Edward Island.

Marinating the corn in the lime juice instead of putting the juice in the sauce is very effective.

SERVES 4

8 ears	very fresh corn		Sauce:
1	ripe lime, freshly juiced	1 cup	mayonnaise (see page 247)
¼ cup	extra virgin olive oil	½ tablespoon	ground cumin
	Sea salt and freshly ground	½ teaspoon	cayenne
	black pepper	½ tablespoon	ancho chili powder

Shuck the corn, wipe clean of all the silk, and rub with the lime juice, olive oil, salt, and pepper. Let the corn marinate half an hour, turning the cobs a few times, and grill it over a medium real charcoal fire for 10 minutes, or until the corn is cooked and slightly caramelized.

Mix all the sauce ingredients together and serve with the hot corn.

SQUASH BLOSSOMS STUFFED WITH MOREL MUSHROOMS AND FRESH CORN

SERVES 4

16	large fresh squash blossoms	1 teaspoon	fresh marjoram leaves
2 tablespoons	melted butter	1 recipe	asparagus sauce (see page 252)
½ cup	dried morels		Salt and freshly ground black pepper
1 cup	fresh corn kernels		
2 tablespoons	butter		

Soak the morels in a cup of water for 4 hours, or until tender. Remove the mushrooms, cut off the base of the stems and discard. Pour 4 tablespoons of the soaking liquid into a small saucepan.

Add the corn, butter, and marjoram, cover, and simmer for 10 minutes. Puree the mixture, using a little more mushroom water if necessary to get a spoonable puree the consistency of thick mayonnaise. Season.

Cut the stems and hard bases from the blossoms, but do not cut away so much of the base that the flowers fall apart.

Preheat the broiler.

Brush a sheet pan with half the melted butter.

Put a spoonful of the mushroom-corn mixture into each blossom. Gently fold the opening of each flower over, pat the blossom into shape, and put it on the sheet pan. Brush the flowers gently with the rest of the melted butter. Broil 5 minutes or so, depending on the heat of the broiler.

Serve immediately with the asparagus sauce spooned over the blossoms.

VARIATION Squash blossoms can be stuffed with olive puree, chopped cooked eggplant, or lentils. They can be covered with raclette cheese and broiled, or served with ancho-chili mayonnaise, or any of the salsas or relishes mentioned on page 243. At the Stars Cafés, we stuffed the blossoms with goat cheese, put them between two sheets (3 inches by 6 inches) of cooked green pasta, and poured fresh tomato sauce (see page 240) mixed with 1 tablespoon of chopped fresh tarragon over the pasta.

LENTIL PILAF

This pilaf method is one I prefer if the lentils are going to be eaten as they are. For soups, gratins, and purees, cook them in boiling water.

SERVES 4 TO 6

1 cup	lentils, de Puy, or beluga	½ cup	aromatic vegetable mix
2 tablespoons	butter		(see page 14), wrapped
1	small onion, peeled,		in cheesecloth
	finely chopped		Salt and freshly ground
2-4 cups	chicken stock, or water		black pepper
	(see page 215)		
1	small herb bundle		
	(see page 16)		

Heat the butter in a 2-quart casserole. Add the onion and 2 tablespoons of water. Cover and sweat for 5 minutes. Add the lentils and cook while stirring for 5 minutes, until the lentils are well coated and slightly toasted.

Add the stock or water to cover the lentils by ½ inch, the herb bundle, vegetable mix, and ¼ teaspoon salt, and cover the casserole. Bring to a boil, lower the heat to a mere simmer, and cook 20 to 30 minutes, or until the lentils are tender, taking care not to overcook them. The lentils should be tender but not mushy. Add more liquid if necessary.

Remove the lentils from the heat and leave covered for 15 minutes. Remove the cover and discard the herbs and vegetables. Season and cover again until needed.

SPICED EGGPLANT AND LENTILS

This dish can be eaten by itself, hot or cold; served as an accompaniment to fish and meats; stuffed into onions or other vegetables; or made into a hot or cold soup.

The lentils should be du Puy lentils from France, which have a wonderful flavor and hold their shape. Even better are the "black beluga" lentils, not only for their texture, appearance, and flavor, but because they can be cooked in no time at all. It's worth the time and energy to visit some specialty food stores or search the Internet to find these wonderful lentils.

If you use large (non-Japanese) eggplants, you'll need to cut them in half lengthwise, score them 1 inch deep on the cut side, press kosher salt into the cuts, and leave them face down on a rack for one hour. Then rinse them and cook according to the recipe.

SERVES 4 TO 6

10	Japanese eggplants	1 tablespoon	chopped ginger
1	large red onion, peeled, chopped	1 teaspoon	chopped garlic
		1	orange, zested and juiced
1 tablespoon	fresh thyme leaves, chopped	1 tablespoon	Indian spice mix (see page 38)
1 cup	cooked lentils (see page 127)	2 tablespoons	extra virgin olive oil
½ cup	fresh cilantro leaves, chopped		Salt

Preheat the oven to 350 degrees.

Sear the eggplants over gas burners (or a wood or charcoal fire), turning them constantly, for about 5 minutes each. Remove the stems from the eggplants and put them in an ovenproof dish. Add the onion, thyme, and 2 pinches salt. Add ¼ cup water, cover, and bake 30 to 40 minutes, or until they are tender but still holding their shape. Take them out of the oven to cool.

When the eggplants are cool, put them on a board and chop until almost pureed. Put the eggplant in a bowl, then add the lentils and all the other ingredients. Mix, let sit for 2 hours for all the flavors to mingle, season, and mix again.

WINTER SQUASH IN WHITE TRUFFLE OIL

I use butternut squash in this recipe, but you could use acorn, turban, or hubbard as well, or pumpkins, as long as they are small enough to handle.

I don't usually like ruining the advantages of a delicious inexpensive ingredient with an expensive one, but there is something magical about winter squash perfumed with white truffles, and the small amount of oil used will not break the bank.

SERVES 4 TO 6

1	small butternut squash
1 tablespoon	butter
1 tablespoon	fresh white truffle oil
	Salt and freshly ground white pepper

Peel the squash, cut it in half lengthwise, and scoop out the seeds and all the membrane.

Cut each half lengthwise into halves again. Slice on a vegetable cutter (a mandoline or Japanese vegetable slicer), so that the slices are evenly ⅛ inch thick. They should all be the same size, about 2 inches across.

Boil in salted water for 5 to 8 minutes, or until just tender. Drain and put the squash in a bowl. Add the butter and white truffle oil. Season and toss together in the bowl gently, so as not to break up the pieces. Serve.

VARIATION If you want to go entirely mad, as at Christmas, then toss the cooked squash in 2 tablespoons of cream (instead of the butter), salt, and white pepper, and shave fresh white truffles over it.

Savoy Cabbage with White Beans and Mushroom Butter

I think that plain cabbage with lashings of butter and freshly ground Malabar black pepper is sublime by itself as a first course, but it is also one of the best vegetable garnishes in anyone's repertoire. I use Savoy cabbage because it's my favorite for both appearance and flavor.

In this recipe, I use fenugreek (*Trigonella foenum-graecum*), which is one of the most characteristic aromas in curry powder. It smells a bit like spicy celery, and it flavors this dish superbly.

SERVES 4 TO 6

2 pounds	Savoy cabbage		½ tablespoon	lemon zest
1 cup	cooked white beans (see page 33)		¼ cup	mushroom hash (see page 17)
1 tablespoon	finely chopped fresh garlic		¼ cup	butter
1 teaspoon	ground fenugreek			Salt and freshly ground black pepper
2 tablespoons	chopped fresh Italian parsley			

Cut the cabbage in half from top to bottom. Cut out the core, and slice across the halves at 1-inch intervals. Wash the cabbage in cold water and drain.

Put the beans, garlic, fenugreek, parsley, and lemon zest in a bowl.

Mix the butter and mushroom hash together very well (or puree in a food processor until smooth).

Cook the cabbage in a large pot of boiling salted water, 5 to 10 minutes, until tender. Drain well in a colander, and then put the hot, drained cabbage in the bowl with the other ingredients. Add the mushroom butter and toss to mix everything together. Season and serve immediately.

VARIATION   Do nothing except toss the hot drained cabbage with ¼ cup of the Montpelier butter on page 246.

THE BLACK BEAN CAKE

This recipe appeared in my first book, *Jeremiah Tower's New American Classics*, and when people heard I was doing a new book, everyone said, "Make sure to include the black bean cake!" And that bit about Liz Smith. So here they are.

I think that the columnist Liz Smith's farewell to Rock Hudson—"So long, big boy, have a good rest"—is what I would like on my tombstone, but it will probably be: "He invented the black bean cake."

It is simple, beautiful, easy, fast, and inexpensive. But it has never been imitated with any success, despite many tries, because no one has ever believed what the secret is: let the cooked black beans drain overnight, uncovered, so they dry out. The worse they look before grinding, the better the final result. And you cannot use a food processor—they must go through a meat grinder (or a food mill, but that's too much work).

SERVES 4

3 cups	black beans	1 tablespoon	milk
1 tablespoon	ancho chili powder	¼ cup	rendered duck fat, lard,
1 tablespoon	ground cumin		or pure vegetable oil
1	small fresh hot green		(canola, peanut, or
	chili, stemmed, seeded,		safflower)
	finely chopped	¼ cup	fresh tomato relish
½ cup	cilantro leaves,		(see page 243)
	coarsely chopped	12 sprigs	cilantro, washed,
¾ teaspoon	salt		spun dry
½ cup	sour cream		

Cook the beans as directed for white beans (see page 33), but before you grind them, let them drain for at least 6 hours, preferably overnight. Don't worry if they look terrible after sitting that long. Save the liquid for soup.

Put the cooked beans through a meat grinder into a bowl. Add the chili powder, cumin, fresh chili, cilantro leaves, and salt, and mix all the ingredients to form a paste.

Roll the paste into four equal balls. Put each ball between two pieces of waxed paper and press them with the palm of your hand into neat rounds ⅛ inch thick. Put the rounds in the refrigerator for 30 minutes to firm up (they can stay in the refrigerator for up to 24 hours).

Just before cooking the bean cakes, whisk the sour cream and milk together until smooth.

Heat the duck fat (or lard or vegetable oil) in a nonstick pan or on a griddle. When the pan is hot, put in the cakes and cook 2 minutes on each side. Put the cakes on warm plates with a spoonful of sour cream on the center of each cake. Spoon the relish onto the sour cream. Garnish the plates with the cilantro sprigs.

VARIATION   In Manila, we served the cakes with pieces of suckling or roast pig skin with a cilantro–banana flower salad dressed in lime juice and sesame oil.

MY BAKED BEANS

There are five secrets to taking little dried white pea (or navy, or cannellini) beans to ethereal heights of gastronomy: 1) soaking, parboiling, and cleansing (de-gassing) as on page 33; 2) cooking them twice; 3) cooking them slowly; 4) using a half-glazed (inside) earthenware bean pot; 5) letting them sit overnight after the second cooking and then reheating them.

Great baked beans cannot be rushed, making them a perfect, made-in-advance party food. The mystery of why earthenware does its usual magic with beans is just that, a certified mystery.

SERVES 6 TO 10

4 cups	dried cannellini beans, cooked (see page 33)	¼ cup	molasses
¼ pound	dried apricots	1 tablespoon	powdered mustard
½ cup	dark rum	½ bottle	Pickapeppa or your favorite "steak" sauce
4 tablespoons	chopped fresh garlic	¼ cup	red wine vinegar
1 tablespoon	powdered ginger	8 strips	smoked bacon
½ tablespoon	ancho chili powder	1 cup	stout or dark ale
½ cup	dark brown sugar		Bean cooking liquid

Soak the apricots in the rum for 2 hours, drain, saving the rum and chop them.

Preheat the oven to 325 degrees.

Put the beans in a big mixing bowl. Add the apricots and rum, the garlic, ginger, ancho chili powder, brown sugar, molasses, mustard, Pickapeppa sauce, and vinegar.

Mix well and put in the bean pot. Layer the bacon on top of the beans. Pour in the stout and enough bean-cooking liquid to cover the beans by 1 inch. Cover and put in the oven. Bake 2 hours, topping up with liquid as it disappears.

When cool enough to handle, take out the bacon and chop. Add the chopped bacon to the beans and mix. Stir salt and pepper into the beans if needed. Cover and refrigerate overnight.

To serve, add 2 cups of the cooking liquid or chicken stock, and heat the beans uncovered for 30 to 45 minutes at 350 degrees, or until the beans are heated through.

GRILLED LEEKS CATALAN STYLE (*ESCALAVADA*)

One of my first cookbooks, Irving Davis's *A Catalan Cookery Book: A Collection of Impossible Recipes*, was printed the year I bought it in Paris in 1968. Only 165 copies were printed, so it could not have turned out to be very influential, but it was for me. It gripped me then as totally as it does now.

During my first years at Chez Panisse, I relied a lot on this book for inspiration, and from it I developed the recipe for rabbit with prunes (see page 211)—a dish falling culinarily somewhere between Normandy and Spain, and for which this leek dish would be a wonderful accompaniment.

Escalavada means "braise" in the original meaning of the word, or to cook on glowing wood fire embers. Davis cooks the vegetables right on the embers, and when they are cooked, scrapes off the burnt skin, chops them all up, and serves them with olive oil, salt, and chopped garlic. My saucing the leeks is taking an American liberty.

I must stress that you should use wood or real charcoal in the fire, not briquets, and that the sauce can be made in a mortar, food processor, or chopped by hand and mixed into the liquid ingredients, but never in a blender.

SERVES 4 TO 6

8	leeks, trimmed to 4 inches of green leaves, slit at the top, washed		Sauce:	
			3	salted anchovies (see page 42)
¼ cup	extra virgin olive oil		6	whole almonds, skinned, lightly toasted
1 tablespoon	finely chopped garlic			
8	leaves bergamot (genus *Monardia*), or fresh oregano		1	ripe tomato, grilled, skinned, seeded, chopped
			½ tablespoon	sweet paprika
1 teaspoon	orange flower water		3	leaves fresh mint
¼ cup	dry white wine		2 tablespoons	medium sweet sherry
½ cup	herb flowers		½ ounce	bittersweet chocolate (one 1-inch square)
			1	small almond biscotti

Cook the leeks in boiling salted water for 5 minutes. To make the marinade, mix together the oil, garlic, bergamot (or oregano), orange flower water, and wine. Drain the leeks well and while still hot put them on a platter and pour the marinade over them. Set them aside for 1 hour, turning them twice.

Wipe the marinade off the leeks into a bowl. Add the marinade left in the leek dish, and put the leeks back in the dish. Add the sauce ingredients to the marinade in the bowl, mix together, and grind in a mortar or food processor until a coarse paste is formed.

Season the leeks and grill over a low fire until tender. When the leeks are cooked, put them on a platter and spread the sauce over them. Garnish the dish with the herb flowers.

VARIATION   This sauce is good on any grilled vegetables, but especially those in the onion family.

COWBOY-STYLE FIRE-ROASTED ONIONS

If you were a Catalan cowboy, you would roast the unpeeled onions in the coals without wrapping them. This version is easier. Use a mild sweet onion hybrid of the Yellow Granex type: Maui (Hawaii), Vidalia (Georgia), or that European onion transplanted to Washington State, the Walla Walla Sweet.

If you are baking or spit-roasting meats, quarter a few of these onions and put under the meat. All the juices will drip down onto them, the fire will cook them, and then you will want to throw away the meat and eat the onions by themselves with a great glass of draft Pilsner Urquell.

Eat them whole as a course with warm tomato-shrimp sauce (see page 237); serve them as is with grilled meats; or chop them up to make a sauce with lemon juice, extra virgin olive oil, and chopped rosemary.

SERVES 4

4	large red onions, peeled	1 tablespoon	cumin seeds
4	bay leaves	8 slices	smoked bacon
1	dried chipotle chili, quartered, seeded	1 cup	Pickapeppa sauce
			Freshly chopped Italian parsley
4 sprigs	fresh thyme		Salt

Preheat the oven to 375 degrees.

Dig out 2 teaspoons of the center of the onion with a small spoon or a grapefruit knife. Reserve the scooped-out onion pieces.

Put a bay leaf, a piece of the chipotle, a thyme sprig, and some cumin seeds in each of the cavities. Wrap each onion in two slices of bacon. Put each onion in a piece of foil large enough to wrap it, and spoon ¼ cup Pickapeppa sauce over each. Put the scooped-out onion on top. Season.

Wrap each onion and cook in the embers of a cooling wood (or charcoal) fire, in a wood oven, or in a skillet covered with aluminum foil in a regular home oven. If cooked this way you can omit the step of wrapping each onion individually.

Cook for 60 minutes, or until the onion is very tender. Unwrap, remove the bay leaf, chili, and thyme, and continue with whatever the onion is to be used for. Just before serving the onions, sprinkle with the parsley.

Fresh Morel Mushroom Stew with Fava Beans and Peas

I can't say that I initiated the first "foragers" at Chez Panisse in 1973, because they invented themselves: a couple of them came to the back door, at first for cash or trade in dinners. When the word got out that we would look at anything brought in from forest, field, or ocean (even a few times from the plains of Montana), lots more people showed up. Soon we were telling them what we wanted, and commissioning them for special or commercially unavailable ingredients.

The back of the mushroom forager's hatchback car was the most inspiring, filled with chanterelles, matsutake, boletus (even the toxic *Amanita muscaria*), and morels.

In the kitchen, the morels were the most trouble since they served as high-rise condos for all sorts of crawling things. I was forced to use cream to finish any dish they were in, so that I could see anything red with lots of feet floating to the surface—my last chance to act before the dish was picked up by the waiters, who were trained to look again before putting the plate down in front of the customer.

SERVES 4 TO 6

2 pounds	fresh morels	½ cup	fresh twice-peeled fava beans (see page 122), split (about 2 pounds of pods)
4 ounces	finely chopped pancetta or bacon		
1 tablespoon	butter		
1 tablespoon	freshly chopped garlic,	½ cup	heavy cream
1 teaspoon	fresh winter savory or fresh thyme leaves chopped	1	egg yolk
			Salt and freshly ground black pepper
½ cup	chicken stock (see page 215)		
½ cup	shelled fresh young peas		

Cut ¼ inch off the base of the stem of the morels (which may be full of sand). Slice the morels in half lengthwise and put into a sieve to shake out any critters and all the sand.

Sauté the bacon over a low fire, about 10 minutes, until all the fat is rendered. Take out the bacon and drain, discarding the fat. Wipe out the pan with paper towels, then add the butter. Melt the butter over medium heat, and as soon as it is melted add the savory and garlic. Stir them together and cook over medium heat 1 minute only. Add the morels and a pinch of salt, and toss or mix with the garlic and savory, cooking for another 2 minutes. Add the chicken stock, cover, and cook 5 minutes, or until the combined mushroom juices and chicken stock is reduced to about half a cup (⅛ inch in a 10-inch pan).

During these last few minutes of cooking the morels, boil the peas and favas in salted water for 5 minutes. Drain and add to the morels. Turn off the heat under the sauté pan with the morels and favas.

Whisk the cream and egg together and pour into the morels. Add the bacon and heat again gently, constantly tossing or stirring, only until the sauce just begins to thicken. Do not boil. Season and serve immediately.

BAKED POTATO WITH SMOKY EGGPLANT-LENTIL PUREE AND INDIAN SPICED BUTTER

I am indebted to the superb *Joy of Cooking*, but one of its recipes made me sit back in horror: potatoes baked after being covered in "rosin" ("rock rosin" from "any dance supply store") touted as being "far superior" to any other baked potato because cooking the potatoes in the rosin produces a much "flakier" result. Such claims have to be taken seriously by any lover of baked potatoes, but do they really mean "rosin" as we know it?

They do say not to eat the skins—I should hope not. They say to perform this only out of doors, and that a potato cooked this way "will send the spirits soaring." I take exception to this statement because if I can't eat the skins, my spirit will stay lead-weighted to the ground.

I prefer to use rock salt since you can still cook inside in the kitchen and because the salt draws out moisture, flaking the potato.

For baked potatoes use only mature potatoes grown for that purpose, like large Idahos.

SERVES 4

4	large Idaho potatoes	1 cup	spiced eggplant and lentils (see page 128)
½ cup	butter		
2 tablespoons	Indian spice mix (see page 38)	2 tablespoons	chopped fresh basil leaves
2 tablespoons	melted butter	1 tablespoon	orange Sichuan pepper salt (see page 42)
2 cups	rock salt		

Mix the ½ cup butter and the spice mix together and let sit 1 hour to meld the flavors.

Preheat the oven to 400 degrees.

Wash and dry the potatoes, then brush them with melted butter. Fill a shallow ovenproof dish with 1 inch of rock salt, and place the potatoes on top. Put the dish of potatoes in the oven. After 20 minutes prick each potato with a fork, and continue cooking, 40 to 60 minutes in all, depending on the size of the potatoes, until the fork meets no resistance when stuck into the center of a potato.

Heat the eggplant mix in a double boiler and keep warm.

Remove the potatoes from the oven, cut each potato open lengthwise, push each end to open, spoon some eggplant-lentil mix on top, and then put a spoonful of spiced butter on top of that. Sprinkle the basil on the butter. Pass both the remaining eggplant-lentil mix and the spiced butter, and also the flavored salt to sprinkle on top of the potato.

VARIATIONS Use almost any of the sauces in the Sauces chapter. Or the vegetable ragout on page 118. I would not refuse guacamole, a pile of deep-fried fresh little anchovies topped with Montpelier butter (see page 246), pesto by itself, blue cheese mixed with whipped cream, or gobs of black or white truffle butter.

Try also a ragout of braised pigs' feet with morels, or just morels themselves, or lobster (or crab or prawn) rémoulade, warm shrimp sauce (see page 237), smoked salmon scraps ground with butter in a mortar with lots of black pepper, a sweetbread stew, or leftover ham chopped up and mixed with cream and Dijon mustard. And so it goes. (My choices would be creamed salt cod [see page 174] or cooked white beans with white truffles.)

Oven-Roasted Root Vegetables

Like fruits, which improve by concentrating their flavors with a bit of oven drying (see page 138), commercial vegetables can slim down and improve their flavor by losing a bit of their irrigation water. I recommend root vegetables, which are full of starches and sugars (since things like fennel, which I have seen treated this way, just get tough and boring)—the exception to the rule being pumpkin or any of the hard squashes such as hubbard, acorn, butternut, or turban.

You can use celery root, onions, carrots, Jerusalem artichokes, beets, sweet potatoes (yams), potatoes, salsify, swedes (rutabagas), parsnip, and turnips.

For those with a wild streak, you can also forage and use the root stalks of bulrushes, cattails, spatterdock (water lily), pickerelweed, burdock, groundnut, and daylily.

Using a wood oven produces the most flavorful results with these vegetables. So flavorful, in fact, that customers at our café in Oakville would make an entire meal of them. Obviously, we did have a wood oven, and used wood as well as old grapevine roots to fuel it, but since almost no one in America has one at home, I suggest using a covered grill with the least smoke possible, although a little makes the vegetables taste better.

SERVES 4 TO 6

2	celery root, peeled, cut in six wedges each	4 sprigs	fresh thyme
4	parsnips, peeled, and any core removed	16	small carrots, peeled, tops removed
2	large Walla Walla Sweet, Vidalia, or Maui onions, peeled, quartered	½ cup	extra virgin olive oil
			Salt and freshly ground black pepper

Preheat the oven to 325 degrees.

Put all the ingredients in a bowl, season, and toss together. Cover and leave 2 hours, tossing the vegetables together a couple of times to spread the marinade ingredients evenly around.

Put the vegetables in a baking pan, and cover and cook for 1 hour. Remove the cover and cook for another 1 to 2 hours, or until the vegetables are tender. If some finish before the others, remove them and put back in the bowl. If using a covered grill, put the vegetables on a metal baking sheet, and grill them on that.

Serve as they are, or with lemon juice and more olive oil.

VARIATIONS When we made this dish for the 1992 anniversary of the Chappellet Vineyards in Napa, we tossed the hot vegetables with a little white truffle oil, put them on platters, and then covered the vegetables with a field of borage flowers and shredded red and yellow wild rose petals to complement the young Chappellet Cabernet Sauvignon. Or you could serve the vegetables with garlic mayonnaise (see page 248) or Montpelier butter (see page 246).

Oven-Dried Fruit for Roasted Meats, Game, and Poultry

Whenever a recipe calls for fruit to accompany meat, game, or poultry (as in duck with pears), this is the best way I know to bring out the flavors of the fruit, giving a commercial product a whole new lease on life, as if it were ripe fruit fresh from a farm in Oregon or Long Island. The process is oven drying, slowly evaporating all that Colorado River irrigation water from the fruit without cooking it.

SERVES 4

4	pears
1 tablespoon	salt
1 cup	sugar

Preheat the oven to 300 degrees.

Slice the pears in half lengthwise. Rub each half with a pinch of salt. Put parchment paper on a tray just large enough to hold the pears, and spread the sugar on the paper. There should be a ⅛-inch layer. Put the pear halves cut side down on the sugar and bake for 1 hour. Remove, take the core and stem out of the pears, and proceed with any recipe using the fruit as a garnish.

VARIATION Do the same thing with halved apples, peeled sliced pineapple, quinces, plums, apricots (especially, since they tend to be the most ruined by growers), peaches, and figs.

GRILLED MUSHROOM CAPS

Use portobello or field mushrooms, although if you can find and afford them, fresh cèpes (porcini or any boletus) or *matsutake* would be by far the best.

The old tradition of "mushrooms under glass" is still worth noting: the mushrooms were served on toast with an herb butter sauce, and came to the table under a glass dome. When the dome was raised in front of the diners, the aroma was released all around the table. Not a bad touch, any time.

SERVES 6

6	large portobello or field mushroom caps	¼ cup	olive oil
½ tablespoon	fresh thyme, finely chopped	1 cup	Italian parsley leaves
1 teaspoon	finely chopped fresh garlic		Salt and freshly ground black pepper

Rub the mushroom caps all over with a mixture of the thyme, garlic, and olive oil. Cover and let marinate for an hour.

Start a charcoal fire or heat the broiler. Cook the mushrooms over medium heat for 5 minutes and then turn them over and cook for another 5 minutes. Rake away the fire so that the heat is low (or turn down the broiler), and continue to cook another 15 minutes, or until the mushrooms are very tender. In the last five minutes of cooking, throw the marinade ingredients on the fire to smoke the mushrooms a bit.

VARIATIONS The mushrooms are delicious with nothing added, or perhaps just a mixture of equal parts chopped garlic chives, lemon zest, and Italian parsley. The real secret is not the garnish but the slow cooking of the mushrooms. But a foie gras sauce, with or without black truffles, would be awfully good, and a lobster or prawn rémoulade would be wonderfully over the top! And if you are not nervous about beef marrow, then by all means poach 1-inch-thick slices in salted water for 3 minutes, roll the slices in black butter, put on top of the mushrooms, season, and put under the broiler for 2 minutes. Finish by sprinkling with a little sea salt.

CAULIFLOWER WITH WHITE TRUFFLE SAUCE

The only white truffles worth the expense are from the area around Alba in the Piedmont region of Italy. Since their season is from September (dicey) to the end of December (heavenly) and they must be eaten within a week of being dug only fresh and not frozen, it is excusable to go slightly mad each year as I do, and set off in mid-November for Alba.

I have eaten the white ones, such as the *Tuber texense*, from elsewhere. As far as I know, the first time they were served in a restaurant in America (with little success) was at Chez Panisse, after Linda Guenzel (who wrote the first Chez Panisse cookbook) saw some squirrels doing cartwheels on her mother's lawn in Texas and scooped a few truffles up herself and brought them back to us. But they, like the ones from Oregon, are really no good, smelling of pine sap and tasting the same. I have never tried the African dessert truffles (*Terfezia*), beloved by imperial Romans, but I think I will stick to Italy.

I first tasted white truffles at Harry's Bar in Venice. I was there with Alice Waters on a little "honeymoon" of ours at the Gritti Palace. Even after two days at the Gritti, we had enough money to tiptoe into Harry's. Of course, it was truffle season, so—after nearly bankrupting ourselves on those divine sandwiches at the bar, washed down with Bellinis—we had to try the famous tagliarini with white truffles. The waiter had the bowl of truffles at the table as the pasta arrived, and with a truffle slicer in hand, he proceeded to slice along at the normal rate. Unknown to me was the fact that I was supposed to say "stop" after about five passes of truffle over the pasta. Being an employee of the incomparable Harry, the waiter stopped, paused elegantly, and told me how much each slice cost. I looked at Alice and she at me. We shrugged, as in "you only live once (and can afford to eat here only once)" and waved him on for more slices.

Since then, I have eaten them on fried eggs, possibly the best way of all; I have had those eggs on pizza then covered with truffles; I have doused fresh white beans and cipollini onions with them; I have put eggs in ramekins and covered the eggs with cream and white truffles; I have made club sandwiches with them; I have put them on all sorts of vegetables like mashes of potato, cardoon, cauliflower, artichoke, white beans, and fennel; I have steamed lobster meat in a buttered puree of white truffles; and I have put them in fish soup.

I wanted to give a recipe for a puree of cardoons in which are sunk coddled eggs, brought to the table in a gratin dish to be covered with white truffles, but thought that might be a bit over the top, even for me. Another dream of a dish, which I had during the last white truffle season, was cornmeal crêpes stuffed with Jerusalem artichokes swamped in a *bagna cauda*, and covered with a blizzard of white truffles. This was at the wonderful Ristorante Centro in Priocca, near Asti in the Piedmont.

But I have decided on cauliflower, not only because I love it, but because anyone can find it and afford it, and because this recipe is wonderful even without the truffles. Of course the obvious thing is to load up the puree with butter and cream, so the challenge here was to leave them both out.

The secret with cauliflower is to cook it quickly in a lot of salted water and then to use it right away. Always break it up into small flowerets so that they cook quickly and at the same rate.

SERVES 4

1	cauliflower, stemmed, cored, broken into 1-inch flowerets	1 small pinch	ground cardamom
		½ cup	extra virgin light yellow olive oil
4	cloves garlic, peeled		Freshly ground white pepper
5	salted anchovy fillets (see page 42)		White truffles
1 teaspoon	freshly grated lemon zest		

Put the cauliflower in 8 quarts of boiling salted water and cook for 5 minutes. Add the garlic and cook another minute or more until the cauliflower is tender when pierced with a fork.

Drain the cauliflower well in a colander, pick out the garlic cloves and place them in a small mixing bowl and then immediately, while still hot, put the cauliflower through the coarse blade (¹⁄₁₆ inch) of a food mill, right into a warm serving bowl. Mix in a little salt (not too much—remember the anchovy) and keep warm.

Put the anchovy filets, lemon zest, and cardamom in the mixing bowl with the garlic and mash them all together with a fork. Then beat in the olive oil with the fork until the puree is just barely mixed.

Pour the sauce over the cauliflower, shave as many truffles over the dish as you can afford, and then grind the pepper over that.

VARIATIONS Instead of the expensive truffles, try saucing the cauliflower with the asparagus sauce on page 120 or the nasturtium sauce on page 253.

STEAMED BLACK PERIGORD TRUFFLES (*TUBER MELANOSPORUM*) WITH POTATOES

Truffles are expensive, but if used effectively that money can go a long way. A whole egg-size black truffle, costing sixty to a hundred dollars, will provide six to eight people with a special-occasion feast they will never forget. And anyway, as Colette says in *Portraits et paysage*, "If you love her, pay her ransom regally, or leave her alone."

Truffles are best when fresh, but unlike anything else (except pastry, meat and fish essences, and ice cream) the black ones do very well when frozen. Freeze them while they are at their peak of freshness, wrapping each truffle separately in two layers of odorless plastic wrap, then in aluminum foil, and putting them in a sealed, dated container in the freezer

It is important to remember that they work well frozen *only* if you put them in whatever they are flavoring *while still frozen* and leave them there for an hour or two. Only in this way will frozen truffles retain their crisp texture and flavor, as well as infusing whatever they are in. Truffles preserved in Madeira make superb truffle-flavored liquid, but soft truffles and canned truffles (unless of the premium quality of the Pebeyre family in Cahors) are a total waste of money.

SERVES 4

4	small fresh black Perigord truffles, brushed to remove sand	12	fingerling potatoes (same size as truffles)
2 cups	unsalted mixed white veal and chicken stock	2 tablespoons	extra virgin light yellow olive oil or unsalted butter
8 sprigs	fresh thyme		Salt and freshly ground black pepper

Put the stock in the bottom of a steamer that has a tight-fitting top. Then put the thyme in the top part of the steamer. Cut the potatoes in half and put them on top of the thyme, and the truffles on top of the potatoes. Season.

Cover and simmer for 30 minutes. Remove the truffles and potatoes and keep warm. Whisk the butter into the stock, taste for seasoning, and pour over the truffles.

VARIATION When Mark Franz left Stars in San Francisco to open his own restaurant, Farallon, I threw a party for him and 25 guests in our private dining room. Each person had a truffle two inches in diameter, and I added a little Madeira to the steaming liquid.

VEGETABLE STOCK

This aromatic broth is a poaching liquid for fish, shellfish, and vegetables.

The wine is added halfway through the cooking, because if added at the beginning the acid in the wine would prevent the vegetables from cooking and giving up their flavor to the broth.

You can use a food processor to chop up the vegetables into ¼-inch pieces (although I would cut the onions by hand)—it is less work, and allows maximum contact of the water and vegetables, thus ensuring the shortest cooking time, which, as with fish stock, is desirable to keep the freshest possible flavors.

MAKES 1 GALLON

1	large onion, peeled, chopped	1 sprig	fresh thyme
		2 sprigs	fresh parsley
1	carrot, peeled, chopped	1 tablespoon	salt
1	leek, chopped, washed	1 gallon	water
1 stalk	celery, chopped	1 cup	dry white wine
1	bay leaf		

Put the vegetables, herbs, and salt in a pot with the water. Bring to a boil, skim, and simmer, uncovered, for 20 minutes.

Add the wine and simmer another 20 minutes.

Strain through a fine sieve into a bowl, discarding the vegetables, and let cool. Store in the refrigerator for no more than 3 days, but it can be frozen in covered containers for up to a month.

VARIATIONS For salmon-poaching stock, the white wine can be changed to a young red wine, and for other flavor variations infuse fresh ginger, fennel tops, lemon grass, or fresh herbs in the simmering broth for the last 10 minutes before straining.

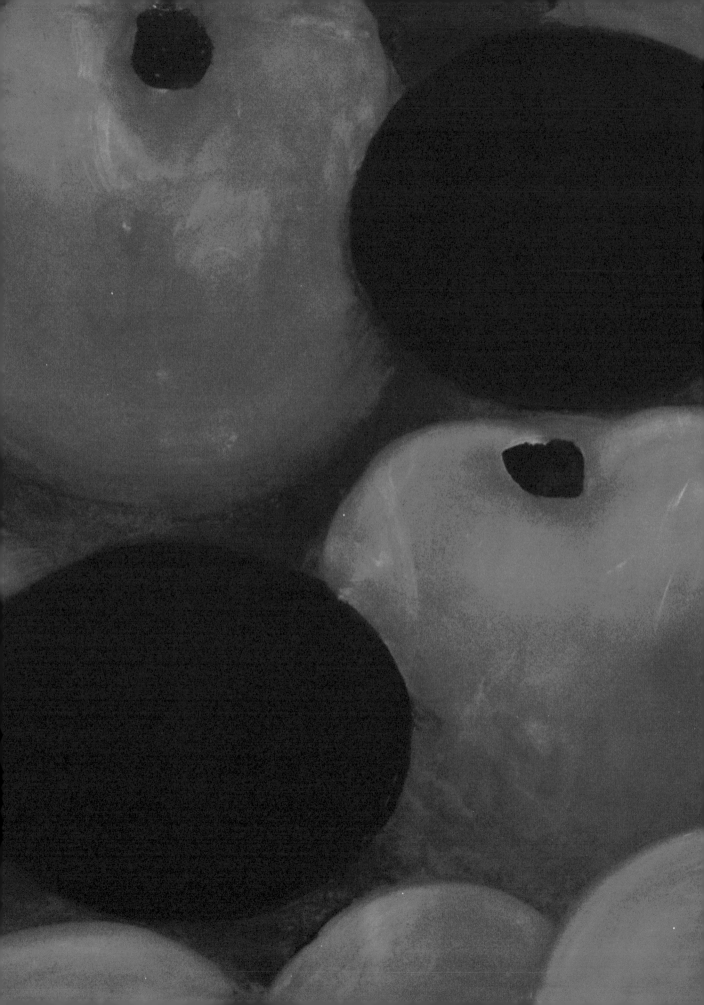

CHAPTER SIX
PASTA *and* GRAINS

PASTA DOUGH

FAST AND EASY SPAGHETTI WITH WARM SHRIMP SAUCE

CANNELLONI WITH SALT COD AND FRESH TOMATO SAUCE

RICOTTA DUMPLINGS WITH FAVA BEANS AND SAVORY

CAPELLINI WITH MUSSELS AND JT'S "AMERICAINE"

LINGUINE WITH CHICKPEAS, POTATOES, WHITE BEANS, GARLIC CLOVES,
AND RED CHILI FLAKES

RAVIOLO OF CRABMEAT WITH SHELLFISH BUTTER SAUCE

CORNMEAL AND POLENTA

POLENTA WITH WILD MUSHROOMS

BLUE CORN ENCHILADAS WITH HUITLACOCHE AND SQUASH FLOWERS

SQUID- OR CUTTLEFISH-INK RISOTTO

FRESH PEA RISOTTO WITH SQUASH BLOSSOMS

KEDGEREE

KASHA

COUSCOUS WITH MINT AND CHILI-INFUSED QUINCE

PASTA DOUGH

The proportions for this recipe will depend on the type of flour used and the size of the eggs, but 4 ounces of flour to 1 egg plus a yolk is my general rule, and bread flour or good semolina flour is the best.

The secret to making pasta by hand is a long, slow kneading until the texture of the dough is like satin.

YIELDS 1½ POUNDS

1 pound	flour, plus extra for kneading
4	large eggs
4	egg yolks
1 teaspoon	salt
2 tablespoons	olive oil

Put the flour in a bowl, then make a well in the center of the flour and add the eggs, the additional yolks, salt, and olive oil. Mix the eggs and oil gradually into the flour.

Gather the dough into a ball, dust with flour, and knead it on a lightly floured surface until the dough is dry, elastic, and smooth. Wrap in a towel or non-smelling plastic wrap and refrigerate for 1 hour.

Cut the dough into pieces and roll out by hand or in a pasta machine. Cut into the shapes you need.

Fast and Easy Spaghetti with Warm Shrimp Sauce

Spaghetti is one of the greatest fast foods in the world, even if served just with superb olive oil, freshly ground Sumatran black pepper, and freshly grated real Parmesan cheese. But whether served this simply, or simply with exotic ingredients like razor clams steamed in garlic and white wine or heirloom eggplant baked in a wood oven, buy the best quality durum wheat spaghetti you can find.

You can use Parmesan cheese in this dish, but in general cheese on seafood makes the seafood taste a bit "past it," so I don't recommend using the two together.

SERVES 4

8 ounces	spaghetti
2 tablespoons	extra virgin olive oil
1 teaspoon	freshly ground black pepper
2 cups	warm shrimp sauce (see page 237)

Put the spaghetti in lots of boiling salted water and cook until just tender all the way through, about 10 minutes. Drain the pasta well and return it to the pot. Add the olive oil and pepper and toss together with the spaghetti.

Put the pasta in a heated bowl, and add half of the sauce. Mix the sauce and the spaghetti together, season, and pass the rest of the sauce.

VARIATIONS For a shorter version of this dish, chop up four seeded Meyer lemons and mix them with ½ cup extra virgin olive oil, 1 teaspoon salt, ½ tablespoon very coarse black pepper (see page 39), 2 tablespoons chopped fresh tarragon leaves, and 4 ounces grated Parmesan cheese. The explosion of flavors when the sauce hits the hot pasta is breathtaking. Or use salt-preserved lemons (see page 43) mixed with fresh lemon, or Meyer lemon and arugula or rocket. Or use the Mediterranean oil and vinegar sauce on page 238 or even the Asian-inspired one on page 238, or the nasturtium sauce (see page 253), the asparagus sauce (see page 252), or fresh tomato sauce (see page 240).

Cannelloni with Salt Cod and Fresh Tomato Sauce

I don't know why one never sees cannelloni anymore. Probably they are considered too old-fashioned, and in the past always received a thick béchamel or white sauce, plus a little mediocre cheese and tomato paste. But when cannelloni are cooked properly, they can be one of the finest, subtlest, and most ethereal of all pastas.

This recipe can be made a few hours in advance of the final cooking and generates at least two cannelloni per person.

SERVES 4

1 recipe	pasta dough (see page 146), rolled out 1/16-inch thick	2 tablespoons	finely chopped salt-preserved lemon (see page 43), or finely grated lemon zest
1 cup	creamed salt cod (see page 174)	½ cup	basil leaves, finely chopped
2 cups	fresh tomato sauce (see page 240)		Salt and freshly ground white pepper
½ cup	heavy cream with a pinch of salt	2 tablespoons	butter

Preheat oven to 375 degrees.

Cut the rolled-out pasta into 4-inch by 3-inch rectangles. Cook in batches of 6 in 8 quarts of gently simmering salted water until almost tender. Remove with a skimmer, dip the pieces of cooked pasta into iced water for a minute, and then drain them on both sides on dishtowels.

Lightly butter an ovenproof 2-inch-deep gratin dish just big enough to hold the rolled-up stuffed pieces of pasta with ½-inch space between them.

Lay the shapes out on a flat surface, and put 2 tablespoons of cold creamed cod ½ inch off one of the long edges, and ½ inch away from each end, and roll up. Place seam side down in the dish. Up to this point the cannelloni can be made 2 hours in advance, if they are tightly covered and refrigerated.

Warm the tomato sauce. Add the lemon and basil to the salted cream and whip it until it just holds its shape on the end of the whisk. Then fold the cream into the tomato sauce. Salt and pepper the sauce lightly if it needs it, then pour the sauce over the cannelloni. Put the dish in the oven and bake for 15 minutes, or until heated through.

VARIATIONS For other sauces, think about a puree of fresh wild mushrooms, or an artichoke puree with some dried wild mushroom puree mixed in, or any kind of leftover meats chopped up and mixed with herb-flavored sour cream. For other stuffings, think squash blossoms filled with blue cheese stuffed inside the cannelloni (or use just the blue cheese). And don't forget a stuffing made from half pureed and half chopped braised sweetbreads mixed with tongue and black truffles, with a creamed puree of Jerusalem artichoke sauce on top and more black truffles on top of that—a dish that is perfect for Christmas Eve, since when you're on your second bottle of champagne, all you have to do is put the dish in the oven and listen for the timer.

Ricotta Dumplings with Fava Beans and Savory

I have tried forever to like the classic heavy potato and flour gnocchi, but have given up. These ricotta dumplings, which I first tasted at the Zuni Café in San Francisco (thank you Judy Rogers) changed my mind about gnocchi, but only if they are made like this.

The recipe calls for savory because its higher purpose is to be cooked with fava beans (although tarragon is a good stand-in). In the south of France, and now in northern California, they know that winter savory (*Satureja montana: poivre d'âne*, or "donkey pepper") is finer than the summer one.

MAKES 24 DUMPLINGS

2 cups	fresh ricotta cheese		½ tablespoon	finely chopped fresh winter savory leaves
¼ cup	white flour			Salt and freshly ground black pepper
1 teaspoon	salt			
5	egg yolks			
3 pounds	fresh young broad or fava beans in the pods		4	nasturtium flowers, stemmed, shredded
4 tablespoons	melted butter			

Mix the ricotta, flour, salt, and yolks together. Refrigerate 1 hour. Take out and form into little *quenelle* shapes with two small soupspoons heated in hot water: mound one with the ricotta, smooth out the mound with the other hot spoon, and slip off the spoon. Roll the dumplings on floured grease-proof paper and store covered in the refrigerator until ready to serve (up to 3 hours).

Take the fava beans out of the pods and then peel the green skin off the beans. Cook the beans in 4 quarts of boiling salted water for 5 minutes, scoop them out with a strainer, and put them in a bowl. Add the butter and savory, a pinch of salt, and lashings of freshly ground black pepper.

Put the dumplings into the same pot of barely simmering water in which the beans were cooked, and simmer for 10 minutes. Lift the dumplings out of the water, and put them in warm soup plates. Spoon the savory butter from the beans over the dumplings, and then the beans around them. Garnish with the flowers.

VARIATION Instead of butter or the flowers, use the nasturtium sauce (see page 253), or one made with ½ cup cream, the savory, and ¼ cup chopped cooked bacon, all in which the beans have been cooked for 10 minutes over low heat.

Capellini with Mussels and JT's "Américaine"

One of the great sauces for lobster and crayfish is the shellfish sauce called either *Américaine* or *Armoriaine*. Which name to use is a debate in France as long and complex as a local tax issue. Let's settle on the position that it comes not from America, but Armorica (Brittany), and just because it has tomatoes in it does not mean it is really *sauce Provençale,* another red herring in the whole debate. The point of the sauce is the flavor of the shells of lobster, or prawns or crab or whatever shellfish you use.

If you have shellfish essence, you do not need the step in the recipe with the shells.

SERVES 6			
6 ounces	capellini	2	cloves garlic, chopped
3 pounds	mussels, washed, bearded	½ cup	dry white wine
4 tablespoons	extra virgin olive oil	1 cup	rich fish-shellfish stock
1 pound	lobster or prawn shells, crushed (or 2 cups shellfish essence, see page 188)	2	large tomatoes, chopped (see page 47)
		6 tablespoons	butter, cut in ½-inch cubes, kept cold
4 tablespoons	chopped white onion	2 tablespoons	heavy cream
2 tablespoons	chopped celery	¼ teaspoon	cayenne
2	sprigs fresh tarragon		Salt

Heat 2 tablespoons of the olive oil in a chemically nonreactive 3-quart pot. Add the shells and stir around in the hot oil for 10 minutes. You can flame the shells with 2 tablespoons of brandy if you want some fun, but it is not necessary.

Remove the shells and put them in a bowl and set aside. Add the onion, celery, tarragon, garlic, and ¼ cup water to the pot. Cover and sweat 10 minutes. Do not brown. Add the mussels, white wine, and fish stock, cover, and cook over high heat until the mussels open, about 5 minutes, shaking the pan hard a couple of times. Remove the mussels and let them cool.

Put the tomatoes and lobster or prawn shells in the pot and simmer the liquid uncovered for 20 minutes. While the liquid is simmering, take the mussels out of their shells and discard the shells.

Strain the simmering stock through a very fine sieve or cheesecloth, discard all the debris, and reduce over medium heat for 15 minutes, skimming off any scum. The sauce can be made in advance up to this point.

Bring the sauce to a simmer, and whisk in the butter, cream, and cayenne. Season, and keep warm in a double boiler, but do not let it boil.

Add the mussels to the sauce for about 2 minutes, or until they are heated through, heating the sauce a little more if necessary, but do not overheat the mussels.

Meanwhile, cook the capellini in boiling salted water for 5 minutes, or until tender. Drain, put in a bowl, add the olive oil and half the sauce (but not the mussels), and mix gently together.

Serve the pasta immediately on warm plates and pour the rest of the sauce and the mussels over the pasta. Let your guests see and savor the aromas of this whole serving process.

Linguine with Chickpeas, Potatoes, White Beans, Garlic Cloves, and Red Chili Flakes

There are three things to remember here: multiple starches really complement each other; whole garlic cloves cooked until soft are a mild and wonderful vegetable by themselves; and the two peppers, red and black, also complement each other. You can cook this dish from scratch or use leftover beans.

SERVES 6

8 ounces	linguine	1 tablespoon	rosemary leaves, finely chopped
½ cup	chickpeas, cooked (as for white beans; see page 33)	¼ cup	grated Parmesan
		½ tablespoon	freshly ground black pepper
30	cloves garlic, peeled	1 cup	cooked white beans (see page 33)
3	medium boiling potatoes, peeled, cut in ½-inch cubes	2 tablespoons	red chili flakes
			Salt
½ cup	extra virgin olive oil		
1	bunch Italian parsley, stemmed, leaves coarsely chopped		

Cook the linguine and garlic cloves in 8 quarts of boiling salted water for 5 minutes, then add the potatoes. Boil another 5 to 10 minutes or until the pasta is tender and the garlic and potatoes are soft enough to squeeze easily between your fingers. If the pasta finishes first, lift it out with tongs into a bowl.

While the pasta is cooking, put the olive oil, parsley, rosemary, Parmesan, and black pepper in a warm bowl big enough to hold all the pasta.

When the pasta is almost done, add the peas and beans for 30 seconds to heat them through. Drain the linguine with the peas and beans, reserving ½ cup of the liquid, and put the pasta and vegetables in the bowl. Add the reserved cooking liquid, and toss all of it together, adding salt to taste.

Sprinkle the chili flakes all over the top of the pasta.

RAVIOLO OF CRABMEAT
WITH SHELLFISH BUTTER SAUCE

I like making one big raviolo per person for a first course—or two for a main—because they are easier to keep track of while they are cooking. If you are standing there with hungry family or guests behind you and you have to shuffle sixteen to twenty ravioli into simmering water, then watch them like a hawk so they don't burst from the water boiling too vigorously, or stick to the bottom of the pan from the water not boiling vigorously enough, you would wish you were cooking these larger ones. The big ones also hold for up to twenty minutes in warm (not hot) fish stock mixed with a little butter or olive oil.

I like wonton wrappers, the large very thin square ones, since they cook quickly, can be bought in the size you want them, and are consistent. Buy only the best quality fresh crabmeat.

SERVES 4

¾ cup	crabmeat, picked through for shell fragments	1	medium ripe red tomato, chopped (see page 47)
¼ cup	heavy cream	1	medium yellow tomato, chopped (see page 47)
1 teaspoon	fresh white onion juice (from pureed onion, sieved)	1 tablespoon	fresh tarragon leaves, chopped
8	wonton wrappers, 3 by 3 inches	6 ounces	butter, cut in small pieces, kept cold
1	egg, beaten		Salt
¼ cup	shellfish essence (see page 188)		Freshly ground white pepper

Mix the crab, cream, and onion juice. Do not beat. Taste for salt, but it may not need any. Add salt if needed and a pinch of white pepper.

Lay out four wrappers, and put one-quarter of the crabmeat in the center of each wrapper. Moisten the edges and the crabmeat with egg, and then put another wonton wrapper on top of each one. Press down on the edges of the top wonton so that they meet the bottom one exactly and create a firm seal.

Cook the filled wontons gently in 4 quarts of simmering salted water for 5 minutes or until the edges can be pinched through easily with your fingernail.

While they are cooking bring the shellfish essence to a boil. Then add the tomatoes and tarragon, turn down the heat, and while the essence is simmering, immediately whisk in the pieces of cold butter until all the butter is incorporated. The sauce must be smooth and hot, but do not let it boil again once you've started to add the butter. Taste the sauce for seasoning.

Lift the ravioli out of the water with a sieve/skimmer, let the sieve rest for a few seconds on a towel, then put one raviolo on each of the four hot plates, and pour the sauce over them.

VARIATIONS For a different stuffing, use the mint-sage-rosemary pesto sauce instead of crab (see page 244), and sauce them with the warm shrimp sauce (see page 237) or Mediterranean sauce (see page 238).

CORNMEAL AND POLENTA

Polenta is made from cornmeal, coarse or fine, and is cooked in stock or water.

Debates rage over whether polenta should have a thick or thin texture, but it's really a question of what it is going to be used for. If it is to be sauced with a mushroom ragout, for example, it should be on the thick side. As a bed for grilled chicken or little game birds, it should be thinner.

Polenta can be kept in a double boiler for hours. If it thickens too much, add more stock or water. Leftovers can be sliced and grilled or fried.

YIELDS 8 CUPS

2 quarts	chicken stock (see page 215) or water
2 cups	coarse ground yellow cornmeal
1 tablespoon	salt
4 tablespoons	butter

Bring the stock or water to a rolling boil. Add the salt. Pour in the cornmeal very gradually in a steady stream while whisking. Passing it through a sieve works well. Continue to vigorously whisk the liquid and cornmeal together until all the cornmeal is incorporated and there are no lumps.

Then use a wooden spoon to stir constantly and scrape around the bottom corners of the pot where the polenta will try to stick and burn.

Cook over medium-low heat, stirring slowly and constantly, for 45 minutes. Taste for salt, stir in the butter, and hold in a double boiler until needed.

HOLDING SOFT CORNMEAL OR POLENTA

One can keep stirring in more liquid to keep the polenta soft, but there is another way, as I found out totally by mistake, when reheating leftover polenta.

Cook the polenta the day before, pour it into a bowl, and let it firm up. Brush the top of the polenta with melted butter or olive oil to prevent a skin from forming. An hour before using, break the polenta up and heat it with a cup of stock or water. Once smooth and held in a double boiler, it will never firm up again.

GRILLED POLENTA

Spread the just-cooked polenta out on a buttered and then chilled cookie sheet or sheet pan, brush with butter, cool, cut it in shapes, then grill it over charcoal *very* slowly for 30 minutes, basting it occasionally with herb oil.

The polenta becomes crusty on the outside and stays voluptuously soft on the inside, especially if you mix ½ cup blue cheese with the polenta before pouring it into the pan.

POLENTA WITH WILD MUSHROOMS

The first time I had polenta was when I was nine and on an Italian ship sailing from Australia to Genoa. I loved all sorts of hot cereals, and thought polenta was the same thing, so insisted they serve it to me for breakfast, with caramel. Much later (although still remembering with fondness the sugared polenta), I graduated to one of the greatest dishes in the world, polenta with mascarpone covered with freshly grated mounds of white truffles and lashings of ground black pepper.

For this dish, I put the cold mascarpone under the hot polenta, creating a surprise as the cream melts slowly out from under the polenta, as well as a contrast in temperatures.

For a faster and easier version (30 minutes to prepare), omit the cèpe salad on top of the cooked mushrooms and use just the white domestic and portobello field mushrooms to sauce the polenta.

SERVES 4 TO 6

1½ cups	polenta meal	2 large	cèpes, *matsutake*, or
6 cups	water		Caesar's *Amanita*
2 tablespoons	mixed fresh herb leaves,		mushroom caps, cooked
	finely chopped		as on page 139, sliced in
1 cup	mascarpone (or double		⅛-inch thick pieces, and
	cream, see page 27)		kept warm
¼ pound	butter	1 tablespoon	balsamic vinegar
2 tablespoons	finely chopped fresh garlic	2 tablespoons	chopped fresh Italian parsley
2 pounds	fresh wild and domestic	3 tablespoons	hazelnut oil
	mushrooms, sliced		Salt and freshly ground
½ cup	chicken stock (see page 215)		black pepper

Cook the polenta as directed in the recipe on page 153, and keep it warm in the top of a double boiler until needed. Stir in more water if it gets too thick. Mix in 4 tablespoons of the butter just before serving.

Mix the herbs with the mascarpone and keep chilled.

Melt 2 tablespoons of the butter in a sauté pan. Put the garlic in the pan and cook for 2 minutes, without letting it brown. Add all the mushrooms (except the cèpes), toss them in the garlic butter, add a pinch of salt, and cook over medium heat for 2 minutes. Add the stock, turn up the heat, and cook another 5 minutes. Add the remaining butter and stir until all the butter is incorporated into the sauce. Add pepper and more salt if necessary. Keep warm.

Put the vinegar, parsley, and hazelnut oil in a mixing bowl. Add the warm cèpe slices and mix gently together. Season.

Put the herb cream in the center of each plate, and spoon the polenta over the cream. Then spoon the mushroom sauce over the cream, and place the warm cèpe salad on top of the mushroom sauce.

VARIATION I love polenta with fresh young white sweet corn kernels off the cob (one-third the quantity of the cooked polenta), which are put in the polenta for the last 5 minutes of cooking. Then I stir in 2 tablespoons of a butter mixed with blanched and pureed chives, and garnish it all with chive or sage flowers.

BLUE CORN ENCHILADAS WITH HUITLACOCHE AND SQUASH FLOWERS

In Mexico, there is no need for black truffles—they have huitlacoche, the ambrosial black fungus that grows on corn, and it is indeed food for the gods, even if it is as hideous as it is delicious. Diana Kennedy calls its flavor "an inky, mushroom flavor that is almost impossible to describe" (although she does it well). If you have ever had squid or cuttlefish ink, think of the fungus variation of that.

You can find huitlacoche (or *Ustilago maydis*) in a can, and if you are ever at the Chino Ranch in southern California, you can find it fresh in their cornfields.

One of these rich enchiladas per person might be enough.

SERVES 4

4	fresh blue corn tortillas, as thin as possible	1 tablespoon	fresh marjoram leaves, finely chopped
4 ounces	huitlacoche puree (canned)	1 tablespoon	sour cream
¾ cup	fresh white Mexican cheese (queso de Oaxaca)	8	fresh squash blossoms, ⅛-inch stem end cut off
¼ cup	heavy cream		Salt and freshly ground black pepper
1 teaspoon	ancho chili powder		
pinch	ground cumin		

Mix the huitlacoche with the cheese, cream, chili powder, and cumin.

Mix the marjoram with the sour cream, season, and stuff this herb cream into the blossoms.

Melt one-fourth of the butter in a frying pan large enough to hold a tortilla, and warm a tortilla for a minute on each side in the butter. Repeat with the other three tortillas.

Divide the huitlacoche mixture amongst the tortillas, placing it just off center to one side. Roll up the tortillas and put them seam side down in an oiled, ovenproof 3-inch-deep gratin dish.

Put two stuffed blossoms on top of each enchilada, and heat them in the oven for 7 to 10 minutes, until the enchiladas are heated through and the cream inside the blossoms is hot and melts down over the enchiladas.

Serve immediately.

SQUID- OR CUTTLEFISH-INK RISOTTO

This *risotto nero* belongs to the family of risotto that has the flavoring element cooked along with the rice for the whole cooking time rather than being added during the last few moments of cooking. But the cuttlefish ink adds a delicate perfume to it as well, so in order to keep this intact (it would cook off after five minutes of cooking), I like to finish the risotto with an ink butter.

Of course, the black risotto is delicious with squid or cuttlefish cooked in with the risotto (*risotto di seppie*), but this risotto is delicious by itself, although there are many possible additions, like lobster or sliced tiny artichokes stewed in olive oil. See also the Variations below.

If you are not getting your ink from fresh squid or cuttlefish, the squid ink can be bought in 1-ounce packages at specialty stores (see Resources, page 280).

SERVES 4 TO 6

4 ounces	squid ink		2 sprigs	fresh thyme
6 cups	fish stock (see page 187)		1 ½ cups	Carnaroli or Vialone rice
4 tablespoons	butter			(or Arborio)
2 tablespoons	olive oil		½ cup	dry white wine
1	large shallot, peeled, finely chopped			

Bring the stock to a simmer.

Mix half the ink thoroughly with the butter.

Put the olive oil, shallot, and thyme in a 4-quart saucepan and cook over low heat, stirring constantly, for 5 minutes. Add the rice, and stir with the shallots and oil for another 5 minutes, or until the grains of rice are coated and slightly translucent.

Turn up the heat to high, add the wine, and cook while stirring for 2 minutes. Remove the thyme sprigs. Turn the heat down to medium, and start adding the stock, ½ cup at a time. Dissolve the remaining half of the ink in the second ½ cup of stock before adding it. As each ½ cup of stock is absorbed, add another ½ cup, and keep on cooking like this, with the rice and stock simmering gently (adjust the heat if you need to), and stirring constantly, until the rice is cooked, no less than 20 minutes, and probably no more than 30.

You will know the rice is cooked when the rice as a whole is creamy and each grain is tender. If at this point you need to add a bit more stock, do so; and if there is too much stock at this point, turn the heat to high and stir like crazy until the excess liquid is gone. If you run out of stock at the end, add boiling water until the rice is cooked.

Remove the pot from the heat, and stir in the ink butter. At this point, stir ¼ cup of stock or boiling water into the risotto, to give it an even more voluptuous (*all'onda*, "like a wave") texture. Check the seasoning, and serve.

VARIATIONS I like the richness of this risotto with the richness of shellfish like lobster, mussels, or crab; and with mussels in a saffron shellfish butter sauce, it is superb.

FRESH PEA RISOTTO WITH SQUASH BLOSSOMS

This risotto, in contrast to the black risotto, is flavored with elements that should not be added until the end of the cooking of the rice, keeping the flavors fresh and their colors bright. This risotto is finished with peas and a butter mixed with fresh pea puree. Asparagus, fava beans, green beans (*haricots verts*), and fresh herbs like basil are examples of other ingredients and flavors that need to be added only at the last minute.

SERVES 4 TO 6

2 cups	shelled fresh peas	2 tablespoons	olive oil
4 tablespoons	unsalted butter	1	large shallot, peeled,
½ cup	mascarpone, sour cream,		finely chopped
	or double cream	1½ cups	Carnaroli or Vialone rice
	(see page 27)		(or Arborio)
2 teaspoons	freshly ground	½ cup	dry white wine
	black pepper	6 cups	vegetable stock
1 tablespoon	freshly grated lemon zest		(see page 143)
8	squash blossoms, stemmed		Salt

Cook the peas in 4 quarts of boiling salted water for 5 to 8 minutes, or until tender. Drain in a sieve, and put on a cold cookie sheet in the freezer until they are cool (10 minutes).

Put ½ cup of the cooked peas in a food processor with the butter, and puree. Take the puree out and put it through a sieve, discarding the debris and saving the pea butter.

Mix the mascarpone, pepper, and lemon zest and stuff into the blossoms.

Put the olive oil and shallots in a 4-quart saucepan, and cook over low heat for 5 minutes, stirring constantly. Do not let the shallots brown!

Add the rice, and stir the rice with the shallots for another 5 minutes or until the grains of rice are coated and slightly translucent.

Turn up the heat, add the wine, and cook while stirring for 2 minutes. Turn the heat down to medium, and start adding the stock, ½ cup at a time.

As soon as the stock is absorbed, add another ½ cup, and keep on cooking like this, with the stock and rice simmering gently, and stirring constantly, until the rice is cooked, no less than 20 minutes, and probably no more than 30.

Preheat the boiler to high.

After the last ½ cup of liquid is added to the risotto and it starts to be absorbed, add the cooked peas. Finish the risotto with the pea butter, seasoning, and last few tablespoons of hot vegetable stock (or boiling water if you have run out of stock).

Put the blossoms under the broiler for 1 minute, and then put 2 on top of each serving of risotto.

VARIATIONS If you can find pea tendrils (the actual end of the plant's new branches and not the horrible pea shoots), soften them in butter and a little water for 2 minutes, and fold them into the risotto with the peas. I have also stuffed the blossoms with foie gras mousse, and the foie gras melting over the risotto is spectacular.

KEDGEREE

This grand pilaf is one of the many good things that came out of Anglo-Indian cookery and is an example of one of the first "fusion" dishes. The word comes from the Hindi *khichri*, a breakfast rice that contains cooked lentils and a lot of butter with fried onions on top. If you were rich in the fifteenth century, you fed it to your elephants as well.

Kedgeree made my first reputation as a cook when I was twelve. I cooked it for the family Sunday breakfast, as a change from our usual, either haddock or huevos rancheros. All I remember is everyone asking me, "How did you do that?" "Easy," I thought privately, "I'd do anything to avoid eating that smoked haddock in milk and onions again." Years later, when I cooked the haddock for myself, it was fine, and I realized my mother had been cooking the fish too fast, letting the milk boil, and toughening the fish to dryness.

This is a modern version of the classic Anglo-Indian dish. It is an amazing leftover the next day, cold, with even colder beer.

SERVES 4 TO 6

1½ pounds	undyed smoked haddock fillet (or very good quality kippers)		4	hard-boiled eggs (see page 67), shelled, quartered into wedges
1	white onion, peeled, cored, finely chopped		1	bunch cilantro, stemmed, leaves chopped
2	fresh lime leaves		1	ripe lime, juiced and zested
2 tablespoons	chopped fresh garlic		1 teaspoon	finely chopped ginger
4 tablespoons	unsalted butter		pinch	cayenne, salt, and freshly ground black pepper
½ teaspoon	ground cumin			
1 teaspoon	ground turmeric		½ cup	clarified butter (see page 27)
½ teaspoon	ground cardamom		8	lime wedges, seeds removed
6 ounces	rice			

Preheat the oven to 300 degrees.

Put the haddock, onions, lime leaves, and garlic in a 4-inch-deep pan just large enough to hold the fish and add 3 cups water. Cover and simmer gently over very low heat for 10 minutes or until the fish is tender and flaky. Take the fish out and set it aside to cool. Discard the lime leaves, and strain the cooking liquid, saving it as well as the onions.

Melt the butter in the same pan, and add the reserved chopped onions, the cumin, turmeric, and cardamom. Add the rice and cook for 5 minutes, stirring constantly until all the rice is coated with the butter. Add the reserved fish cooking liquid, bring to a simmer, cover, and cook the rice over low heat for 15 minutes, or until the rice is cooked through and tender. Uncover the pan and put it in the oven to keep warm and dry out a bit (but for no more than 10 minutes).

Flake the fish and remove any bones. Put the flaked fish in a bowl with the eggs, cilantro, lime juice and zest, ginger, and cayenne. Mix gently, and season. Take the rice out of the oven, and while hot add to the bowl with the fish and mix gently with the spices, eggs, and herbs. Put the kedgeree on a hot platter and serve with the melted butter and lime wedges on the side.

KASHA

I adore kasha, but I wonder if my personal memories of it are too strong for me to be objective. In my late teens and early twenties, whenever I visited my aunt and Russian uncle, they would fill their table with Russian counts and princes of imperial blood, then serve pheasant cooked in 100-year-old Madeira, perched on nests of wild rice and kasha. The fact that these meals usually occurred in the dripping 100-degree heat in Washington, D.C., in August, only added to the surreal quality of the dinners, something that appealed to and never deterred the Russians. After all, "it was grouse season in Scotland, and pheasant season somewhere."

Unlike wild rice, kasha is cooked using the "pilaf" method, which is to say that the liquid is measured so that theoretically, when the liquid is gone, the kasha is done. But like wild rice, kasha really comes into its own when put back in the oven and toasted again after the first cooking. The extra oven work is worth the added flavor the kasha gets from the toasting.

Use the largest size groats.

SERVES 4 TO 6

1 cup	kasha or buckwheat groats
1	whole egg, beaten
1 teaspoon	salt
4 tablespoons	butter
2½ cups	water
1 cup	chicken, turkey, or duck stock, or a mixture

Preheat the oven to 350 degrees.

Choose a 6-inch-deep covered heavy casserole that will hold the kasha in a 2-inch-deep layer.

Put the kasha in a bowl with the egg and salt, and mix well. Melt 2 tablespoons of the butter in the casserole over medium heat, and add the kasha. Cook while stirring constantly for 5 minutes or until the kasha and egg are dry. Then add the water, cover, put the casserole in the oven, and bake for 20 minutes.

Take the casserole out of the oven, uncover, add the rest of the butter and the chicken stock, and stir well. Put the casserole back in the oven uncovered for another 15 to 20 minutes, stirring and turning it over every 5 minutes, until the kasha is fluffy and dry, the grains separate, and the kasha has a wonderful toasted aroma.

Couscous with Mint
and Chili-Infused Quince

Poor old couscous. Once rarely seen in U.S. restaurants, and now seen everywhere, it remains misunderstood. There is a reason why the hennaed hands of the Berber women look so smooth and beautiful: it's from all that rubbing of warm couscous in clarified butter. This rubbing process is one of the secrets to successful couscous. The other is to never use the instant or precooked kind. As with anything, always buy the real thing of the best quality, and please do not pour cold water over the couscous as some books direct.

SERVES 6

2 cups	couscous		6	quince, quartered, cored, put in lemon water
¼ cup	clarified butter (see page 27)		½ cup	ancho-chili puree (see page 32)
1	1-inch-piece cinnamon stick		2 tablespoons	butter
1 teaspoon	cumin seeds		¼ teaspoon	cardamom
2	bay leaves		1 teaspoon	grated orange zest
1	small bunch fresh mint, stemmed, stems saved, leaves coarsely chopped			Salt

Put the couscous in a bowl and pour 6 cups of boiling water over it. Leave it for 15 minutes, then mix it with a spoon until the mass of couscous is broken up and loose. It will still have some small lumps.

Warm the clarified butter, and pour half of it over the couscous. Work the couscous through your hands, rubbing it backwards and forwards, for 10 minutes. Pour the rest of the butter over the couscous, sprinkle it with a teaspoon of salt, and work it another 10 minutes, or until there are no more lumps. Discard any small lumps that will not go away.

Put the cinnamon, cumin, and bay leaves in a pot with a gallon of water. Put the couscous in a colander (or even better use a couscous steamer) that fits the pot tightly, cover the colander tightly with foil, and simmer the water in the pot for 30 minutes.

Add the mint stems, 1 teaspoon salt, and the quince sections to the water under the colander. Stir the couscous well and put the colander over the steam again. Cover and cook another 20 minutes, this time stirring the couscous well every 5 minutes.

When the quince is tender, take it out of the spice water, drain, and toss it in a bowl with the ancho chili puree, butter, mint leaves, cardamom, and orange zest. Season and put the couscous in mounds on warm plates with the quince sections on top.

CHAPTER SEVEN
FISH *and* SHELLFISH

Fast and Easy Plate-Cooked Fish Paillard with Ginger, Garlic, and Tomatoes

What the black bean cake did for the Santa Fe Bar and Grill in Berkeley, this paillard of fish did for Stars in San Francisco. I developed it with the same purpose: to present, at the opening of a restaurant, a fast, new, easily cooked, foolproof, and easily understood dish. With a little advance chopping and slicing, you can serve this winning dish in five minutes.

I call this dish a "paillard" because the piece of fish is cut like a paillard of veal—in a very thin slice, which is then pounded even thinner. It is so thin that you do not have to use a pan to cook the fish, which is why you can't overcook it—the heat of the plate and the hot sauce poured over the paillard do all the cooking.

The original recipe had lobster butter drizzled over it, and since then it has also featured fresh chilies, Chinese black beans, and most of the other ingredients that recur throughout this book. So feel free to make your own version.

If you cut open plastic ziplock bags or something similar, very lightly oil the insides, and gently pound the fish between the two sides of plastic, the job of pounding is very easy.

SERVES 4

4	2-ounce slices boneless and skinless fillet of salmon, tuna, halibut, grouper, red snapper, sturgeon, sea bass, or albacore, no thicker than ¼ inch	1	2-ounce piece fresh ginger, peeled, finely chopped
		3 cloves	garlic, finely chopped
		⅔ cup	chopped tomatoes (see page 47)
		12 sprigs	fresh cilantro
3 tablespoons	butter		Salt and freshly ground black pepper
1 cup	fish stock (see page 187)		

Preheat the broiler or oven.

Pound the fish slices until they are evenly ⅛-inch thick.

Put four heat-resistant plates in the oven or under the broiler until hot. Remove and brush each one with ½ teaspoon of the butter.

Season the paillards of fish with salt and pepper and put one on each plate. Mix the fish stock, ginger, garlic, and tomatoes in a sauté pan. Bring to a boil and cook 2 minutes. Whisk the remaining butter into the sauce and pour it over the fish.

By the time you garnish the plates with the cilantro, the fish will be done.

VARIATIONS Use sturgeon and garnish the center of the cooked fish with a tablespoon of spiced crabmeat, cooked fish in green goddess mayonnaise (see page 249), or preserved tuna (see page 173) in sour cream mixed with ancho chili puree (see page 32). Or use radish salad as on the sea bass (see page 168). And spoon over the fish your choice of a flavored cream from a puree of chipotle, mixed herbs, or a ginger puree. Or cut open an avocado, dice it, add a teaspoon of cumin and 2 tablespoons lime juice, and put that in the center of the cooked fish.

WHOLE BONED DEEP-FRIED SOLE "COLBERT"

Some dishes never grow old, and although this dish was meant for Dover sole, petrale or any firm-fleshed flatfish will do, even a small halibut or turbot.

This dish is easily done for two, but don't cook it for four, unless you love to deep-fry and are comfortable doing it safely in larger quantities.

The filling can be anything you want: a mixed warm vegetable salad like asparagus, green beans, and fava beans boiled and tossed in butter, or just a sauce, such as rémoulade, tartar, or Montpelier butter (see page 246) or lemon fig relish (see page 243).

Whatever the filling, it is pure pleasure to be able to cut into this whole fish and find no bones.

SERVES 2 TO 4

2	1-pound whole Dover or petrale sole, cleaned, scaled, gills removed	6 cups	vegetable oil (peanut or canola)
1 cup	milk	½ cup	Russian dressing (see page 250)
½ cup	flour, seasoned with salt and pepper	1 tablespoon	chopped chives
4	eggs, beaten	1 tablespoon	chopped fresh Italian parsley leaves
2 cups	fresh white breadcrumbs (see page 32)		

Have the fish seller remove the gills and guts from the sole.

Put the sole, white skin side, upon a clean cutting board that will not slide around on the table (put a damp cloth under it). Then, using a sharp, thin boning knife, cut down the center line along the back-bone from the tail to the head, all the way to the bone. Then insert the knife at a right angle to the cut, between the fish flesh and the bone, and work along the back bone, to within ¼ inch of the sides of the fish. Repeat, freeing the flesh from the bone on the other side of the cut.

Snip the head and tail ends of the backbone with scissors, severing them completely. Now take one end and lift the bone up and away from the fish. Tradition says that you should remove the black skin before doing this, but at home that is easier said than done. If you don't like the black skin, don't eat it. I do.

Rinse the fish in cold running water and pat dry with paper towels. First, immerse the sole in the milk, then put it into the flour on both sides, then into the beaten egg, and finally into the breadcrumbs, patting them into the interior as well. If the flaps do not stay open outward, put toothpicks in them to hold them back. Refrigerate the fish for 10 minutes (or up to 30 minutes) to set the coating.

When ready to serve the fish, heat the oil to 375 degrees and deep-fry the fish for 6 to 10 minutes, depending on the size of the fish, making sure that the flaps stay open and curl up and outwards. Cut into the fish at its thickest part to test for doneness. The fish is done as soon as there is no more translucent flesh at the cut. When the fish are cooked, put them on paper towels for a minute to drain. Serve on heated oval platters just bigger than the fish, sprinkle with the chives and parsley, and spoon some sauce into the center of the fish cavity. Pass the rest of the sauce separately.

The only bones left will be around the edges of the fish, and these are easily scraped aside before eating the fish.

SEARED THAI SNAPPER
WITH BLOOD ORANGE SAUCE

There are many versions of this dish, but all involve an entire fish, boned and flattened out (butterflied), head on with tails trimmed, then cooked and served whole to enjoy the beauty of the fish. It is also easy to eat because there are no bones left between the head and tail.

Whether you use a Thai snapper, red Gulf snapper, golden trout, small Arctic char, or even rock cod (or the fabulous South China Sea's So Mei), the dish is very easy to cook once the boning is done. The garnish can be elaborate (fried spring rolls made out of the fish skin stuffed with ancho chilies and cooked black beans) or simple like one of the compound butters on pages 245–246.

SERVES 4

The Fish:

4	1-pound fresh whole Thai snapper, scaled, cleaned, gills removed
½ tablespoon	chopped fresh thyme leaves
¼ cup	olive oil

The Sauce:

1	blood orange (or half ripe pink grapefruit), juiced, zested
	Salt and freshly ground pepper
¼ cup	extra virgin olive oil

The Garnish:

½ cup	Italian parsley leaves
2 tablespoons	fresh chervil leaves
1 teaspoon	fresh tarragon leaves
1 teaspoon	fresh squeezed lemon juice
3 tablespoons	extra virgin olive oil
	Salt and freshly ground black pepper

Get your fish seller to do this preparation of the snapper, or put the fish on a cutting board that does not slide around on the table (put a damp cloth under it). Using a medium-sized sharp boning knife, insert the knife into the belly cavity, and cut along one side of the spinal cord along the flat backbones ½ inch from the edge that is the "top" of the fish on the outside. Turn the fish over and repeat on the other side of the flat backbones. Turn the fish on its back and gently flatten it out with your hand. With scissors cut the backbone, which is now free of the flesh, at the head and tail ends, and pull the bone out away from the fish. Remove any bones that are left in the sides of the fish.

Mix the fresh thyme and olive oil together and rub over the fish. Cover and refrigerate for 1 hour. Remove from the refrigerator 30 minutes before cooking.

To make the sauce, put the orange juice in a bowl and add a pinch of salt and pepper. Stir to dissolve the salt, and then add the olive oil. Do not mix.

Heat a large nonstick frying pan and cook one or two of the fish, skin side down, for 3 minutes. Flip over and cook another 3 minutes on the flesh side. Drain the fish on paper towels and keep warm while you cook the other fish. Put each fish on a hot oval plate, skin side up.

Pour the orange–olive oil sauce over the fish.

Put the herb leaves in a little bowl, add the lemon juice, olive oil, and salt and pepper, and toss together. Place the salad on top of the fish.

VARIATIONS I have served this dish with a sea urchin–mussel soufflé presented in a cleaned-out sea urchin shell (see page 182), and the fish sauced with a simple chopped garlic–chopped tomato or blood orange sauce with a warm mixed vegetable–white bean salad; or just chopped citrus and extra virgin olive oil mixed together with a simple chopped capellini and warm white truffle salad.

Try mixing blanched pea tendrils, white beans, and thinly sliced cooked asparagus in with the herb salad as a garnish for the fish. If that is too much work, just take leftover cooked vegetables out of the refrigerator, chop them, warm them in a double boiler with a tablespoon of extra virgin olive oil, and mix them into the herb salad. Or add chopped Chinese roast pork from Chinatown and Key or Rangpur lime sections to the herb salad.

Chilean Sea Bass With
Lentils, Radish, and Chervil Salads

This dish was a huge success at my restaurant in Singapore, and was one we served during the Academy Awards in Los Angeles in 1996, as well as on a Crystal Cruise off Vietnam in 1998. In the original, we smoked the sea bass slightly, taking the dish to a higher dimension, but at home and without a smoker, use a covered grill and very low fire. To keep the dish simple, I have left out the crabmeat rémoulade that topped the original.

If you can't get the big watermelon radishes, sometimes called "Beauty Heart," use daikon stained with beet juice, or just the largest normal red ones.

This dish is meant as a first course, but with bigger pieces of fish, it makes a great main course as well. Use real lentils that will hold their shape, such as "beluga" or the French "du Puy," and not split pulses like dahl that fall apart.

Brining the fish makes the bass even more tender and moist than it already is.

SERVES 4

4	4-ounce pieces sea bass fillet, boneless	1 teaspoon	ground cardamom
4 cups	wet brine (see page 22)	1	large watermelon radish, or 6 small red ones, stemmed
½ cup	black beluga or green du Puy lentils		
1	large bunch chervil, stemmed, stems and leaves saved	1 tablespoon	fresh squeezed lime juice
		½ tablespoon	sesame oil
		1 teaspoon	extra virgin olive oil
		½ teaspoon	cracked white pepper
3 tablespoons	butter		Salt and freshly ground black pepper
1 tablespoon	chopped shallots		

Put the pieces of bass in the brine, and refrigerate for 1 hour.

Cover the lentils by 4 inches of salted water and boil them for 20 minutes, or until tender. Drain well. Chop up the chervil stems very finely and add to the lentils, along with the butter, shallots, and cardamom. Mix, season, and keep the lentils warm.

Cook the fish in the smoker grill (or 400-degree oven) for about 10 minutes. While it is cooking, use a vegetable cutter to slice the radishes as thin as paper into a bowl. Add the lime juice, sesame oil, olive oil, cracked pepper, and a pinch of salt; toss together, and let marinate 5 minutes.

Spoon the lentils in the center of hot plates, and put the fish pieces in the center of the lentils. Put the radish salad on top of the fish.

Toss the chervil leaves in the remaining dressing in the bowl used to mix the radishes, and place on top of the radish salad.

VARIATION Garoupa with grilled mushroom hash: use garoupa, red snapper, or salmon, cooking it the same way, or grilling or broiling it. Put the fish on a bed of lentils, and spoon crabmeat or prawn rémoulade, mixed with 2 tablespoons of steelhead caviar, on top of the fish, and on top of that, a tablespoon of portobello mushroom hash.

Marcel Boulestin's Society Salmon

Boulestin was a failed actor, great raconteur, cookbook writer, and superb Soho restaurateur who catered to the louche side of *tout* London society in the 1930s. He is making posthumous waves once again in England. His restaurant, Boulestin's, was a stunning place with yellow walls and curtains in a deeper shade of the same tone, made from silk with a design of Dufy's called "Paris." I mention the color because it was much copied at the time, and also by me at Stars in San Francisco fifty years later. Except I did not have the courage to cover the paint in cheap varnish as he did by mistake, thereby achieving a dark, smoky, old amber color that gave the room a certain stature of age and became the rage for restaurants for the next thirty years.

By the "society" in Society Salmon I mean Douglas Fairbanks and Gertrude Lawrence; the fascist Oswald Mosely and the Mitfords (the Duke of Devonshire reluctantly tagging along); the Baron Schroeder, flavoring his Clicquot with peaches after a polo match; Robbie Ross telling stories of Oscar and Bosie; Lawrence (of Arabia) still brushing the sand out of his headdress; the divinely beautiful young Percy Grainger, pleading with that Catholic duke from up north to keep his hands on his Boulestin omelette instead of his knee; another Percy (this one the page boy Esme Percy) stroking his lyre while still trying to make up his and the admiring customers' minds whether he was Apollo or Aphrodite; and Lady Diana Cooper, her Poiret compact brimming with cocaine, helping out her husband Duff after a particularly strenuous parliamentary question-time.

You can read about all of this in Boulestin's *Ease & Endurance* (1948), a translation of his *À Londres naguère*. He writes of the "near-Eastern origin" of this salmon dish, so loved by his customers, but by none so much as the Levantine bankers sprawled lavishly across the old gold banquettes.

SERVES 4

4	6-ounce pieces fresh wild Atlantic salmon fillets	1 tablespoon	freshly squeezed lemon juice
4 pieces	parchment paper, cut in 12-inch rounds	4 ounces	unsalted butter, cut into 8 equal pieces
4 tablespoons	unsalted butter	2 tablespoons	heavy cream
½ tablespoon	freshly grated lemon zest	4 tablespoons	sevruga or osetra caviar
2	egg yolks		Sea salt and freshly ground white pepper

Preheat the oven to 425 degrees.

Fold each piece of the parchment over in half. Put each salmon piece on a piece of parchment just next to the fold, top each with a tablespoon of butter, and season. Fold over the other half of the paper and fold the edges together, making little overlapping folds, starting at one end and progressively folding as you go.

Put the packages on a sheet pan and bake for 15 minutes. Remove them from the oven and let sit for 5 minutes.

Put the egg yolks, lemon juice, 1 tablespoon of cold water, and the butter in the top pan of a nonreactive double boiler, and whisk over boiling water for 2 minutes, until all the butter is incorporated. Whisk in the cream, then, off the heat, gently fold in the caviar.

Open the bags and slip each piece of fish with all its juices out onto hot plates. Serve with the caviar sauce.

GRILLED BACON-WRAPPED SALMON WITH BASIL MASHED POTATOES AND SWEET RED ONION SAUCE

Salmon and bacon are made for each other. A really easy way to cook them together is to put fresh basil leaves on top of a salmon fillet, cover with bacon strips and lots of freshly cracked black pepper, and cook in a hot (preheated) broiler. The salmon comes out moist and perfumed with basil and the flavors of the bacon. As perfect as that is, this dish, which adds basil mashed potatoes and red onion sauce, is my new favorite.

SERVES 4

4	6-ounce pieces salmon fillets, boneless, skinless	½ cup	fish or shellfish stock (see page 187)
1 bunch	fresh basil, stemmed, stems saved, leaves washed	6	medium boiling potatoes, peeled, quartered
2 tablespoons	olive oil	1 cup	milk, or more if needed
8 slices	apple-wood smoked bacon, ⅛-inch thick	¼ cup	heavy cream
		4 drops	sesame oil
2	large red onions, peeled, cored, finely chopped	1 tablespoon	freshly squeezed lemon juice
1 sprig	fresh thyme	½ cup	mixed fresh herb leaves (Italian parsley, chervil, tarragon)
8 tablespoons	butter, cut into 8 equal pieces		Salt and freshly ground black pepper

Chop the basil stems, and moisten them with 1 tablespoon of the olive oil. Put the salmon in a shallow dish or bowl and pack the oiled basil stems around them. Marinate in the refrigerator for 2 hours.

Take the salmon out of the dish and wipe off the basil stems, saving them to put on the fire when you are grilling the salmon. Flatten the pieces of salmon slightly with the palm of your hand, and then with your hands form a 3-inch circle with each of the salmon pieces, the side of the salmon that held the skin on the inside of the circle. When the salmon has taken on a "medallion" shape, wrap 2 slices of bacon around the outside edges of each salmon medallion, securing them with wooden toothpicks.

Put the onions in a saucepan with the thyme and 1 tablespoon of the butter. Add 2 tablespoons water, cover, and sweat 5 minutes over low heat. Remove the thyme sprig, add the stock, and simmer until reduced by half.

Blanch the basil leaves in boiling water for 1 minute, pushing the leaves under the water surface so that they do not blacken. Drain and refresh under cold water for a few seconds, and then puree immediately in a small blender with a tablespoon of the blanching water. Add 2 tablespoons of butter and blend until a smooth green. Remove the basil butter and put it in the refrigerator.

Cook the potatoes and mash them through a ricer or food mill into a saucepan. Add the milk and beat it into the potatoes until just incorporated. Then whip the cream and fold it into the potatoes, and keep warm over a double boiler, for no longer than the time it takes to cook the salmon.

Grill or broil the salmon, turning once, for 3 to 4 minutes each side. Heat the onion sauce and whisk in the remaining 5 tablespoons of butter. Season and keep warm. Whisk the basil butter into the potatoes, season them, and put a bed of the potatoes on each of four warm plates, the salmon on top and the onion sauce over the fish.

Mix the oil and lemon juice together and dress the herbs, season, and put the herbs on top of the salmon.

VARIATIONS Serve with a warm spinach salad (see page 92), and a sauce of sabayon made with fish stock (see page 187) and flavored with a tablespoon of freshly ground black pepper; the garnish could be polenta finished with blue cheese, made into sticks and grilled. The salmon is also wonderful with buttered white beans (see page 33) flavored with chopped sage and a whisper of cardamom, then mixed with an equal quantity of cooked and sliced artichoke bottoms and 2 tablespoons of chopped cooked bacon, and sauced with a preserved lemon vinaigrette. Or you could flavor the white beans with just white truffle oil and nothing else. Or make a shellfish essence with mussels (see page 188) and chop up the cooked mussels to put in a mussel hollandaise made with the essence. Or serve grilled salmon with cooked black beans (see page 131), your favorite fried Thai rolls, and a buttered curry sauce, as we did at my first "fusion" restaurant in 1990, Speedo 690.

VARIATIONS on the mashed potatoes: Use bell pepper purees (see page 39), red, yellow or both (separately), to flavor the mashed potatoes, and accompany the basil-flavored ones. Or use basil mashed potatoes side by side with ones flavored with mushroom hash (see page 17).

POACHED TURBOT WITH OYSTER HOLLANDAISE

The first thing I do when I arrive in France is find a restaurant that serves plainly poached turbot and hollandaise. Heaven is having a huge sauceboat of hollandaise all to myself, tasting it on the turbot, and then sopping it up with boiled Channel Island potatoes.

No other fish can compare, unless you sell your portfolio, fly to Hong Kong, and have So Mei (the flesh is a cross between turbot and foie gras). Turbot used to be scarce in the United States, but they are available now, often small ones that are still big enough to serve two.

SERVES 4

1	2–3 pound piece turbot	2 cups	hollandaise sauce
4 tablespoons	butter		(see page 254)
3 tablespoons	finely chopped shallots	1 teaspoon	freshly grated lemon zest
1½ cups	fish stock (see page 187)	24	fingerling-style potatoes
1 cup	parsley stems, sage stems,	1 tablespoon	chopped Italian parsley
	other fine herbs	½ tablespoon	chopped fresh chervil
10 medium	fresh oysters, shucked,		Salt and freshly ground
	oyster juices and liquids		white pepper
	reserved		

Cook the oysters in their liquid for 2 minutes and drain, saving the oysters and their liquid separately.

Make a hollandaise sauce as on page 254, but cook the egg yolks with the oyster-cooking liquid as well as the lemon juice. Then chop the cooked oysters and put them and the lemon zest in the finished sauce. Keep the hollandaise warm.

Choose a pan just large enough to hold the piece of fish with about 2 inches free on all sides. Melt 2 tablespoons of the butter in a pan. Add the shallots, 2 tablespoons of the fish stock, and the herb stems. Cover and sweat 5 minutes over low heat, not letting the stems color.

Add the fish, black skin side down, and pour in the fish stock to cover the fish. Bring to a very low simmer. Cover the pan and cook until the fish is done, about 10 minutes. Remove the fish from the stock and drain it for a minute.

While the fish is poaching, boil the potatoes until tender, peel while still hot, and toss with the remaining butter and chopped herbs. Season and keep warm.

Take the black skin off the fish. Serve the turbot with the potatoes and the oyster hollandaise, and with boiled and buttered tiny green beans (*haricots verts*) if you just have to have another vegetable.

VARIATION For a New Orleans or Creole flavor, add ½ teaspoon of Tabasco or other hot sauce to the hollandaise.

PRESERVED PEPPERED TUNA

This idea came to me at the wonderful restaurant at the entrance to the harbor of St. Tropez where, because everyone there was a foodie and the tuna was delicious, we sat around for hours embroiled in the debate over tuna names. Since the names for tuna (especially the one known as albacore) change from country to country, I will not get into that debate here, but stick to my belief that the only good cooked tuna is either in a can or, in this case, a jar.

Use 2 to 3 inch tall preserving jars, the ones with the red rubber strips and clamp-down tops. The tuna should fit with a ½-inch space on the sides and 1 inch on top. To serve it, all you have to do is put a jar in front of each person. You can use skipjack, Spanish mackerel, or bluefish if the pieces are big enough and at least 3 inches thick. But whether tuna or one of these others, be sure to use the fattiest fish and tuna you can.

SERVES 4

4	6- to 8-ounce pieces fresh fatty tuna, cut 3 inches thick	1 tablespoon	fresh rosemary leaves
		4	bay leaves
¼ cup	black peppercorns	8	cloves garlic, peeled, crushed
1 tablespoon	sea salt	½ cup	mild black olives, pitted, chopped
8	salted anchovy filets (see page 42)	2 tablespoons	grated lemon zest
4 sprigs	fresh thyme	4 cups (approx.)	extra virgin light yellow olive oil
8	fresh sage leaves		
8 sprigs	Italian parsley		

Grind up the peppercorns and salt and rub all over the tuna pieces. Let sit 30 minutes.

Put an anchovy fillet in the bottom of each jar. Then divide half the thyme, sage, parsley, rosemary, bay, and garlic equally among the four jars. Place a piece of tuna in each jar, then add the olives and lemon zest. Divide the remaining herbs equally on top of each piece of tuna and the remaining anchovy fillets, and pour enough of the olive oil over each piece of tuna to cover it by at least ½-inch.

Close the jars and put them in a water bath with the water coming up to the necks of the jars. Cover and simmer very gently for 2 hours. Test to see if the fish is tender (timing will depend on the kind of fish you are using) and cook more if necessary. For salmon cook only 30 minutes.

Serve at room temperature with a sauce made from extra virgin olive oil and lemon juice (see page 237), or with Russian dressing (see page 250), or rémoulade (see page 251). The tuna makes a perfect Niçoise salad—make sure to use the cooking oil to dress it.

CREAMED PUREE OF SALT COD

Puree of salt cod or *brandade* is what the legendary Henri Soule—of New York's once famous Le Pavillon—thought "the epitome of culinary perfection." His love for it must have come from his mother who lived in a village near Bayonne and served it with "sliced potatoes, vinegar, oil, garlic, and chopped parsley" (from *On the Town in New York* [1973] by the Batterberrys).

A passing glance at the *Larousse gastronomique's* classic garnishes for this dish shows it to be one of the glories of classic French regional cooking: served in a bowl layered with a ragout of crayfish tails and truffles; mixed with truffles tossed in hot butter (I would serve it with the truffled sandwiches on page 76); or served in a mound covered with roasted peppers (see page 39) and slices of tomato fried in extra virgin olive oil. Not bad.

But the simple regional recipes call for a lot of handwork in shredding the salt cod after it is poached—so much work, in fact, that it makes *brandade* a huge challenge for most home cooks. Unless you use the following procedure, that is.

One day in the early 1970s at Chez Panisse in Berkeley, I was eyeing the countertop mixer, then worth its weight in gold, and jealously guarded by the pastry chef. One of those lightbulbs in my head went off, and I figured out a way to make the otherwise tedious preparation of this dish a lot easier and a great deal more fun. Here is the secret.

This puree is basically a fish mayonnaise, so use the same mixing techniques (see page 247).

SERVES 4-6

1 pound	salt cod fillet (not the whole fish), cut into 1-inch cubes	1 cup	heavy cream
¾ cup	extra virgin light yellow olive oil	1 tablespoon	fresh garlic puree (see page 37) Salt and freshly ground white pepper

Soak the cod pieces in cold water twice, each time for 20 minutes. Then poach them in unsalted water for 30 minutes, or until just tender and falling apart.

Drain and save a cup of the liquid (save the rest for leek and potato soup).

Put the cod, while still hot, in the food mixer, and using the "whip" attachment, turn the mixer speed to medium-slow to flake the fish, scraping down the sides of the bowl every 5 minutes with a rubber spatula. Once or twice, take out the whip, mix the cod together, and continue flaking for a total of about 30 minutes, or until the salt cod is smooth.

In separate saucepans heat the olive oil and the cream until just too hot to touch. With the machine still on low speed, add a quarter of the hot oil, then the garlic puree, and then a quarter of the cream, continuing to alternate between the oil and hot cream. Halfway through the process of adding the oil and cream, turn the speed to medium. Then if the puree is separating slightly, turn the speed to high for a minute, adding only cream. Make sure the cream and oil stay hot.

The final consistency should be mayonnaise-like, so plan to add the last quarter of the cream as the last addition (so that you can omit the remaining oil, depending on the texture). Season, as it may need salt and certainly pepper. Keep warm but not hot in a double boiler or water bath, covered, until ready for use (up to an hour).

HOW TO COOK A LOBSTER

Killing a lobster before cooking is the humane thing to do and I believe it keeps the lobster meat more tender. Hold the lobster (claws secured with elastic bands) with a gloved hand at the front of the tail and back of the main body, and with the other hand cut a half-inch-wide and inch-deep slit into the shell, jiggling the knife backwards and forwards to sever the spinal cord. Leave the lobster for ten minutes before cooking it.

Before cooking a lobster, please remove the elastic bands from the claws, a procedure sadly forgotten most of the time. What could be worse than getting residual rubber flavor from the claws on your hands and then into your mouth when eating a whole lobster? Or poaching a lobster in rubber water?

If you have live lobsters and are not going to eat them for two days, the best way to keep them is to put them in boiling water for two minutes, then in a colander covered with ice until they are cold. Then refrigerate. When you are ready to eat the lobsters, go ahead with the cooking method suited to the dish, taking into account the two minutes the lobsters have already been cooked.

I give two methods to cook a lobster for two different end results. The first is for lobster meat that is to be cooked further (by itself as on page 177, or to be included with other ingredients as with a risotto, heated in a bisque, or mixed in a shellfish ragout). The second is for lobster to be eaten whole and fully cooked, hot or cold.

METHOD 1: COOKING LOBSTER TO BE REHEATED

Put the lobsters in a pot and pour in cold water to cover them by 6 inches. Turn the heat to high and cook until the water is just about to boil. Turn off the heat and let the lobsters sit according to the times below. Then remove the lobsters, put them in a colander, and cover them with ice to stop the cooking and cool them.

1-pound lobsters:	1 minute
2-pound lobsters:	3 minutes
3-pound lobsters:	4 minutes

The meat yield will depend on the time of year and the thickness of the shell, but generally a 1-pound lobster yeilds 6 to 8 ounces, a 2-pound lobster 18 to 20 ounces, and a 3-pound lobster 1½ pounds.

METHOD 2: COOKING LOBSTER COMPLETELY TO SERVE WHOLE (HOT OR COLD), OR IN SALADS

Put the lobsters in a pot and pour cold water over them to cover by 6 inches. Turn the heat to high and cook until the water is about to boil. Turn off the heat and let the lobster sit according to the times below. Then remove the lobsters. For cold lobster meat, put the lobsters in a colander and cover with ice to cool them down and stop their cooking.

1-pound lobsters:	7 minutes
2-pound lobsters:	12 minutes
3-pound lobsters:	20 minutes

REMOVING LOBSTER MEAT

Take the lobster apart and remove the meat from the shell over a bowl so that you save all those flavorful juices. As you remove each piece of the meat, put it on a large plate or platter so that the pieces lie flat and separate from one another. Save all the shells for soup, sauces, and fish and shellfish stews; if not using them right away, put them in sealed plastic (odorless bags or containers) and freeze.

First, twist off the small legs, cutting off and discarding the bits of feathery gill sticking to the knuckle ends. Keep the legs on the platter with the lobster meat.

Twist off the two claw arms and twist off the claws. With a pair of scissors or poultry shears, cut down the length of the (knuckle) arms, and pull out the meat.

Twist off the flaps at the end of the tail and reserve (big ones have wonderfully juicy lobster meat inside). Twist off the tail and cut through the soft shell on the underside of the tail with a knife or scissors, being careful to cut only the shell and not the tail meat. Hold the tail in both hands on the table and break it open. Lift out the meat. Make a ⅛-inch-deep cut down the center of the outside curve of the tail meat and pick out the intestinal tract.

Crack the claws with a mallet. Move the small, lower part of the claw around and slowly pull it away from the larger part of the claw. With luck it will come away and leave the thin meat of the little claw intact. Now all you have to do is get the big shell off the meat, so very gently pull out (or cut out, shake out, or lift out) the claw meat in one piece if possible. If the lobster is in a soft shell-stage, you can use scissors to cut away all the shells from the lobster meat.

Lift the main shell (the curved top with eyes and feelers) off the central body of the lobster, scoop out any of the white fat clinging to the shell, and reserve it (frozen or refrigerated) for sauces. Remove the mouth sac at the head of the shell and discard. Scoop out any dark green eggs (if the lobster is female), and the liver, or tomalley (green, and both male and female have it), and reserve (frozen or refrigerated) for sauces. Keep the shell either for stock or for display. The white main body part has the feathery lungs, so remove those and discard. Rinse off what is left of the body and save for lobster or shellfish broth.

LOBSTER IN LOBSTER SAUCE

Few things are more glorious than lobster steamed in butter and served with just its cooking juices. If the lobster is very fresh, it needs nothing except this aromatic vegetable support for the sauce, and maybe a little fresh chervil. The "bodies" are the part the legs are attached to.

SERVES 4

2	2-pound live Maine lobsters, prepared as in Method 1 on page 175 and lobster meat removed (see page 176), keeping the meat, lobster shells, lobster fat, bodies, legs, and juices	1 tablespoon	fresh thyme flowers
		1 sprig	fresh tarragon
		4 cups	fish or shellfish stock (see page 187)
		8 tablespoons	French (Normandy) butter Coral from the lobster if available
2 tablespoons	peanut or canola oil	¼ cup	chopped tomato (see page 47)
¼ cup	white wine		
½ cup	aromatic vegetable mix (see page 14)	2 tablespoons	fresh chervil leaves, chopped

Pound and crack the lobster shells and cut up the bodies. Heat the vegetable oil in a large saucepan and when the oil is hot add the shells and bodies. Cook over high heat, stirring constantly, for 5 to 10 minutes, or until the shells are totally red. Turn down the heat and let the pan cool for 2 minutes, then pour the wine into the pan and cook another 5 minutes.

Add the lobster juices, vegetable mix, and herbs and cook another 5 minutes, stirring all the time. Then add the stock and bring to a boil. Turn down the heat to a simmer, and skim off any scum that rises to the surface of the stock. Simmer for 45 minutes. Strain, and force all the juices out of the debris in the strainer.

Simmer the strained lobster stock until it is reduced to 1 cup of liquid.

Cut the lobster in serving portions, slicing the claw meat lengthwise so that there are two complete claw halves, and the tail meat across the tail into ½-inch-thick medallions.

While the stock is reducing, mix the butter with the coral (and any of the fat from the shells) and keep cold. Ten minutes before serving, cut the butter into 8 pieces. Bring the lobster stock to a simmer, add the tomatoes, and whisk the butter pieces one at a time into the simmering reduced lobster stock until dissolved. Strain the sauce through a very fine sieve and keep hot, but never boiling. Warm the lobster tail meat in the sauce for 1 minute. Lift it out and put it on a heated flat serving dish. Then add the claw and knuckle meat and pour the hot sauce over the lobster. Sprinkle the lobster with the chopped chervil.

BAKED WHOLE LOBSTER
WITH GREEN GODDESS BUTTER

The point of baking a whole lobster in its shell is that it cooks in its own juices, cooking just long enough for the shell to cook through and fill the lobster meat with flavor, but not long enough to toughen the lobster. For cooked lobster to remain tender it needs to be subjected to only gentle heat and low temperatures.

Use either a covered grill or an oven, but in either case, cook the lobster on a fireproof tray or baking sheet.

SERVES 4

2	2-pound live Maine lobsters	4 tablespoons	butter
¾ cup	green goddess butter (see page 249)	¼ pound	green beans (*haricots verts* variety)
6 ounces	capellini pasta	1 small	celery root, peeled, cut in ⅛-inch sticks
½ cup	mushroom hash (see page 17)		Salt and freshly ground black pepper
¼ cup	chopped tomatoes (see page 47)		

Kill the lobsters as explained on page 175, let them sit for 10 minutes, and preheat the oven to 450 degrees.

Meanwhile, insert a ¼-inch tip with a circular end into a pastry bag and fill it with the green goddess butter. Squeeze three quarters of the butter into the head cavities through the hole made to kill the lobsters. Make another small hole in each of the four claws (if the claws are too hard, make a hole in the joint between the claw and the arm), and fill each claw equally with the remaining butter.

Put the lobsters on a tray or baking sheet, then put the tray in the oven (or on top of the grill and then close the top) and cook for 10 minutes. Turn the oven off and let the lobsters sit in the turned-off oven with the door open.

Meanwhile, boil the pasta in salted water until tender (5 to 8 minutes), lift it out with a strainer, and put it in a metal bowl. Add the mushroom hash, tomatoes, and 2 tablespoons of the butter. Season, toss gently together, and keep warm over hot water. Cook the beans and celery root in the pasta water for 5 minutes. Drain and put them in another bowl with the remaining butter. Season and mix until the butter evenly coats the vegetables.

When the lobsters are just cool enough to handle (with a towel), put them upside down on a table or cutting board. Using a large chef's knife, cut lengthwise exactly down the centers of the lobsters. Save any juices in a small bowl and add them to the pasta.

Remove the stomach, head sac, and intestinal tract from the tail. Loosen the tail meat and turn it so that the red skin side faces upward, putting each lobster tail in the shell of the other so that the tails fit in this other direction. Put the pasta in the head cavities, the vegetables on top of the pasta, and pour any butter left in the pasta and vegetable bowls over the tail pieces.

VARIATIONS Serve with boiled fingerling potatoes mixed with the celery root and green beans, all tossed with fresh black truffle butter; with cooked lentils added to the pasta; or with a grilled portobello mushroom hash mixed with ⅓ its volume of cooked sweet Italian sausage chopped very finely and put on top of the vegetables. To be fancy, take the claw meat out and put it on top of the vegetables and then put the sausage-mushroom hash on top of the claw meat. The simplest variation is to coarsely chop up ½ cup of fresh lovage leaves and toss them with the pasta, 2 tablespoons butter, and 2 tablespoons of coarsely chopped Italian parsley.

BAY OR SLIPPER LOBSTER WITH OYSTER AND CAVIAR SAUCE

I have used bay or slipper lobsters (both are "flat" lobsters of the *Scyllaridae* family) instead of spiny lobsters (*langouste* or crawfish, all names for the same kind of lobster of the family *Paniluridae*), which, although the most glorious looking (some are as colorful as peacocks), are impossible to cook unless they are out of their water and into your pan in less than an hour.

The slipper (*Scyllarides latus*) is from the Mediterranean and eastern Atlantic and is bigger than the Indo-Pacific bay lobster (*Thenus orientalis*), which in Australia is called a "bug," as in Moreton Bay bug or, in the south of Australia, the Balmain bug (a slightly different species).

I prefer the Moreton Bay, but they are both the origin of the ubiquitous "lobster tail" in America and, quite frankly, are a waste of time when frozen. When fresh and cooked gently, they are a dream.

This preparation is for lobster taken out of the shell and reheated, a method that allows you prepare the dish partially in advance.

SERVES 4

4	1½-pound slipper lobsters, cooked (Method 1), and shelled, juices saved (see page 175)
8	large fresh oysters, shucked, juices saved
½ cup	heavy cream
2 tablespoons	cold butter, cut in 4 pieces
2 tablespoons	sevruga caviar

Preheat the oven to 400 degrees. Simmer the oysters in their juices and the lobster juices for 5 minutes. Puree the cooked oysters in a food processor very gently for a minute and then put the puree through a fine nylon sieve. Lightly butter (1 tablespoon) a shallow ovenproof gratin dish, and arrange the lobster meat in one layer in the dish.

Put the oyster puree in a nonreactive pan and heat without boiling. Stir in the cream. Remove the pan from the heat and whisk in the butter. Pour over the lobster and heat in the oven for 5 minutes. Take the gratin dish out of the oven and let it cool for a minute. Sprinkle the caviar over the lobster, and serve.

VARIATION You could heat the lobster meat in its juices in the gratin dish, spoon a cup of oyster hollandaise (see page 254) over the lobster, and put the dish under the broiler for 2 minutes to slightly brown the top of the sauce.

Lobster with Fresh White Cannellini Beans

At my rented villa in Chiesanuova, I often cook the best things I find at the main market in Florence. One especially good day yielded fresh cannellini beans already shucked, cipollini onions already peeled, salted fat belly from wild boar, and flowering sage. I added garlic, olive oil, and black pepper, and we ate one of the best meals I have ever tasted.

A few months later in Galicia (northwestern Spain), I had a similar dish, minus the wild boar, but packed with lobster and lobster sauce. We swooned.

SERVES 4

1	3-pound Maine lobster	¼ cup	fresh tarragon leaves
2 cups	shucked fresh white cannellini beans		Salt
12	cipollini onions, peeled	½ cup	lobster butter (see page 189)
2 tablespoons	butter		
2 cups	fish or shellfish stock (see page 187)		

Cook the lobsters as in Method 1 on page 175. Then follow the directions on page 176 for removing the lobster meat, cutting the lobster meat into chunks, but keeping the claws intact. Reserve any juices and coral, and mix them with the lobster butter.

Preheat the oven to 400 degrees.

Put the onions, butter, stock, tarragon, and a pinch of salt in a casserole, cover, and cook over low heat for 10 minutes. Put the beans in a sieve and immerse them in boiling salted water for 5 minutes. Let them drain for a minute, and while still hot, add the beans to the onions, cover the casserole, and continue cooking another 10 minutes or until the beans are just tender. Take off the heat and stir in the lobster butter and the lobster meat without the claws. Season.

Put all of the bean-onion-lobster mix in a large 2-inch-deep oven-proof gratin dish. Put the claws in the center, and bake for 5 to 10 minutes, just until the lobster meat is heated through.

VARIATIONS Instead of the lobster, my personal favorite would be blood sausage grilled until crisp, sliced into 1-inch pieces, and tossed into the beans with a cup of cooked fresh fava beans and a tablespoon of red chili flakes. Try that on a winter night! Chicken wings, boned Chinese "drumstick" style and then curried (use the Indian spice mix on page 38), would also be very good.

MUSSELS IN *CATAPLANA*
WITH MINT-OLIVE TOASTS

This dish saw its first light when a line cook—drawing on the traditional combination of saffron and mussels, but wanting something new that reflected the current interest in Indian food, the Far East, and Mexico—made curried creamed mussels with a cilantro pesto drizzled over the top. It was fantastic. This recipe, however, is less rich, and less complicated since you cook the ingredients together all at once.

Mussels vary in size, but twelve to fifteen per person should do for a first course. One often hears that mussels still unopened after a brief cooking are no good, or downright dangerous, as in dead. I have always seen those as the ones hanging most strongly onto life. It is the floaters (when washing them) or any that gape and don't close when handled that should be discarded. You can store the mussels in salted water after cleaning them, but "bearding" kills them, so do that as close to cooking as possible. Scrub the mussels and then just before using them, beard them by pulling off the piece of mussel hanging outside the shell.

If you don't have a *cataplana* (a Spanish, tin-lined cooking vessel, which looks and operates like a big clamp, hinged at one point), which I don't expect anyone to have, just use a covered thin metal saucepan. The point is for the mussels to cook very quickly, and then be presented in the pot (since the finished sauce is made there) with all their steamy perfumes.

SERVES 4 TO 6

The Toasts:			
1 tablespoon	chopped fresh mint leaves	¼ cup	extra virgin olive oil
½ cup	black olives, pitted	8	baguette slices, ⅛-inch
2 tablespoons	fresh orange juice and the		thick and 6 inches long,
	finely grated zest of one		cut on the bias
	orange		

The Mussels:			
		2 cups	fish stock (see page 187)
4 pounds	fresh mussels	½ cup	dry white wine
1	medium red onion, peeled,	2 tablespoons	ancho chili puree
	cored, finely chopped		(see page 32)
2 sprigs	fresh thyme	½ cup	garlic mayonnaise
2	bay leaves, crumbled		(see page 248)

Preheat the oven to 400 degrees.

TO MAKE THE TOASTS:

Put the mint, olives, orange juice, and oil in a food processor and puree until just a bit of texture remains. Spread the bread with the puree, and bake for 10 minutes. Keep warm.

If you are using a *cataplana*: put all the ingredients for the mussels except the mayonnaise in the *cataplana*, and clamp down the lid. Cook over high heat on top of the stove for 7 to 8 minutes, shaking the *cataplana* three or four times. Open carefully at the table, check for seasoning, stir in the garlic mayonnaise, and serve with the hot olive toasts.

If you are using a saucepan with a lid, combine all the ingredients except the mussels in the pan and cook covered over high heat for 2 minutes. Add the mussels and cover the pot tightly. Cook over high heat, shaking the pot every minute or so, until all the mussels open, about 5 minutes. If 1 or 2 mussels are reluctant to open, don't overcook the others while waiting for those to cook—just pry them open with a knife. Take the lid off the pot at the table, check to see if the broth needs salt, stir in the garlic mayonnaise, and serve with the hot olive toasts.

SEA URCHIN SOUFFLÉ

This may seem like an obscure recipe, but sea urchins are back in vogue and they are not always eaten raw at sushi bars. I recently prepared this recipe in Galicia as a first course, before a lunch of lampreys cooked in a sauce finished with their blood (like a true *coq au vin* or jugged hare). But the first time I cooked a sea urchin soufflé was in 1975. Jim Beard had told me that if he had to choose four restaurants in the United States to revisit, they would be the Four Seasons and the Coach House in New York, Tony's in Houston, and Chez Panisse—"but before writing this in my column I want you to cook for me out of your own home kitchen." I didn't have any money at the time, and didn't have a home or a kitchen, but a rich Texan college mate of mine, John Sanger, had both, so I borrowed his.

I was very nervous to be cooking for Jim with no professional backup staff to make me look good; and up to the morning of the day of the dinner, I still couldn't decide what to serve. I wandered around Chinatown in San Francisco, looking for my usual inspiration from the markets. When I saw several deep-sea urchins, each the size of a large grapefruit, I knew I must have them.

Once I bought them, I was faced with the problem of what to do with them. From somewhere in the dark recesses of my mind (perhaps from one of my favorite books, *La Bonne cuisine du Comte de Nice* by Jacques Médecin, or Jean-Noel Escudier's *La Véritable cuisine Provençale et Niçoise*) came a memory of a recipe for sea urchin sauce that could be used as the basis for a soufflé. "Right," I thought. "Soufflés they will be." By the time all this occurred to me, it was too late to buy individual soufflé dishes, so the shells would have to do.

With Jim and the other guests waiting at the table, my heart was in my throat as I opened the oven door. But when I did, I saw the scheme had worked. The spines were intact, a wonderful ocean smell wafted into the kitchen, and best of all, the soufflé mixture had risen above the crater-like openings of the shells, puffy, pink-beige, and beautiful. I rushed them to the table.

Jim tried a spoonful. No word was said. He looked up slowly, fully aware of his massively theatrical effect and, rolling his eyes slowly around the room, said: "My God, that is the best thing I have ever tasted."

4	large sea urchins		2	egg yolks
4 tablespoons	butter		4	egg whites
2 tablespoons	flour			Salt and freshly ground
1 cup	fish stock (see page 187)			black pepper

Using scissors, cut a hole around the inside perimeter of the underside of each sea urchin. Discard the cut shell and clean out the inside of the remaining shell, leaving only the orange-colored roe that sticks vertically to the shell in sections.

When the shell is perfectly clean, scoop the roe into a bowl. When all the roe is out, rinse the shells thoroughly in cold water and dry the inside surfaces with paper towels. Puree the roe through a clean sieve.

Preheat the oven to 400 degrees.

To make the soufflé base, melt 1 ounce of the butter in a saucepan. Add 1 tablespoon of the flour and cook over low heat for 5 minutes, stirring all the time. Heat the fish stock, add it to the butter-flour mixture, and whisk until smooth. Cook over low heat (or in a 325-degree oven) for 30 minutes, whisking every 5 minutes and skimming off any scum that rises to the surface. Let cool to room temperature.

Beat the egg yolks with the pureed roe and mix into the cooled soufflé base. Rub the insides of the shells with the remaining butter and dust with the remaining flour. Beat the egg whites with a pinch of salt until stiff, then fold them into the soufflé base and spoon that into the shells. Put the shells on a sheet pan (or in a pan with rock salt to hold the urchins steady if the spines are more than an inch long, the salt preheated for 10 minutes in the 400-degree oven) and put the pan in the oven. Cook until the soufflés have risen and are slightly browned on top, about 20 minutes. Serve immediately.

HOT BIMINI STONE CRAB CLAWS

In 1980, at the Santa Fe Bar & Grill, we celebrated the great culinary region of Miami and the Florida Keys by serving stone crab claws with green goddess mayonnaise (see page 249) mixed with chopped hard-boiled eggs, dollops of caviar, and pink pomelo sections.

Today I would not be so over the top as to have pomelo and caviar together on the same plate, but would serve the claws as inspired by the best hot crab I have ever eaten, the mangrove crab at Casa Armas in Manila—cooked in butter, salt, and black pepper. Of course, this recipe is delicious without the pomelo also.

SERVES 4 TO 6

24	jumbo stone crab claws		1	large pomelo, peeled, sections cut in half lengthwise
²/₃ cup	clarified butter (see page 27)			
2 tablespoons	kosher salt		1 tablespoon	chopped fresh mint leaves
2 tablespoons	freshly ground black pepper		1 tablespoon	hellfire sauce (see page 241), or use chili vinegar
¼ cup	chopped fresh garlic		2 tablespoons	almond oil (or peanut oil)

Heat the butter in a sauté pan over high heat until hot but not smoking. Add the crab claws, toss with the butter, and add the salt and pepper. Continue heating while tossing for 2 minutes. Add the garlic, turn down the heat to medium, and cook and continue tossing another 3 minutes, or until the claws are heated through.

Pour the claws onto a heated platter.

Mix the pomelo sections with the mint, hellfire sauce, and oil, and arrange on the plate around the crab.

SHELLFISH MIXED GRILL

Cooking any shellfish in its shell improves it because the flavor of the shell permeates the meat. Here from the grill you get the three irresistible flavors of salt, smoke, and cooked chilies.

Although I use prawns, crabs, and scallops in this recipe, you can easily substitute lobster, mussels (which you can cook in a deep-fry basket on top of the grill), razor clams, oysters, or any other shellfish. Cooking shellfish in the shell preserves all the juices, and as they cook, the smoke from the wood or charcoal gives the shellfish a wonderful taste. Use the leftover shells to make stock for a gumbo that is unbelievable.

You will need 8-inch bamboo skewers soaked in water.

SERVES 4 TO 6

1	Dungeness or similar crab	6 sprigs	fresh fennel tops, chopped
2	1½-pound Maine lobsters	¼ teaspoon	saffron threads
16	fresh prawns or shrimp in the shell	1 cup	olive oil
		1 tablespoon	ground cumin
8	sea scallops in their shells, cleaned, leaving roe and the muscle intact	¾ cup	mayonnaise (see page 247)
		½ pound	unsalted butter
1 clove	fresh garlic, peeled, finely chopped	4 tablespoons	freshly squeezed lemon juice
4	fresh serrano chilies, seeded, stemmed, coarsely chopped	½ cup	tomatillo salsa (see page 239)
		16	lemon wedges
6 sprigs	fresh thyme		Salt and freshly ground black pepper

Divide the crab in half by holding the claw and legs on each side of the crab in one hand and smashing the underside of the crab against the edge of a table or sink. Then twist the two sides in alternate directions, pulling the body away from the top shell. Clean out the body parts, removing the gills and other debris. Scoop out and save the white crab fat and green liver from the shell, wash the shells, and put the liver and fat back in.

Crack the crab claws and legs with a cracker or the flat side of a heavy knife, being careful to keep the pieces intact.

Kill the lobsters, remove the tails, and put skewers through them lengthwise to straighten them out. Take off the claws and legs.

Thread 4 skewers with 4 shrimp each.

Mix the garlic, chilies, thyme, fennel, saffron, oil, salt, and pepper together. Put the marinade in a big bowl and gently toss all the shellfish in the marinade. Marinate for 1 hour, turning the shellfish several times.

Meanwhile, mix the cumin and mayonnaise together and let sit for 1 hour, allowing the flavors to develop.

Start the fire in the grill (or preheat the broiler).

Add the butter to the crab fat and liver in the crab shell. Put the shells on the grill until the butter is hot and bubbling, at which point the liver and fat will be cooked. Put on a warm part of the fire or in a low oven to keep warm.

Put the crabs and lobsters on the grill and cook 3 minutes. Turn them over and put on the shrimp and scallops. Grill everything until just cooked through, about 2 minutes on each side for the shrimp, 4 minutes for the scallops, and 8 to 10 minutes total for the crabs and lobsters.

Add the lemon juice to the hot butter-filled crab shells, passing them with the rest of the sauces; spoon the cumin mayonnaise and the tomatillo salsa into little ramekins and put one of each on 4 warm plates. Put the shellfish on the plates and serve immediately. Pass lemon wedges and hot, damp napkins.

VARIATIONS At the Peak Café in 1990 and then again later in Singapore, I used my ketjap manis marinade: 2 tablespoons ketjap manis sauce, ¼ cup lime juice, ¼ cup sesame oil, ¼ cup olive oil, ¼ cup chopped green chilies, ¼ cup chopped fresh garlic, 1 teaspoon salt, and 1½ teaspoons ground black pepper. Another possibility is pimento sauce: for each cup of melted butter, add 1 tablespoon chopped serrano chilies, 1 tablespoon chopped fresh garlic, one chopped and pureed roasted pimento or red bell pepper (see page 39), 2 tablespoons fresh lime juice, salt, and pepper.

FISH STOCK

The best fish to include in a light stock to be used for cream and butter sauces are sole, turbot, halibut, and trout. For fish soups and hearty stews, use whatever non-oily fish bones and heads you have: the fish already mentioned plus bass, grouper, snapper, haddock, etc.

Despite what most cookbooks tell you, fish stocks should be brought to a boil as fast as possible so that all the albumin coagulates and rises to the surface for skimming.

Simmer for no more than 30 minutes (or the stock will taste "fishy" and stale).

The vegetables have to be finely chopped so that they cook entirely in this short time, and the acid from the wine is necessary if you are to use the stock for making butter sauces, but add it only after the vegetables have given up most of their flavor (it impedes this process if added at the beginning).

Any leftover stock can be frozen for up to a month.

YIELD 1 GALLON

5 pounds	fish carcasses	1 sprig	fresh tarragon or
1 cup	finely chopped celery		chervil, or ½ tea-
1 cup	finely chopped onion		spoon dried leaves
2	bay leaves	½ teaspoon	salt
1 sprig	fresh thyme or ½ teaspoon	1 gallon	water
	dried leaves	1 cup	dry white wine
2 sprigs	fresh parsley		

Wash the fish carcasses, removing the gills from the heads and, under running water, scrape away any blood from the backbone.

Put the celery, onion, herbs, and salt in a pot. Add 1 cup of the water, cover, and sweat the mixture over low heat for 10 minutes. Do not let any browning occur.

Add the fish carcasses and remaining water. Bring to a boil over high heat. The moment it boils, lower the heat to a bare simmer. Stir the bones around very gently for a few seconds so that any coagulated albumin trapped at the bottom will rise to the surface. Skim off any scum, avoiding floating vegetables or herbs. Simmer uncovered for 20 minutes.

Add the wine, and simmer another 10 minutes. Remove from the heat, let sit for 5 minutes, then carefully ladle all the stock into a fine strainer set over a container. Do not press down on any fish in the strainer. Pour the last of the stock into the strainer and discard the debris. Immediately refrigerate the stock uncovered. When cold, cover and keep refrigerated or frozen until needed.

QUICK SHELLFISH STOCK

Fresh mussels are the secret to a 10-minute rich shellfish stock. Cook them with either fish stock or clam juice (bottled) and water, plus a little white wine and fresh herbs. Serve the mussels themselves for a salad, hot first course, or chopped up into mayonnaise for a sauce to serve with grilled fish.

MAKES 3 CUPS

2 pounds	fresh mussels, washed
3 cups	fish stock or 1 cup clam broth and 2 cups water
2 sprigs	fresh thyme
2 sprigs	fresh parsley
½ cup	dry white wine

Put all the ingredients in a pot, cover, and bring to the boil over high heat. Cook 10 minutes and strain. Decant the strained stock into another container, leaving ⅛ inch of the old behind along with its sand.

SHELLFISH ESSENCE

Essences are good for using in cream and butter sauces, for mixing with lemon juice and oils for salad dressing, or reduced and added to butter to make a shellfish butter.

This recipe works for lobster, shrimp, or prawn shells (crab shells don't give up much flavor or color and are usually too hard to process), and is one we developed at Stars in San Francisco in the early 1980s. I have since seen this method only in the restaurants of people who worked there, but it could be as old as the Hobart mixer. In the nineteenth century and early twentieth, the shells were processed in huge mortars with a pestle, but that practice disappeared along with slavery in the kitchen.

Classically, any essences made from shells (the classic *sauce Nantua*, for example) call for cooking the shells in the oven. Tossing raw shells in hot olive or canola oil in a frying pan for a few minutes until deep red is passable, but I hate the flavor the shells tend to get (with the inevitable overcooking) in the oven. Boiled or sautéed shells give a much subtler flavor.

If the shells are not cooked, steam them covered in a little stock, or toss them in hot oil for 5 minutes over medium heat.

MAKES 4 CUPS

4 cups	cooked lobster shells (from 3 lobsters), or shrimp shells
4 cups	fish stock

If using shrimp shells, grind the shells in a food processor just enough to break them up. If using lobster shells, just put them in the bowl of an electric mixer fitted with the dough hook or paddle, and turn on the mixer at the lowest speed possible for 15 minutes. Wrap some aluminum foil around the top of the bowl and the mixer arm to keep the lobster shells from jumping out of the bowl as they are being crushed. After 15 minutes, add 1 cup of the stock, turn the speed up one notch, and mix for another 10 minutes.

Add the remaining fish stock and mix on low speed until the shells are completely broken up in small pieces and the stock in the bowl has turned red, about another 15 minutes. The long mixing time is necessary to break up the shells gradually and extract the full flavor and color.

Scrape out all the shells and any essence sticking to the sides of the bowl into a sieve placed over a bowl.

Strain completely, pressing down on the shells, reserving the liquid and discarding the shells.

Refrigerate for up to 2 days or freeze for up to a month.

SHELLFISH BUTTER

Use the same method as for shellfish essence, but add 1 pound of room temperature butter for the last 30 minutes of processing the shells in the mixer. Cook the buttered shell liquid 5 minutes, strain, and refrigerate the liquid. When it is cold, lift off the butter from the top and use it to enrich sauces, or season it and put it on grilled fish. Use the liquid for shellfish essence.

This butter freezes well and will hold for a month.

CHAPTER EIGHT
POULTRY, FEATHERED GAME, RABBIT, and FOIE GRAS

FAST AND EASY CHICKEN BREAST

Each whole chicken breast is actually two pieces when off the bone, and very often each breast half is called the breast, leading to confusion in recipes of how many pieces of breast meat are being called for.

This recipe calls for one boned half breast (no wing bone attached) per person, making it a very economical dish. The breast meat is flattened out and cooks in a few minutes, so it is fast, and once you get the hang of pounding out the chicken meat, it's easy. And, of course, these chicken "steaks" can be broiled, as well as grilled.

SERVES 4

2	large chicken breasts, skinned, boned (4 boned half-breast pieces)	1 tablespoon	finely chopped fresh mint leaves
4 tablespoons	ancho chili powder	4 tablespoons	extra virgin olive oil
¼ cup	canola oil	4	large fennel bulbs, trimmed, halved lengthwise, cored
6 tablespoons	unsalted butter	8	lime wedges
3	anchovy fillets (see page 42), chopped		Salt and freshly ground black pepper
½ tablespoon	finely grated orange zest		

Put the chicken pieces between two pieces of heavy plastic, and with the side of a cleaver or mallet pound them out evenly until ¼ to ⅜ inch thick. Mix 1 tablespoon of the chili powder and the canola oil in a shallow pan or platter just large enough to hold the four flattened breast pieces in one layer. Dip the chicken in the mixture and marinate for 3 hours, turning once.

Make ancho butter by putting the butter, ½ teaspoon of salt, and the remaining 3 tablespoons of the chili powder in a food processor and blending it until the butter is smooth and the chili totally incorporated. Let the chili butter stand for at least 2 hours to develop its flavors. If you refrigerate the butter, bring it to room temperature, whisking it to get the right smooth texture before using.

Start a charcoal or wood fire, or preheat the grill or broiler.

Put the anchovies, orange zest, mint, and olive oil in a bowl big enough to hold the fennel. Boil the fennel in salted water for 10 minutes or until tender, drain well, and while still hot put it in the bowl and gently mix with the marinade. Season the fennel.

When ready to serve, grill or broil the fennel over medium heat for 5 minutes per side. Then move it to the edge of the grill and keep warm.

Salt the chicken pieces and cook them on a hot charcoal grill or under a broiler for 2 minutes per side. Serve the chicken with a squeeze of lime and the ancho butter on top (or pass it separately) and the fennel with the marinade spooned over it.

VARIATIONS By all means use turkey, goose, game, or duck to make these little "steaks," the turkey served with mole sauce and the duck or goose with cooked white beans tossed with blanched pea tendrils, chopped garlic, parsley, and a pinch of cardamom.

ROAST CHICKEN

When I cooked roast chicken on TV for Julia Child, she kept saying, "Don't forget to mention salmonella, dear." Well, I didn't mention it, but hinted that using the lemon juice cleans everything up, as well as making the chicken taste wonderful. So I will not talk about that subject here either—except to say always use a cutting board and wash it well along with everything else that has been in contact with uncooked poultry—nor add much more to the millions of words already written about roast chicken.

But I do know that roast chicken can be one of the world's greatest and easiest dishes if you buy chicken that has as much pedigree as possible (organic, cage free, range-roaming, and so on) and has never seen a plastic covering (if it has, let the chicken dry out for three hours before cooking); wash the chicken with fresh lemon juice half an hour before cooking it; and let the chicken rest for twenty minutes after cooking and before carving.

I think turning the chicken over on its sides and onto its back (and then back again) when it is hot either in or from the oven is a lot of dangerous work for most people, so I start the chicken in a covered casserole just large enough to hold it (2 inches of free space all around) and then uncover it for the last cooking to crisp the skin.

Serve with the oven-roasted vegetables on page 137 or the oven-baked fruits on page 138, or with both.

SERVES 4 TO 6

1	4-pound fresh roasting chicken	¼ cup	olive oil
2	whole lemons	1 cup	mixed fresh herbs (rosemary, thyme, basil, etc.)
1	head fresh garlic cloves, separated, skin on, smashed with a cleaver		Salt and freshly ground black pepper
4 slices	bacon (wood smoked if possible), finely chopped		

If the chicken comes in a plastic bag, take it out, rinse it under cold water inside and out, pat dry inside and out, and let sit uncovered in the refrigerator for 3 hours. Take it out and let it come to room temperature before cooking.

Preheat the oven to 450 degrees.

Cut the lemons in half and squeeze the juice over and inside the chicken, and then rub it in. Season the cavity of the chicken, then put the lemon halves and garlic cloves in the cavity.

Loosen the skin of the breast at the rear of the chicken, and gently insinuate all your fingers under the skin, moving down the sides and up to the front. Then take the bacon in your fingers and push it under the skin evenly all over the breast.

Rub the chicken with the olive oil, then sprinkle with salt and pepper. Stuff half the herbs in the cavity and put the other half in the casserole. Put the chicken in the casserole, cover, and put in the oven.

Cook at 450 degrees for 15 minutes, then turn the oven down to 350 for another 20 minutes. Uncover, turn the heat to 400, and finish cooking the chicken for 15 minutes. Insert a skewer in the thighs to see if the juices run clear. When they do, remove the chicken and let it rest for 20 minutes in a warm place (on the open oven door with the oven turned off).

Put the chicken onto a hot platter. While the chicken is resting, strain the juices in the casserole and remove the fat floating on top. Wipe any fat out of the casserole with paper towels, and pour the defatted juices back in the casserole. Heat the casserole on the stove and stir the juices to dislodge any of the bits that are stuck to the casserole. You can use chicken stock or red or white wine to help with this process if there are not a lot of juices. Season the juices and serve them with the chicken.

VARIATIONS Stuff mushroom hash (see page 17) mixed in equal quantities with the bacon under the skin, or use chopped fresh black truffles and bacon. And see the tagine on page 49.

BRAISED CHICKEN IN A CASSEROLE WITH CHESTNUTS AND SAUSAGES

This dish was originally created for older squab, but I love this easier version with chicken. You can also use duck (wild or domestic) instead.

In England, the little sausages I love to put with poultry are called chipolata, and are the same size as American breakfast sausages, though not as highly seasoned. The latter will work well, and if you want to add a real zinger, use lamb merguez sausages, which are full of red pepper.

Serve this dish in the winter with mushroom hash mixed in equal quantities with mashed potatoes, and in warmer (but still chestnut) weather with a warm potato salad of your choice, like the *pommes de terre à la provençale* in Alexandre Dumas's *Le Grand dictionnaire de la cuisine* (1873), served hot, or see James Beard's Bacon Potato Salad in his *American Cookery* (1972).

SERVES 4

1	large roasting chicken	12	chipolata-type sausages
½ cup	dry brine (see page 22)	16	small boiling onions, peeled
4 slices	bacon, chopped	2 sprigs	fresh tarragon
1 cup	aromatic vegetable mix (see page 14)	12	roasted chestnuts, double-peeled, broken into quarters
1	herb bundle (see page 16)		
1 cup	dry white wine	1 tablespoon	grated orange zest
4 cups	rich chicken stock (see page 215)	½ tablespoon	orange Sichuan pepper salt (see page 42)

Put the chicken in a mixing bowl and pour the marinade salt over it. Rub the salt over the chicken and marinate 1 hour, then wipe off all the salt.

Preheat the oven to 375 degrees.

Put the bacon in a heavy casserole just large enough to hold the chicken with 2 inches all around, and cook the bacon over medium heat until it has rendered most of its fat. Take the bacon pieces out with a slotted spoon, leaving the fat in the casserole. Turn the heat up slightly and brown the chicken on all sides in the casserole, for about 8 minutes. Be careful not to let anything burn. Take the pot off the heat, remove the chicken, wipe out the casserole with paper towels, and put the bird back in. Add the cooked bacon, vegetable mix, and herb bundle.

Turn the heat to medium, and when the casserole is hot, pour in the wine. Boil for 1 minute, then cover the casserole and sweat everything for 10 minutes. Add the stock, bring to a boil and immediately put the casserole in the oven and cook for 1 hour, or until the chicken is tender.

Cook the sausages in a pan over medium heat for 5 minutes, turning them once or twice. Put them aside on paper towels to drain, wipe the fat out of the pan, and add the onions and tarragon. Add ¼ cup water and a pinch of salt, cover, and cook over medium heat for 10 minutes, or until the onions are just tender when pierced with a fork.

Take the chicken out of the casserole, strain the braising juices, and simmer in another pan to reduce a bit and clean of all the fat (see page 30). Put the chicken back in the casserole and add the onions, sausages, and chestnuts. The dish can be prepared several hours in advance up to this point if you want.

Thirty minutes before serving, stir the orange zest into the reduced sauce and pour it back over the chicken in the casserole. Correct the seasoning. Reheat the chicken in the casserole on top of the stove or in a 350-degree oven, but do not let the sauce boil.

Carve the chicken, and pass the salt separately to be sprinkled over it.

VARIATION Serve with the lemon and fig relish on page 243.

TRUFFLED CAPON ROASTED ON A SPIT

The dish made famous by the greatest and most modest of masters, Alexandre Dumaine of the Côte d'Or in Saulieu, was one that people like the Aga Khan, Orson Welles, and Grace Kelly would travel far to enjoy, defining the Michelin term "worth the journey." Dumaine's dish was a whole capon, or sometimes a *poularde*, but always "a chicken which has been reared and fed in an exemplary manner for most of its life, then confined and fattened for the table." Dumaine stuffed his bird with whole fresh black truffles, stuffed some under the skin as well, then encased and sealed the chicken in a pig's bladder for poaching in aromatic broth. The chicken was then brought to the table in the bladder and opened in front of the rapturous guests, releasing a cloud of rich chicken and truffle vapors. In France, you can still order this spectacular dish at the restaurants of Paul Bocuse near Lyon, or Georges Blanc in Vonnas.

This recipe, which Ken Hom recently cooked for me in Catus, France, is a bit easier, especially since I don't know where to get that bladder. You will need a grill with a spit and a cover, like a Weber. Or cook the capon in the oven as for a roast chicken, although it may take an extra thirty minutes to cook.

SERVES 6 TO 8

1	6-pound fresh capon with liver		1	4-ounce fresh black truffle, sliced ¼-inch thick
2	whole lemons		¼ cup	fresh lovage leaves (or the leaves of the heart of celery), chopped
2–3 cups	2-day-old country-style bread, crusts removed, cut in 1-inch cubes			Sea salt
1 lobe	duck foie gras, cleaned and denerved (as on page 212) then cut into ½-inch cubes			Freshly ground pepper

Cut the lemons in half and squeeze the juice inside and all over the capon and season its cavity.

Put the bread, foie gras, truffles, and whole lovage leaves in a bowl and mix them all together. Season and put the stuffing in the cavity of the capon. Sew up the cavity opening, and let the chicken develop the flavors of the stuffing for 3 hours in the refrigerator.

Start a real charcoal or wood fire. When it is ready, put the capon on the spit over the fire and lower the cover of the grill.

Cook for 1½ hours, or until the juices from the thigh of the capon run clear. Let the capon sit 30 minutes in a warm place before serving.

CHICKEN POT PIES WITH FIRST-CROP GARLIC AND WHITE CORN

For this dish, you can use either the leftover meat from any roast poultry (the roast chicken, the capon, or little chickens on pages 193–199), or chicken cooked specifically for the recipe.

Because any variation of this dish will improve in taste and complexity if cooked the day before (add the vegetables just before the final heating), this recipe calls for braised chicken legs and thighs, since they (unlike the breast meat) can be reheated without drying out

Of course, you can make the crust with a dough (see page 274 for short crust, but omit the sugar). If you do, remember to cut out circles of pastry the same size as the inside diameter of the little casseroles so that steam can escape around their edges and prevent the pie crusts from becoming soggy, and to paint the underside of the raw dough with egg wash to seal it against steam.

But I prefer a buttered toast "crust" that is added only at the reheating time. It stays really crisp and seems to me to be a lot lighter than a dough crust (though perhaps not as comforting).

Twenty garlic cloves are not too many, since the garlic in this recipe is mild-flavored, first-crop garlic in addition to the fact that any garlic cooked this way becomes mild.

You will need four "pots" each of 3-cup capacity and about 4 inches deep.

SERVES 4

4	chicken legs with thighs	4 slices	white bread, ½-inch thick, cut in rounds to just fit inside the pots
2 tablespoons	ground cumin		
2 tablespoons	vegetable oil	2 tablespoons	melted butter
1 cup	aromatic vegetable mix (see page 14)	1 tablespoon	freshly squeezed lime juice
6 cups	chicken stock (see page 215)	1 tablespoon	fresh tarragon leaves, finely chopped
20	fresh garlic cloves, peeled		
½ cup	fresh white corn kernels (from 3–4 ears)		

Put the chicken in a shallow dish and sprinkle both sides of the legs and thighs with the cumin and rub it in. Cover the dish loosely, and marinate the chicken in the refrigerator for 4 hours.

Preheat the oven to 350 degrees.

Heat the oil in a heavy casserole, season the chicken, and sear it in the casserole over medium heat for 1 minute on each side. Add the vegetable mix, and cook for another 2 minutes while stirring constantly. Add the stock, stirring to loosen anything sticking to the bottom of the casserole, and bring to a simmer. Cover the casserole and put it in the oven for 45 minutes to 1 hour, or until the leg meat is tender.

Take the casserole out of the oven. Remove the chicken and let it cool. Strain the braising liquid, skim off and discard any fat, and put the strained liquid back in the casserole. Bring to a boil, reduce the heat, and simmer for 10 minutes, taking off any more fat or scum. Let cool.

When the chicken is cool enough to handle, remove the bones. Cut the chicken into 1-inch chunks, and when the sauce has cooled slightly, add the chicken. The dish can be prepared in advance up to this point.

Preheat the oven to 400 degrees.

Put the garlic cloves in 2 quarts of salted boiling water and cook them for 10 minutes. Then add the fresh corn and cook another 2 minutes. Drain the garlic and the corn and add them to the chicken.

Bake the bread rounds in the oven for 5 to 8 minutes, or until completely dry and just golden. Remove the toasts and brush them on one side with the melted butter.

When ready to serve, add the lime juice and tarragon to the chicken and heat it (without letting it boil). Portion the chicken and its sauce into the individual "pots." Put the toast rounds, buttered side up, on top of the chicken in the pots, and then place them on a baking sheet and bake in the oven for 10 minutes.

VARIATIONS To flavor the sauce, use 2 tablespoons of huitlacoche mixed with ½ cup heavy cream. And instead of the legs and thighs, use sixteen chicken wings (which to me are the best part of the chicken), cooked in the same way (but for less time), boned but not cut up. The recipe is also very good with leftover turkey or with duck legs and thighs.

GRIDDLED POUSSIN CHICKEN WITH WHOLE HOMINY

The little (1-pound) chickens called poussin by the English and French make a perfect one-per-person bird, and when flattened out and cooked weighted on a griddle or in a heavy skillet, they are easy, no work, no worry, just crisp and delicious.

Whole hominy is the only canned vegetable or grain I ever use—both the yellow and the white. Do not even think of making hominy at home—even if "nixtamalization" (the process, as practiced first by the Aztec and Maya of Central America, involves soaking the ripe corn kernels and then cooking them with wood ashes and lime or lye, which removes the outer skin) is something you've always wanted to do. Buy the cans!

Before using, always empty the cans of hominy into a colander, rinse under cold water for two minutes, and drain.

SERVES 4 TO 6

4	1-pound chickens	½ cup	chicken stock (see page 215)
8 stems	fresh sage, stemmed, stems and leaves saved, leaves finely chopped	2 tablespoons	ancho chili puree (see page 32)
¼ cup	olive oil	2 tablespoons	butter
1	small can white whole hominy, drained, rinsed	½ bunch	fresh chives, chopped into 1-inch lengths
1	small can yellow whole hominy, drained, rinsed		

With a knife, scissors, or poultry shears, cut down each side of each chicken's backbone to remove it. Place the cavity surface of the chickens on a cutting board and give them a couple of hits on the breast to flatten them completely. Tuck the wing tips under the wings. Then put the chickens in a shallow dish, and rub them all over with the sage stems and then with 2 tablespoons of the olive oil. Marinate for 2 hours covered in the refrigerator, turning them a couple of times.

Wipe the sage stems off the chickens, and season them. Pour the remaining olive oil into a hot heavy skillet or onto a griddle, and add the sage stems. Put the chickens skin side down on the stems, and put a weight (bricks on top of a cookie sheet, plate with can on top, etc.) of at least 5 pounds on top of the birds. Turn the heat to medium-low, cook for 15 minutes, turn the chickens over and cook for another 10 minutes, then again for 5 minutes on the other side to crisp the skin.

After the chickens have cooked for 15 minutes, heat the hominy with the chicken stock. Add the ancho chili puree, butter, and sage leaves, and stir until all the hominy is hot and coated with the chili sauce. Season.

Serve the chickens on a bed of the hominy and to garnish, sprinkle the chives over the chickens.

QUAIL WITH BLACK-EYED PEAS

At The Inn at Little Washington, Patrick O'Connell marinates his quail in Coca-Cola, saying that it tenderizes them, as well as giving flavor and caramelizing the skin. Now I have had chicken in Coca-Cola at Korova in Paris with its inventor, the incomparable Frederick, the wife of the equally incomparable Pierre Hermé, so I can wax enthusiastic about a sauce made with Coke and cooked with poultry.

But I want to introduce you to another unusual cooking method for poultry that ensures full flavor and a silky texture. Poaching white-fleshed poultry in fat or oil (olive if you can afford it) cooks it in a way that gives you the texture of Chinese "velvet" chicken, and makes it difficult to overcook as long as the fat *never* boils. An added bonus is that the chicken can rest in the warm fat for up to thirty minutes without overcooking.

I first saw fresh black-eyed peas in a supermarket thirty-five years ago in Cambridge, Massachusetts, when Julia Child was standing there holding up a bag of them and staring at it. Somehow, we got into a conversation about frozen goose versus fresh goose and which type was easiest to cook, and then she wanted to know what I would do with the black-eyed peas. "I don't know," I replied. She looked at me kindly.

Later, as an accompaniment to baked ham, I tried them hot with a sherry vinegar vinaigrette mixed with chopped, broiled, apple-wood smoked bacon, and fell in love. Buy the fresh black-eyed peas in the plastic bags and rinse them before using. Even better, look for their more noble cousins, the kind you find fresh in the summer in Alabama.

SERVES 4

4	whole fresh quail	1 teaspoon	freshly ground white pepper
2 cups	wet brine (see page 22)		
2 ounces	fresh ham, finely chopped	1½ cups	fresh black-eyed peas, rinsed and drained
1 tablespoon	fresh tarragon leaves, finely chopped	1 cup	young fresh peas
6 cups	water-rendered duck or chicken fat (see page 30), or olive or peanut oil	½ cup	chicken stock (see page 215)
		¼ cup	extra virgin light yellow olive oil
1 tablespoon	freshly grated lemon zest		Salt
½ tablespoon	fresh sage leaves, finely chopped		
2 tablespoons	fresh Italian parsley leaves, finely chopped		

Put the quail in the brine and refrigerate for 2 hours. Remove them from the brine and pat dry.

Mix the ham and tarragon together, and, lifting up the skin on the breasts of the quail, push this mixture under the skin all over the breasts. Tuck the wings under the quail.

Put the quail in a casserole just large enough to hold them side by side, and pour the fat over them. Heat the fat to about 180 degrees, to the point where you can still put your finger in it for a second, cook 15 minutes and turn off the heat, leaving the quail in the fat for another 15 minutes.

Mix the lemon zest, sage, parsley, and black pepper in a bowl.

Cook the black-eyed peas in boiling salted water for 3 minutes and then add the fresh green peas, cooking them together for another 5 minutes. Drain and put the mixed peas in a pot with the chicken stock and the olive oil. Bring to a boil, season, and turn down the heat just to keep them warm.

Cut the wings (all but the bone closest to the body) off the quail. Put the two peas in the center of hot plates, put the quail on top, and sprinkle each quail with the sage and lemon mixture.

LAVENDER HONEY–GLAZED DUCK BREAST WITH BLACKBERRIES AND WATER CHESTNUTS

Pairing fruit and duck hearkens back to older classics like duck with hot Morello cherries or with the bitter oranges of Moorish Andalusia fame. For me, it's a tradition that still makes sense because the sweet acid of the fruit is a perfect foil to the richness of the duck.

The duck breast itself can be grilled, broiled, or sautéed. The points to remember are that the initial cooking on the bone renders out the fat, and that the final cooking is really just heating, letting the breast remain pink.

The honey flavors the skin and also helps to render out the fat, allowing the skin to become crisp. If you cannot get lavender honey, buy the best floral honey you can find, warm it, and infuse it with lavender flowers or rosemary leaves for ten minutes and then strain.

This recipe is even better if you smoke the breasts slightly first.

SERVES 4

2	whole duck breasts (on the bone), first wing bone left on	1 tablespoon	freshly ground coarse black pepper
½ cup	dry brine (see page 22)	8	large fresh water chestnuts, peeled, sliced ⅛-inch thick
6 cups	chicken or duck stock (see page 215)	1 cup	fresh blackberries
¼ cup	Malmsey Madeira	1 tablespoon	butter
¼ cup	lavender honey	16 sprigs	watercress
			Salt and freshly ground black pepper

Rub the duck breasts all over with the salt mixture, and let sit for 30 minutes with the skin side down in the remaining salt.

Preheat the oven to 450 degrees.

Place the breasts skin side up on a rack set on a sheet pan or roasting pan. Put the pan in the oven and bake for 10 minutes to render some of the fat from under the skin. Take the duck out of the oven and cool.

When the duck is cool enough to handle, carefully cut each half breast off the bone in one piece. You will have four pieces. Save the breast bones. "French" the bones by cutting around the base of the wing bone, and peel off the meat and skin from the bone. Chop off the knuckle end of the bone. The duck can be prepared up to this point a day in advance and refrigerated.

Rinse the breast bones under cold water to get rid of any salt, and then cut or smash them up. Put the bones in a 3 quart stock pot with the discarded wing and knuckle bones. Add the stock and bring to a boil. Lower the heat to a simmer and skim off any scum that rises to the surface of the stock. Simmer for 45 minutes and strain. Rinse out the stock pot. Remove any fat from the surface of the stock. Put the Madeira in the rinsed pot and boil for a minute. Add the stock, bring to a boil, immediately turning the heat down to a simmer, and clean up the sauce as described on page 30. Simmer the sauce for 30 minutes, reducing it down to 1 cup.

Meanwhile, put the honey and pepper in a little bowl and mix them together. Brush the honey-pepper mix onto the skin side of the all the duck breast pieces.

Heat a frying pan to medium heat and put the duck pieces skin side down in the pan. Cook for 3 minutes, then turn the heat down to low (or put in a preheated 350-degree oven) and cook until the duck is medium rare, 3 to 5 minutes more. Let the duck rest in a warm place for 5 minutes so that the juices are reabsorbed into the meat.

While the duck is resting, bring the sauce to a boil and add the water chestnuts. Simmer 1 minute, add the blackberries, and take off the stove. Stir in the butter and season.

Immediately pour the sauce with the blackberries and water chestnuts out onto four hot plates, then slice off the wing joints and slice the breasts across on a diagonal about ⅛ inch thick. Fan the slices on the plates, put the watercress in the center and stand the wing joint in the watercress.

VARIATIONS Use peeled and thinly sliced Jerusalem artichokes—steamed in butter and water for 5 minutes—instead of, or as well as, the water chestnuts. Or instead of the berries and water chestnuts, use mandarin orange sections, with ¼ cup chopped pecans or black walnuts, cooked and chopped duck livers and 1 tablespoon of coarse black pepper. Or serve the duck with very garlicky cooked white beans (see page 33) and lemon and fig relish (see page 243). Or serve with fresh fava beans and fresh morels steamed in butter, garlic, and a little chicken stock.

FAST AND EASY PRESERVED DUCK LEGS WITH CHESTNUTS

There are two ways to go with this most glorious and easiest of fast foods—either served with something rich like potatoes cooked in water-rendered duck fat and truffles or wild mushrooms, or with something acidic with a bitter edge that will cut and act as a foil against the richness of the duck such as a fruit or a salad.

You can serve this dish without the gizzards, but they are truly delicious! And as for the chestnuts, buy them from a street vendor on your way home. Or to make this dish really fast and easy, buy the very best quality chesnuts in jars and toast them in a 325-degree oven for ten minutes before using them. Or eat these fast food ducks with your favorite green salad and be done with it!

SERVES 4

4	fat-preserved duck legs (see page 15)		8–10	fresh chestnuts, roasted, double-peeled, coarsely chopped
2	large Winesap or other tart apples		1 tablespoon	orange Sichuan pepper salt (see page 42)
2 tablespoons	freshly squeezed lemon juice		2 tablespoons	fresh herb flowers
12	duck gizzards cooked in duck fat (see page 15)			Freshly ground black pepper
¼ cup	Muscat wine (or Riesling)			

Preheat the grill or broiler to medium.

Peel the apples, quarter them, and remove the cores. Chop them into ⅛-inch dice and put them in a bowl with the lemon juice. Mix well.

Season the duck legs with pepper and grill or broil them for 5 minutes on the flesh side and 8 minutes on the skin side. Warm the gizzards in ½ cup of the fat from the preserved duck leg jar without letting it boil.

While the duck legs are cooking, put the apples in a nonstick frying pan, turn the heat to high, and cook for 5 minutes, tossing or stirring them constantly. Add the wine off the heat and flame it. Add the chestnuts and cook another 2 minutes while mixing them with the apples.

Put the apple-chestnut mix in the center of hot plates. Then put the legs on top, spoon any of the dressing and chestnuts left in the pan around the plates, along with the gizzards. Sprinkle the gizzards with the flavored salt, pepper, and the herb flowers.

SPICED DUCK SICHUAN STYLE

The problem with cooking a whole duck (or goose, turkey, or any large game bird) is that you want the breast to be slightly pink (so that it's not dry), but the leg and thigh cooked all the way through and tender. That is why the two parts of the duck are usually cooked separately.

This Chinese poaching method allows you to cook the whole duck, and have the breast, though not pink, still tender and moist. This method also gets rid of all the fat, but leaves the skin moist (though not crisp). Chinese chefs will then deep-fry the whole duck in a wok full of hot oil, which crisps the skin while leaving the breast meat moist and tender. It is the best of all worlds with duck, but the frying part is not recommended outside of a professional kitchen.

We served this at an AMFAR benefit in Napa Valley in 1998 to celebrate the Napa vegetable harvest, and included young red onions, fresh white beans, diced celery root, and squashes cooked separately, and then tossed together with olive oil, herbs, and cooked chopped pancetta.

Keep the poaching liquid and make an amazing soup by straining it and adding fresh ginger, herbs, and vegetables.

SERVES 4 TO 6

1	whole duck	2	whole cloves
½ cup	fresh ginger, roughly chopped	2	stalks lemon grass
		4	bay leaves
2	bunches scallions, roughly chopped	1	ancho chili
		6 sprigs	fresh thyme
1	small bunch celery, chopped	6 sprigs	fresh tarragon
		1 bunch	fresh cilantro, chopped
2	heads fresh garlic, roughly chopped	1 tablespoon	turmeric
6	star anise	1 teaspoon	ground cardamom
1 tablespoon	coriander seeds	2 tablespoons	salt

Choose a pot that will just hold the duck and enough liquid to cover it by 2 inches.

Put the duck in the pot, and add all the ingredients and water to cover by 2 inches. Remove the duck and bring the water to the boil and simmer 15 minutes. Put the duck back in and bring the water back to the boil. Skim off any scum that rises to the surface. Reduce the heat to a low simmer, and cook the duck for 1 hour, or until it is tender (the legs move easily on the body, but by no means are we at the point that the meat is falling off the bones).

Do not overcook the duck, as it will continue to cook as it cools in the broth (in order to maximize its flavors and moistness). When the duck is cool, carve it into legs/thighs and breasts with one wing bone on, and either grill, broil, or sauté. Serve with the black-eyed peas on page 200 or the caramelized sugar and ginger sauce on page 227.

Oven-Roasted Squab with Imperial Roman Sauce

Although this recipe uses an oven, use a smoker if you have one, or a grill with a cover, especially if it has a drip pan with water in it under the rack holding the birds. In this way, the liquid keeps a moist vapor around the squab. The sauce, smoking, and boning can be done a few hours in advance, with the boned halves resting in the reduced squab broth. Be careful when reheating them not to let the broth boil or the squab will become tough and overcooked.

The sauce is from the great inspirational cookbook of the imperial Roman author Apicius, *Cookery and Dining in Imperial Rome*, although in the original Latin the title is more like "Current Ingredients and the Art of Cooking." The sauce was originally to be served on hard-boiled eggs, and not even cranes' and plovers' eggs at that, as expected of Romans.

A plain watercress salad, the sweet corn timbale on page 123, the winter squash slices in white truffle oil on page 129, or the onions cowboy–style on page 134 (heated and glazed under a medium heat broiler for ten minutes), would all be delicious with this smoky squab and its Apician sauce.

You will need some soft white string for trussing the squabs.

SERVES 4

The Squabs:

4	whole fresh squabs	6 tablespoons	extra virgin olive oil
12 sprigs	fresh thyme, stemmed, leaves chopped	4 cups	white veal stock or mixed veal and chicken (see pages 215)
½ teaspoon	salt		
½ teaspoon	freshly ground pepper		

The Sauce:

4 ounces	pine nuts, lightly toasted	1 teaspoon	coarsely ground fresh black pepper (like Tellicherry)
2 tablespoons	extra virgin olive oil		
2 tablespoons	coarsely chopped fresh lovage leaves (or tender celery)	2 tablespoons	squab broth (see below)
		½ teaspoon	sea salt
2 tablespoons	wild flower or herbal honey		

If there are heads and feet on the squab, chop them off and keep them to include in the squab broth.

Take some string and tie up the legs of the squabs, trussing them around the backs of the birds. Put the thyme, salt, pepper, and the olive oil in a bowl and add the squab. Rub all over with the mixture. Cover loosely and leave at room temperature for 2 hours.

Preheat the oven to 425 degrees.

Put the squabs in a baking pan in the oven, cooking them for 15 minutes.

Take the birds out of the oven and set them aside to cool. When the birds are cool, slice the two halves of the birds off the carcasses, leaving the first wing bone attached to the breast. Cover the boned halves loosely.

Chop up the carcasses and put them in a saucepan large enough to hold all the bones (plus feet and heads) and the stock. Pour the stock into a pan, bring to a boil, skim off any scum that rises to the surface of the stock, and simmer for 30 minutes. Strain and degrease the sauce, reducing it and cleaning it as you go (see page 30) until you have 1½ cups.

While the squab broth is reducing, make the Apician sauce. Put the pine nuts into a mixing bowl, add the olive oil, and leave for 30 minutes. Then add the lovage, honey, and pepper, and crush one-third of the pine nuts with a fork. Add 2 tablespoons of the squab broth from the simmering pot, mix it in briefly, and taste the sauce for salt.

Put the squab pieces in a sauté pan large enough to hold them side by side in one layer. Heat them in the oven for 5 minutes, or until the squab is heated through.

Put the squab halves onto warm plates, spoon some sauce next to them, and pass the rest of the sauce separately.

VARIATIONS Marinate little chickens, or even breasts of large roasters, for 5 hours in a marinade of one-third Scotch whiskey and two-thirds olive oil, with lots of fresh thyme and 2 tablespoons of crushed juniper berries, and you will get a taste of a wild game bird such as grouse. Then roast or smoke them as above and serve with the same sauce.

GRILLED GUINEA FOWL WITH WATERCRESS SALAD

It is best to do as little as possible to this wonderful bird (which tastes the way most chickens in the world should), but getting a crisp skin with a young bird that takes very little cooking is a problem. This recipe, which calls for fast cooking, is inspired by a recipe for *poulet d'Inde* (either turkey or guinea fowl) in a cookbook from 1651, *Le Cuisinier François*, of La Varenne, which uses raspberry vinegar to glaze and finish off the grilled bird.

With the acid flavor on the skin of the guinea fowl, I have purposely left any acid out of the dressing for the watercress.

SERVES 4

1	large fresh guinea fowl (3–4 pounds)	3 tablespoons	walnut oil
½ cup	fresh raspberries	2	bunches watercress, washed, spin-dried
¼ cup	olive oil		Salt and freshly ground black pepper
4	sprigs fresh thyme		
1 tablespoon	grated lemon zest		

Cut out the backbone of the guinea fowl and flatten it as for the poussin chicken on page 199.

Sieve the raspberries into a bowl, and discard the seeds in the strainer. Add the olive oil, thyme, and lemon zest to the bowl and mix them together with the sieved raspberries. Put the guinea fowl in the bowl and rub the marinade all over the bird, leaving it in the marinade skin side down. Cover loosely and marinate for 2 hours in the refrigerator.

Take the guinea fowl out of the refrigerator and let it come to room temperature. Start a real charcoal or wood fire, or preheat the grill or broiler.

Brush half the marinade on the guinea fowl skin, and grill or broil for 8 minutes. Turn over the guinea fowl, brush with the rest of the marinade, and grill another 5 minutes. Finish the cooking, skin side to the fire, for another 3 minutes, or until just barely pink in the thickest part. Let rest 15 minutes in a warm place.

Put a pinch of salt and a few grindings of pepper in a bowl, and whisk in the walnut oil. When ready to serve the guinea fowl, toss the watercress in the walnut oil dressing and serve with the guinea fowl cut in quarters.

FEATHERED GAME

The feathered game I have cooked and eaten recently are black duck, Canada goose, grouse, partridge, pheasant, quail, and woodcock. All of them are better with five to eight days aging, quail being the exception—it should be cooked "just off the end of the gun." While chickens get every treatment in the book from crayfish butter (Jean Cocteau), to being stuffed with foie gras and sauced with black truffles (Antonin Carême), or with foie gras and cooked in cream (the Aga Khan), game birds benefit most from very simple cooking. One perfect recipe, called *Palombes en Béatitude*, or Blissful Doves, is given in Fernand Point's *Ma Gastronomie*: stuff some doves with diced truffles, foie gras, and pistachios. Roast the birds in the oven, serve them with the pan juices reduced with red wine, and garnish with tiny puff pastry containers filled with currant jelly. That is the spirit and form of a perfect game-bird recipe.

One cold October night, by the Miramichi River in New Brunswick, we had a goose in the oven roasting along with a black duck, while the writer Charles Gaines was rolling a couple of dozen woodcock around on a griddle with a little bacon fat and watching partridge breasts, over which some wild red currant puree had been spread, cooking under the broiler.

If you read a wonderful book by Guy de Valdene called *Making Game*, like him you will probably be convinced that woodcock is king.

CLASSICAL WOODCOCK

8	woodcocks, aged 6 days in their feathers, dressed of feathers only	4 ounces	foie gras in a jar (see page 212)
2 tablespoons	olive oil	1 teaspoon	Dijon mustard
2 tablespoons	butter	8	toasts (see page 31)
¼ cup	brandy		Salt and freshly ground black pepper
2 cups	veal stock		

Preheat the oven to 400 degrees.

Rub the woodcocks with the olive oil and season well. Put them in one layer in an ovenproof dish and cook in the oven for 15 minutes. Take the birds out of the oven. Remove the internal organs (discard the crop) and put them in a small mixing bowl. Let the woodcocks sit for 10 minutes in a warm place, and then cut the two halves off each carcass. Keep the sixteen halves warm in a serving dish.

Chop the carcasses coarsely and put them in a pan with the butter, and cook for 5 minutes, stirring frequently. Pour in the brandy and ignite, stirring the bones constantly. Add the stock and simmer 30 minutes, skimming any scum that rises to the surface. Strain and keep the sauce warm.

Using a spatula or spoon, put the internal organs through a sieve back into the bowl, and mix in the foie gras and mustard. Season.

Pour the hot sauce over the woodcocks to heat the pieces through. Spread the toasts with the foie gras mixture, and serve with the woodcocks.

Peppered Saddle of Rabbit with Foie Gras and Meyer Lemon Oil

Unless you make an old-fashioned country rabbit stew (cooking the rabbit for a couple of hours until all the meat turns very tender and falls off the bone), the same problem exists with rabbit as with poultry: namely, the back part of the rabbit, the saddle, needs far less cooking time than the legs.

Of course, you do not have to have foie gras for this dish—you could just take the sinews out of the livers that come with the rabbit, flatten the livers out, marinate them with the rabbit, and stuff the saddles with this liver instead of the foie gras.

The dish is easier to eat if you bone out the saddle first, but you do not have to.

SERVES 4

4	rabbit loins or saddles		1	large onion, peeled
4 tablespoons	olive oil		2 tablespoons	black peppercorns
2 sprigs	fresh thyme, stemmed, chopped		2 tablespoons	rose or pink peppercorns
			6 tablespoons	unsalted butter
1 sprig	fresh tarragon, stemmed, chopped		¼ cup	chicken stock (page 215)
4	1-ounce slices foie gras in a jar (see page 212)		2 tablespoons	Meyer lemon oil (see page 29) or another flavored oil
4	medium carrots, peeled			Kitchen string
2	medium celery root, peeled			

Put the olive oil, thyme, and tarragon in a bowl and mix. Add the rabbit pieces and rub the mixture all over the rabbit. Let marinate for 2 hours, and then scrape off the marinade into a small bowl. Strain the marinade and save the oil. Put a foie gras slice on the underside of each saddle and fold the belly flaps over. Tie the saddles up with kitchen string.

Cut the carrots, celery root, and onion into ⅛-inch dice.

Preheat the oven to 400 degrees.

Coarsely crush the black and pink peppercorns. Mix the peppers with the saved marinade oil and a pinch of salt, and pat the pepper mix on top of the saddles.

Put the onion, celery, carrots, 2 tablespoons of the butter, and the chicken stock in a pot. Cover and sweat the vegetables over low heat for 5 minutes, taking the cover off for another 5 minutes. Put the rabbit pieces on a sheet pan in the oven and bake for 15 minutes. Turn off the oven and let the saddles rest for 10 minutes with the oven door open.

Stir the remaining butter into the vegetable mixture and spoon it onto warm plates. Put the rabbit saddles on the vegetables, and drizzle with the Meyer lemon oil.

Braised Rabbit with Prunes Catalan Style

This recipe uses the rabbit legs left after you have cooked the saddles in the previous dish (see page 210).

SERVES 4

The Rabbit:

4	rabbit legs and thighs	1	herb bundle (see page 16)
2 tablespoons	olive oil	1 cup	stock, chicken or mixed
½ cup	good brandy		chicken and veal (see
½ cup	dry white wine		page 215)
1 cup	aromatic vegetable mix	4	prunes, pitted
	(see page 14)	2 tablespoons	fresh fennel leaves,
2 sprigs	fresh tarragon,		chopped
	stemmed, stems and	1 tablespoon	finely grated orange zest
	leaves saved		Salt

The Sauce:

1 tablespoon	black peppercorns	1 teaspoon	mild paprika
2 tablespoons	almonds, skinned	½ cup	extra virgin green olive oil
1	clove fresh garlic, peeled		Salt
¼ cup	fresh pine nuts, toasted		

Season the rabbit legs. Put the olive oil in a nonreactive skillet and heat it to medium. Put the legs in the hot oil and turn them a couple of times to lightly brown them on both sides. Turn off the heat, pour in one-quarter of the brandy and flame it. Then add the white wine and cook another 2 minutes. Put the vegetable mix around the rabbit legs, and add the tarragon stems and herb bundle. Cover the pan and sweat over low heat for 15 minutes.

Add the stock, cover, and simmer very slowly until the legs are very tender, about 45 minutes more.

Meanwhile, put the prunes, fennel, orange zest, and remaining brandy in a bowl to marinate while the rabbit is cooking.

When done, remove the legs from the pan and keep them warm. Strain the cooking juices, discarding the vegetables and the herb bundle. Return the juices to the pan, remove any fat from the surface, and reduce by half to make the broth for the sauce.

Meanwhile, in a mortar and pestle or food processor, grind the peppercorns, almonds, garlic, pine nuts, and paprika with the extra virgin green olive oil.

Cut the rabbit legs away from the thighs, and put the 8 pieces in a casserole. Add the reduced broth and any juices that have collected with the rabbit legs. Bring the rabbit up to but not quite a boil. Add the sauce and the prunes to the rabbit, and stir gently. As soon as the rabbit is heated through (no more than 5 minutes), check the sauce for seasoning, and serve.

VARIATIONS The rabbit legs could be braised the same way, and then put in olive oil and fresh thyme to marinate again for 30 minutes before grilling and serving with the lemon-fig relish on page 243. Or, one of the best ways to cook rabbit legs, especially the front ones, is to use the preserved fat method as for duck on page 15, then grill and serve them with the same lemon-fig relish.

WHOLE FOIE GRAS IN A JAR

For me, one of life's great privileges is to have this jar of liver in the fridge.

It is argued, quite rightly, that this conserve of fattened goose or duck liver could age for two years or more, but does anyone have that kind of discipline? I can see cooking this in November for Christmas or New Year's, but that's about the limit of my inner fortitude.

Goose liver is easier to cook (it does not fall apart or melt as easily), but duck is much easier to get and less expensive. So take your pick.

You will need a glass canning jar just large enough to hold the liver.

SERVES 8 TO 10

2 pounds	whole fattened duck or goose liver
½ cup	dry brine (see page 22)
2 tablespoons	fine Armagnac
2 sprigs	fresh tarragon
2	small fresh (or frozen) black truffles

Rinse the liver under cold water and pat dry. Gently pull the two lobes apart and, cutting and pulling, get rid of any tendons, veins, or green parts on the inside surfaces.

Put the liver in a bowl and pat the salt around it. Cover and refrigerate for 6 hours.

Rinse off all the marinade in cold water. Dry the livers and put the truffles between the two lobes and push the lobes together.

Sterilize the jar in boiling water. When it is cool, put the liver inside, stuffing it in if necessary. Add the Armagnac and tarragon.

Seal the jar and put it in a pot of water that is heated to 160 degrees, the water coming all the way up the jar (this is controversial: the French say 70 degrees Celsius, or 150 degrees Fahrenheit, and the Americans say 160–185 degrees Fahrenheit). Cook without boiling for 1½ hours. Remove, let cool, and store in the refrigerator.

CASSEROLE OF WHOLE FOIE GRAS

SERVES 6 TO 8

1	whole fattened duck or goose liver
1	large fresh black truffle, very coarsely chopped
1 cup	fresh chestnuts, roasted in the shell, peeled twice
1 tablespoon	butter
¼ cup	fine Armagnac
½ cup	Malmsey Madeira
	Chive flowers (optional)

Clean and season the liver as in the recipe for the foie gras in a jar (see page 212).

Preheat the oven to 300 degrees.

Put the truffle, chestnuts, and butter in a casserole just large enough to hold them and the liver. Season. Warm over low heat for 5 minutes, and pour in the Armagnac. Ignite, turn off the heat, and burn off the alcohol.

Put the liver in the center of the truffles, pour the Madeira over it, and cover tightly or seal the casserole with a flour and water paste. Bake for 30 minutes, and remove the casserole from the oven. Serve immediately, opening the casserole at the table. Garnish with chive flowers if using.

ROAST CHESTNUT–STUFFED CORNMEAL CRÊPES WITH FOIE GRAS

SERVES 6 (makes 12 to 15 crepes, 6 inches in diameter)

1 cup	foie gras in a jar (see page 212)			
Crêpes:				
¼ cup	fine cornmeal		2	large eggs
¼ cup	all-purpose flour		½ cup	milk
pinch	salt		4 tablespoons	melted butter

Filling:				
1	small red onion, peeled, finely chopped		½ teaspoon	ground cumin
1 tablespoon	butter		1 tablespoon	chopped fresh mint leaves
12	chestnuts, roasted, peeled twice, coarsely chopped		1 teaspoon	coarsely ground fresh black pepper
¼ cup	fresh mascarpone		pinch	salt

Put the cornmeal, flour, and salt in a bowl. Mix in the eggs and then the milk. Beat until smooth. The batter should be the consistency of half-and-half. Add more milk if necessary. Mix in the melted butter.

Let the batter sit for at least 30 minutes.

Stir the batter just before using. Heat a crêpe or nonstick pan and brush lightly with some of the remaining melted butter. Pour in just enough batter to coat the bottom of the pan, and pour any excess back into the bowl.

Cook the crêpe for 2 minutes, turn over, and cook for another minute. Repeat until all the batter is used. Stack the crêpes on a plate.

Sweat the onions in the butter with ¼ cup water, covered, over low heat for 10 minutes. Do not let the onion brown.

Mix the onions with all the chestnuts, mascarpone, cumin, mint, and pepper. Season.

To serve, roll up a crêpe with the chestnut filling and heat in a microwave (or brush with melted butter and put in a 400-degree oven for 5 to 8 minutes). Serve hot with a large spoonful of the foie gras.

WHITE CHICKEN STOCK

For a clear stock, bring the stock to a boil quickly, but be present when it first boils, because you have to immediately turn it down to a mere simmer. That initial boiling will release albumin and blood, which rise to the surface of the water. Skim that all off until there is none left and, with the occasional gentle stirring in the first ten minutes and more skimming, the stock will be crystal clear.

Old boiling hens will give the best stock (and meat for salad), but bones, feet (for gelatinous structure in the stock, important for sauces), and chicken parts are the most economical.

MAKES 5 TO 6 QUARTS

5 pounds	chicken or duck parts (backs, wings, feet, and necks)
5 quarts	water
1	large onion, peeled, chopped into 1-inch pieces
1	large carrot, peeled, chopped into 1-inch pieces
3	stalks celery, washed, chopped into 1-inch pieces
1	large herb bundle (see page 16)
2 tablespoons	salt

Rinse and wash the poultry parts under cold running water. It is important to wash away any blood so that the stock, free of blood and albumins, stands the best chance of being clear when finished.

Put the poultry parts in a pot with the water. Bring to a boil over high heat. The moment the water boils, lower the heat to a bare simmer. Skim off all the scum and fat that rise to the surface of the water. Gently disturb the bones to loosen more blood and albumin, then skim again. Keep skimming and stirring until the stock is clear.

When the stock is clear, add the vegetables, herb bundle, and salt, and simmer, uncovered, for 2 hours. Strain the stock, cool uncovered as quickly as possible, and refrigerate, covered, until needed.

For a richer stock, simmer the strained stock until reduced by one-third.

QUICK CHICKEN STOCK

For a quick stock, just simmer some chicken wings the same way as in the recipe for chicken stock, and you will have a delicious stock in twenty minutes (with the bonus of having the most delicious part of the chicken to eat as well). The wings actually make a good stock even without the vegetables and herbs.

CHAPTER NINE

MEAT

FAST AND EASY "MINUTE STEAK" OF VEAL

GRILLED RIB-EYE STEAKS WITH MONTPELIER BUTTER

PEPPERED FILLET OF BEEF

BRAISED BEEF SHORT RIBS

BRAISED BEEF CHEEKS WITH MUSTARD AND BREADCRUMB CRUST

GRILLED SWEETBREADS WITH MEYER LEMON OIL AND SERRANO CHILIES

BRAISED PIG TROTTERS WITH GINGER AND GINGER FLOWERS

BACON WITH FRESH WHITE BEANS

GRILLED PORK DOUBLE LOIN MEDALLIONS WITH
WATERMELON-PASSION FRUIT SAUCE

PORK TENDERLOIN IN CARAMELIZED SUGAR AND GINGER SAUCE

CHORIZO STEAKS WITH CILANTRO SALAD

ROAST LEG OF PORK WITH BLACK-EYED PEAS AND CANDIED SEKEL PEARS

LEATHERWOOD HONEY– AND SICHUAN PEPPER–GLAZED RACK OF LAMB WITH
EGGPLANT PASTA AND GREEN GODDESS OLIVE OIL AND LEMON SAUCE

INDIAN-SPICED BUTTERFLIED LEG OF LAMB WITH ROASTED ONION RELISH

BRAISED LAMB SHANK STEW WITH CHICKPEAS AND RED CHILI LINGUINE

BEEF OR VEAL STOCK

QUICK BEEF OR VEAL STOCK

FAST AND EASY "MINUTE STEAK" OF VEAL

SERVES 4

1½–2 pounds	veal round, cut in 4 slices ¼-inch thick	1 tablespoon	chopped fresh chives
1 tablespoon	finely grated orange zest	1 tablespoon	chopped black California olives
1 tablespoon	fresh tarragon leaves, chopped	6	fillets salted anchovies (see page 42), chopped
5 tablespoons	extra virgin olive oil		Salt and freshly ground white pepper
1 tablespoon	champagne vinegar		
½ tablespoon	chopped fresh chervil		

Pound out the veal slices with a mallet until they are evenly ⅛ inch thick.

Put the orange zest, tarragon, and 1 tablespoon of the oil in a bowl and mix. Rub this mixture well into the veal slices, and marinate 1 hour.

Wipe the marinade off the slices into a saucepan. Salt the veal only lightly (because of the little bit of salt left in the anchovies). Heat 2 tablespoons of the oil in a sauté pan and cook the veal over medium heat for 2 minutes on each side. Put the veal on a hot platter and keep warm.

Discard any oil left in the pan, and add any juices collected on the veal platter. Add the remaining 2 tablespoons of the oil and the vinegar, chervil, chives, olives, and anchovies. Whisk together, season if necessary, place the veal steaks on very hot plates, and pour the pan sauce over the veal. This is delicious with buttered asparagus.

VARIATIONS Cook the veal in 2 tablespoons of clarified butter (see page 27), and when cooked, keep the steaks warm and discard the butter, adding to the pan ½ cup sliced white mushrooms and 1 tablespoon finely chopped shallots. Season and cook 5 minutes. Add ½ cup heavy cream, simmer 2 minutes, season, and pour the sauce over the little steaks. Garnish with chopped chives. Also use beef, pork, or lamb, all cut from the round of sirloin.

GRILLED RIB-EYE STEAKS
WITH MONTPELIER BUTTER

James Beard asked me to develop a recipe for porterhouse steaks, which are the most luxurious steaks of all, since they have full pieces of the fillet on one side of the bone and the sirloin on the other.

I prefer rib-eyes because they are the richest of all the beef grill/broil cuts, and have the best "mouth-feel." They are very good when you are cooking raw individual steaks, but when cut from a partially-cooked whole rib roast (for steaks with bones) or rib-eye roast (for boneless), they are quicker to cook and more tender since they do not "tighten up" as much as when cooked from the raw steak. The same is true of New York strip sirloin when the steaks are cut from a partially cooked whole strip.

SERVES 4

1	4-rib beef roast
2 tablespoons	olive oil
1 tablespoon	fresh rosemary leaves, finely chopped
	Salt and freshly ground black pepper
½ cup	Montpelier butter (page 246)

Prepare the beef as for the rib roast on page 31, but cook it for only 30 minutes. Take the beef out and let it cool. When completely cool, slice the beef in four portions, cutting between the ribs.

Mix the olive oil and rosemary together and spread on both sides of the four rib steaks. Let the steaks marinate for 30 minutes, then wipe off the rosemary, season the steaks, and grill them for 5 to 8 minutes on each side. Then let them rest on the cool side of the grill or under the turned-off broiler for 5 minutes.

Serve with the room-temperature Montpelier butter.

PEPPERED FILLET OF BEEF

This recipe is best when roasted on a spit, but it can also be grilled, broiled, roasted, or smoke-cooked in a covered grill.

It is perfect served either at room temperature or slightly chilled (if the weather is hot), and is an excellent way to prepare individual pepper fillets in advance to be finished off quickly in the oven, on a grill, or in a broiler at the last minute.

Serve with the cipollini onions and white beans on page 225.

SERVES 6 TO 8			
1	whole beef fillet, trimmed of excess fat and silver skin, tied up with string	¼ cup	white peppercorns
		¼ cup	olive oil
		1 tablespoon	cognac
¼ cup	black peppercorns (Tellicherry, Lampong, or Malabar)	2 tablespoons	fresh thyme leaves, chopped
		1 teaspoon	sea or kosher salt

Grind the peppercorns very coarsely and put them in a small mixing bowl. Add the olive oil, cognac, and thyme, and mix together.

Spread the pepper mix all over the fillet, then cover it and let it marinate in the refrigerator for 4 hours. Take the fillet out and let it come to room temperature.

Preheat the oven to 450 degrees.

Salt the beef, put it on a rack in a pan and then in the oven. Turn the heat down to 400 degrees, and bake for about 30 minutes for medium rare, or until the internal temperature is 125 degrees. Let the fillet sit in a warm place for 15 minutes before slicing.

VARIATIONS If you are partially cooking the fillet to cut it into individual portions before finishing the cooking, cook it only 20 minutes, let it cool, and cut across the fillet to make "medallions" that are 6 to 8 ounces each. Then broil or grill them to order. In Singapore, these medallions were a big hit served with Montpelier butter (see page 246) and asparagus tempura. I love this beef with the ketjap dipping sauce on page 242.

Or slit the fillet down the middle lengthwise without cutting all the way through, and stuff it with ½ cup of a dried boletus (cèpe, porcini) mushroom puree made by soaking the mushrooms in water and then pureeing them. Then tie the whole fillet back up with string, peppering it and cooking it as above.

BRAISED BEEF SHORT RIBS

When James Beard would drill into his socialite students in San Francisco the importance of searing (sealing) meat before braising it, he would also ask, "Why do all that browning with the fat spitting everywhere when you can broil it?" He's right, of course, especially when it comes to veal, which spits like crazy, burning uncovered arms.

With the broiling method, however, one needs a very rich stock, since there are no wonderful caramelized bits stuck to the bottom of the browning pan to enrich the braising liquid and later the sauce. Serve with the oven-roasted vegetables on page 137.

SERVES 4

6 pounds	short ribs from prime or best-quality beef		1 teaspoon	sherry vinegar
			1 tablespoon	lemon zest
2 tablespoons	fresh thyme leaves		1 tablespoon	whole fresh tarragon leaves
1 tablespoon	grated orange zest		2 tablespoons	hazelnut or walnut oil
2 tablespoons	chopped fresh garlic		1 cup	fresh Italian parsley leaves
2 cups	aromatic vegetable mix (see page 14)		1 tablespoon	jasmine-cardamom-chili oil (see page 29) or another flavored oil
3 cups	Cabernet or Zinfandel wine			
6 cups	veal-beef stock (see page 233)			Salt and freshly ground black pepper

Put the thyme, orange zest, and garlic in a small mixing bowl and mix together. Rub the marinade mixture into the ribs. Cover and marinate at least 4 hours in the refrigerator. Take out and let come to room temperature before cooking.

Preheat the broiler to high, and the oven to 300 degrees. Wipe the marinade off the ribs and season them, reserving the marinade. Broil the ribs for 8 minutes on each side. Put the vegetable mix in a heavy nonreactive braising casserole (big enough to hold the ribs in one layer) along with the reserved marinade ingredients. Cook over medium heat for 5 minutes while stirring constantly. Then add the ribs side by side. Add the wine and cook over high heat for 5 minutes. Add the stock and bring to a very low simmer, then put in the oven and braise covered for 1½ hours, or until the ribs are tender.

Remove the ribs, then put in a bowl and cover with a wet towel. Strain the braising liquid into a saucepan and simmer over low heat, slightly off to the side of the burner, skimming off any fat and scum that rises to the top, as explained on page 30.

Keep cleaning the liquid and reduce it to half its original volume. Take off the heat, and pour over the ribs. Let the ribs sit in this sauce overnight if possible (refrigerated), otherwise, let them stay in this sauce until ready to reheat and serve on heated plates.

Put pinches of salt and pepper in a small mixing bowl, whisk in the sherry vinegar, and then the zest, tarragon, and oil. Add the parsley leaves and dress them. Put the hot ribs on hot plates, put parsley salad in center of ribs, and pass the jasmine oil to drizzle over it all.

VARIATIONS Finish the sauce with a puree of fried boletus mushrooms (use ¼ cup) or sliced fresh black truffles. Finish the ribs as for the beef cheeks on page 222 and heat in the oven, or deep-fry and serve with the ketjap dipping sauce on page 242 or just the orange Sichuan pepper salt on page 42.

BRAISED BEEF CHEEKS WITH A MUSTARD AND BREADCRUMB CRUST

At Stars San Francisco, we introduced beef cheeks to a trusting public, though many considered the idea of eating them strange. It was. Then beef cheeks became chic, almost common, and with familiarity and acceptance are more delicious than ever. You will have to special order them.

SERVES 4

The Braising:		The Finishing:	
4	large beef cheeks	¼ cup	Dijon mustard
2 tablespoons	fresh thyme leaves	1 cup	white breadcrumbs (see page 32)
1 tablespoon	orange zest		
2 tablespoons	chopped fresh garlic	4 tablespoons	melted butter
2 cups	aromatic vegetable mix (see page 14)	1 tablespoon	finely chopped fresh thyme leaves
6 cups	veal-beef stock (see page 233)		

Marinate and braise the beef cheeks, using the braising ingredients listed above, following the same technique as for the short rib recipe on page 221.

When they are cool, trim away most of the membrane, leaving just enough to hold the cheek together.

Preheat the oven to 375 degrees.

Brush a ⅛-inch layer of mustard all over each cheek. Put the breadcrumbs, butter, and thyme in a mixing bowl and mix well. Put each cheek into the crumbs and pat them onto both sides until coated.

Put the coated beef cheeks on a rack on a sheet pan in the oven until the cheeks are heated through and the breadcrumbs are golden brown, about 20 minutes.

GRILLED SWEETBREADS WITH MEYER LEMON OIL AND SERRANO CHILIES

The beauty of grilled sweetbreads is that you leave the membrane on (saving all that work of peeling them), so they hold together on the grill. The grilling cooks off the membrane.

SERVES 4

4	whole braised sweetbreads (see page 45)	1 bunch	fresh cilantro, made into sprigs
2 tablespoons	olive oil	2 tablespoons	Meyer lemon oil (see page 29)
1 tablespoon	chopped fresh tarragon leaves	2	fresh green serrano chilies, stemmed, seeded, minced
1 teaspoon	ground cardamom Sea salt		

Mix the olive oil, tarragon, and cardamom together in a bowl. Add the sweetbreads and toss until well coated with the oil. Refrigerate for 2 hours.

Start a wood or charcoal fire, or preheat the broiler.

Salt the sweetbreads and then grill or broil them at medium heat for 8 minutes per side, or until heated through and golden brown on both sides.

Mix the cilantro sprigs with half the lemon oil and the serrano chilies and make nests on warm plates. Put the sweetbreads on the cilantro and serve, drizzling the sweetbreads with the rest of the oil.

VARIATIONS Neil Perry, one of the founders of the fabulous new Australian cooking, has developed a wonderful sweetbread upside-down tart, but you will have to go to his Rockpool restaurant in Sydney for that. At home, use your favorite butter or oil sauce to accompany the grilled sweetbreads. Don't use a wet sauce; you want the sweetbreads to stay crisp. A chili, mushroom, or Montpelier butter will do, as will any of the olive oil and lemon juice sauces in this book.

BRAISED PIG TROTTERS WITH GINGER AND GINGER FLOWERS

No wild or domestic animal we eat is finer or more versatile than the pig, and when properly cooked there is no pork dish, from *andouillettes* ("take some pig guts…" begins Norman Douglas in *Venus in the Kitchen*) to tails, that I have not enjoyed.

If I get started on pigs in general I might have to give you the recipe from Edouard de Pomiane's *Le Carnet d'Anna* (1938) for scrambled eggs with grilled blood sausage—or, from another book of his, boiled snout with a puree of grilled fresh cèpes (boletus)—so let's just do this dish of the feet instead, meant as a warm first course.

SERVES 4

4	pig's feet with shanks	¼ cup	extra virgin olive oil
2 cups	aromatic vegetable mix (see page 14)	2	hard-boiled eggs (see page 67), peeled and chopped in ¼-inch pieces
1	large herb bundle (see page 16) containing 2 star anise	1 tablespoon	freshly squeezed lime juice
4 cups	chicken stock (see page 215)	¼ cup	hazelnuts, toasted, skinned, finely chopped
2 tablespoons	freshly chopped young Hawaiian pink ginger (or galangal)	1 teaspoon	sesame oil
1 tablespoon	finely chopped fresh garlic	1 bunch	fresh cilantro sprigs, washed, spin-dried
1 teaspoon	turmeric	¼ cup	fresh ginger flowers, shredded (if available)
½ teaspoon	ground cumin		Salt and freshly ground black pepper
2 tablespoons	fermented Chinese black beans, soaked twice for 10 minutes, each time in cool water		

Preheat the oven to 325 degrees.

Put the pig's feet, vegetable mix, herb bundle, and chicken stock in a casserole, cover, bring to a boil on top of the stove, and then cook in the oven for 30 minutes. Turn the feet over and continue cooking, turning them every 30 minutes, for another 1½ hours, or until the feet are completely tender.

Remove the feet and cover with a cold wet kitchen towel while they cool. Strain the cooking juices, skim away all the fat, and reduce for 10 minutes (see page 30).

Meanwhile, take all the bones out of the feet, and chop the meat and skin into ½-inch pieces. Put the ginger, garlic, turmeric, cumin, Chinese black beans, cleaned cooking juices, and olive oil in a bowl and mix. Add the pork meat, mix, season, and let sit 15 minutes in a warm place. Then mix in the eggs very gently.

Put the lime juice, hazelnuts, sesame oil, salt, and pepper in a small mixing bowl, whisk together, and then toss with the cilantro sprigs and ginger flowers.

Serve the pork on warm plates with the sauce around, the cilantro–ginger flower salad on top and, if you like, garlic bread dusted with red chili flakes.

BACON

Many cuisines have a host of dishes using bacon and salted pork, and a few using whole chunks of it. In Italy I found wild boar bacon. Around the corner from the villa where I stay in Chiesanouva (outside Florence) is a perfect tiny shop. It has everything, but two things that get me up in the cold autumn mornings are thin focaccia, right out of the wood oven and covered in wild boar pancetta.

Here is the lunch I recently cooked in Tuscany for friends from California and England:

- Smoked salmon
- Hot hard-boiled eggs with black truffle sauce (see page 35)
- Roast chicken (*gallo*) and *collo de gallo* (stuffed cock's neck and head with comb)
- Fresh cannellini, cipollini, and pancetta of wild boar
- Grilled fresh porcini (boletus)
- *Pecorino fresca* and *stagione*
- *Torta di nonna*
- Biscotti with Vin Santo

The wild boar dish took the prize, and if you cannot get wild boar bacon, the dish is still delicious using a slab of apple-wood smoked bacon (perhaps nitrate-free), or a chunk of lightly salted pork belly.

BACON WITH FRESH WHITE BEANS

SERVES 4 TO 6

1 pound	belly bacon, diced into ⅛-inch cubes	1 tablespoon	finely chopped fresh garlic
16	cipollini onions, peeled, some root core removed	½ cup	extra virgin olive oil
8	fresh sage leaves	1 teaspoon	freshly ground black Pepper
2 cups	fresh white cannellini beans		Sea salt

Put the bacon in a 12-inch-diameter heavy casserole. Add ½ cup water, the onions, and four sage leaves. Cover and cook over low heat for 20 minutes.

Put the beans in a fine wire basket and dip in salted boiling water for 5 minutes. Drain, and put the beans on top of the onions. Remove the sage leaves and add four fresh ones. Cover and cook until the beans are done, stirring a few times, about another 10 minutes.

Turn off the heat, add the garlic, olive oil, and black pepper, and let the mixture sit covered for 10 minutes. Remove the cover and put the casserole on high heat to evaporate the juices for about 5 minutes. There should be some "sauce" but it should not be runny. Pass the sea salt for those who think the bacon did not salt the beans enough.

GRILLED PORK DOUBLE LOIN MEDALLIONS WITH WATERMELON–PASSION FRUIT SAUCE

The title of this recipe may sound just too weird, but believe me, it is one of the dishes of which I am most proud, because it is not only stunningly beautiful (the colors on the plate are magnificent) but delicious as well. I developed it in the tropics, so it is a summer dish, and no work at all once the pork medallions are ready for the grill.

In Singapore, I served it with mashed *ube*, a yamlike tuber from the Philippines that when cooked keeps its bright lavender-purple color and tastes like a very rich sweet potato. On top of the medallion I put "spiced tropical fruit chutney," using the little ripe "finger" bananas, rambutans, salak (*Salacca edulis*), mabolo (*Diospyros discolor*, or butter fruit), sweetsop (*Annona squamosa*, also called custard apple or sugar-apple), guanabana (*Annona muricata* or soursop), mangosteens, and lychees, all mixed in with a bit of fresh chili, "pili" nuts (*Canarium ovatum*, an ethereal nut tasting like a cross between a Brazil and a macadamia), and ginger flowers. These fruits are not available outside of Southeast Asia, so I have left out the chutney, but a superb one could be made in the summer with "mango" or "honeydew" nectarines.

Serve with mashed *ube*, mashed sweet potatoes, or cumin-flavored mashed potatoes with a tablespoon of finely chopped Indian lime pickle stirred into them.

SERVES 4

3 pounds	center-cut pork loin on the bone	8	fresh mint leaves
2 quarts	wet brine (see page 22)	½ teaspoon	light sesame oil
4	bay leaves	1 cup	ripe red watermelon, put through a fine sieve
1 tablespoon	allspice berries	¼ cup	extra virgin light yellow olive oil
1 tablespoon	dried thyme		
2 sprigs	fresh basil	1 tablespoon	jasmine-cardamom-chili oil (see page 29)
2 tablespoons	olive oil		Salt and freshly ground black pepper
4–6	ripe passion fruit (depending on size)		

Trim the loin so that there is only ¼-inch of fat on top. Mix together the brine, bay leaves, allspice, and thyme. Put the loin in a pan just large enough to hold it and the liquid and pour the brine over the pork. Let it marinate overnight or at least 6 hours in the refrigerator.

When the pork is fully brined, remove it, wipe it dry, and preheat the oven to 375 degrees.

Season the pork, heat a sauté pan over medium heat, sear the loin, and brown it on all sides, about 5 minutes. Put the loin in a roasting pan just large enough to hold it and cook for 30 minutes. Remove the loin and let it sit for 20 minutes in a warm place, covered with a piece of foil.

Cut the pork loin off the bone and then slice the boneless loin into four equal medallions.

Chop the basil and mix in a small bowl with the olive oil. Rub this basil oil all over the medallions, cover the pork loosely, and marinate for 2 hours.

Cut open the passion fruit, scoop out all the pulp and seeds, and put them through a fine sieve. Keep the sieved juice and put the pulp and seeds in another small bowl. Finely chop the mint and add it to the seeds. Mix in the sesame oil and season.

Grill the medallions over a real charcoal fire at medium heat (or broil on a bed of the basil marinade) for 5 minutes on each side, until heated through. Put the grilled medallions on hot plates. Mix the watermelon juice with a small pinch of salt and the extra virgin olive oil in a small bowl and stir briefly (do not emulsify). Spoon the watermelon sauce around the pork, put the reserved passion fruit seeds on top of each medallion, and then spoon the passion fruit juice erratically onto the watermelon sauce. Put a few drops of the jasmine-chili oil on each piece of pork.

VARIATIONS Serve the pork with prunes soaked in either Armagnac or apple brandy, then heated 5 minutes with ½ cup chopped scallions, 1 tablespoon lemon zest, and 2 tablespoons cream. In Manila and Singapore, we served the medallions with whole hominy heated with fresh sage, ancho chili puree (page 32), and roasted mild green chilies, accompanied by a watercress and pecan salad, or with fried green tomatoes with sweet corn timbale (see page 123).

PORK TENDERLOIN IN CARAMELIZED SUGAR AND GINGER SAUCE

We used to do this in Speedo 690, and now I have updated it with crystallized ginger and jasmine oil.

SERVES 4 TO 6

2	1-pound fresh pork tenderloins, trimmed	6	star anise
1 quart	wet brine (see page 22)	1 cup	chicken stock (see page 215)
1 tablespoon	chopped fresh ginger or galangal (peppery ginger, Thai ginger)	½ cup	sherry vinegar
		1 tablespoon	olive oil
		1 tablespoon	jasmine-ginger-chili oil (see page 29)
1 tablespoon	chopped fresh garlic	2 tablespoons	crystallized ginger, finely chopped
1 large	stalk fresh basil, stemmed, stems chopped, leaves saved	1 teaspoon	sesame oil
½ cup	superfine sugar		Salt and freshly ground black pepper

Brine the pork for 45 minutes, then take it out of the brine and wipe dry. Put the ginger, garlic, and chopped basil stems in a small bowl, mix together, and then rub the marinade into the tenderloins. Cover them and let marinate for 1 hour.

Meanwhile, put the sugar in a 10-inch nonstick sauté pan and heat slowly until it caramelizes and just turns light brown (but beyond gold). Add the star anise. Let the caramel cool for 2 minutes and then add the stock and vinegar, being very careful because it may sputter, and cook until the sugar is completely dissolved in the sauce. Remove the star anise.

Wipe the marinade off the tenderloins, season lightly, rub with the olive oil, and grill them over real charcoal (or broil) for 8 to 10 minutes. Sprinkle them with the jasmine oil, and let them rest 5 minutes in a warm place. Chop the fresh basil leaves. Bring the sauce to a simmer, then turn off the heat. Stir in the ginger, basil, and sesame oil and adjust the seasoning if necessary. Slice the tenderloins and pour some of the sauce over the slices, passing the rest.

CHORIZO STEAKS WITH CILANTRO SALAD

There is hardly any kind of pork sausage that, when made freshly and in small batches, I do not like. And chorizo is one of the grandest of them all.

Stuff this mix into casings and eat them fresh, or hang them to cure; eat it as patties; or do as I somewhat perversely like to do: make chorizo into little meat balls and cook them in chili during its last fifteen minutes of cooking.

Serve with a salad made of cilantro leaves (2 cups) and shredded rose petals (½ cup) dressed in 2 tablespoons tequila, salt, pepper, ½ tablespoon of sesame oil, and 2 tablespoons extra virgin olive oil. Serve with Bloody Marys made with fresh yellow tomato juice, sieved and chilled before mixing.

SERVES 6 TO 10

2½ pounds	pork butt	½ teaspoon	cumin seeds
6 slices	bacon	1 teaspoon	black peppercorns
1	pasilla chili, roasted, seeded, stemmed, peeled	¼ teaspoon	ground cinnamon
		pinch	ground clove
2	ancho chilies, roasted, seeded, stemmed	1 tablespoon	sweet paprika
		2 tablespoons	kosher salt
1	serrano chili, roasted, seeded, stemmed, peeled	1 teaspoon	sugar
		½ cup	fresh cilantro leaves, chopped
1 tablespoon	fresh oregano leaves, chopped		
4 cloves	fresh garlic, peeled, finely chopped	2 tablespoons	best-quality white wine vinegar
		¼ cup	white tequila
1 teaspoon	coriander seeds	1 pound	caul fat

Chop the meat into 1-inch pieces, removing any sinew or connective tissue. Chop the bacon and mix with the meat.

Chop all the chilies together, mix with the oregano and garlic, and then into the meat.

Toast the coriander, cumin, and black peppercorns together and grind finely. Mix into the meat.

Mix all the rest of the ingredients into the meat with your hands.

Cover and refrigerate for 2 days. Then while still cold, put the meat through a meat grinder with a medium-sized (⅛-inch) hole attachment at low speed (high-speed machine work toughens the meat and emulsifies and oxidizes the fat, which then runs out of the meat when it is cooking, drying it out).

Put the ground sausage back in the refrigerator for 2 days, and then make it into patties 4 inches in diameter and 1½ inches thick. Wrap each sausage in caul fat and then grill over charcoal, bake in a wood oven, or fry in a seasoned (or nonstick) pan, cooking 3 to 5 minutes on each side over medium heat.

Roast Leg of Pork with Black-Eyed Peas and Candied Sekel Pears

What an incredibly easy, inexpensive, and delicious cut of pork for a dinner party or buffet! A roast leg of pork eaten cold the next day, in sandwiches with mango chutney, makes cold roast turkey (even with stuffing in the sandwiches) pale in comparison. And the pork makes great hash.

As always with pork, the secret here is brining, which can be a bit of a problem in most refrigerators with a big leg, so buy one that is 8 to 10 pounds.

I love the flavor of fresh turmeric (*Curcuma longa*), and use it here to flavor and color the sweet pears. If you use the powdered turmeric, then as with all spices, ground or whole, use only the freshest.

SERVES 6 TO 8

8–10 pounds	fresh leg of pork ("fresh ham") with skin on	4 cups	fresh black-eyed peas, rinsed, drained
2 gallons	wet brine (see page 22)	1 cup	chicken stock
½ cup	fresh sage leaves, chopped	½ cup	sour cream
5	Seckel or Bartlett pears, halved, oven-dried (see page 138)	1 tablespoon	orange zest
		½ tablespoon	lemon zest
1 tablespoon	fresh turmeric, peeled, pureed in 2 tablespoons water (or 1 teaspoon powdered)		Salt and freshly ground black pepper

Brine the leg for 24 hours refrigerated (or iced).

Preheat the oven to 400 degrees.

Wipe the leg dry, and score the skin just down to the fat layer, in a 1-inch grid. Rub in at least 2 tablespoons of black pepper and the sage leaves.

Put the pork in a pan and bake for 15 minutes. Reduce the heat to 325 degrees and cook about 20 minutes per pound, or until the internal temperature is 140. Fifteen minutes before the baking is finished, turn the oven back up to 425 degrees, crisping the skin to make "cracklings." Remove the pork and let it rest on a platter on the door of the turned-off oven for 30 minutes.

Meanwhile, pour 1 cup water into the roasting pan, and simmer while scraping the pan. Put the pears in a pan and sprinkle with the turmeric. Sieve the pan juices and pour over the pears. Simmer for 10 minutes while basting the pears.

Boil the peas in 4 quarts of salted water for 2 minutes. Drain and put in a saucepan with the chicken stock. Simmer the peas for 5 minutes, or until tender. Add the sour cream and the two zests, and stir until incorporated. Season the peas with a little salt and a lot of freshly ground black pepper.

Slice the pork leg, and serve it with the peas and pear halves, spooning any pear juices over the pork.

LEATHERWOOD HONEY– AND SICHUAN PEPPER–GLAZED RACK OF LAMB WITH EGGPLANT PASTA AND GREEN GODDESS OLIVE OIL AND LEMON SAUCE

The best way to cook rack of lamb is over a wood or charcoal fire, seared on high heat the first ten minutes, then over a slow fire ten minutes, then left for thirty minutes at the edge of the heat to rest and continue cooking. Follow this procedure and the lamb will be the most flavorful and tender you have ever tasted. But by all means use whatever grill or broiler you have.

The lamb is served with spiced eggplant and lentils (see page 128) stuffed into pasta tubes and sauced with green goddess olive oil and lemon sauce (see page 249).

SERVES 4

2 pieces	rack of lamb (10–12 chops total), trimmed and "Frenched"	6	large pasta tubes (manicotti), cooked in salted water until barely tender
¼ cup	Sichuan peppercorns	1 tablespoon	olive oil
½ cup	leatherwood honey (or any floral honey)	½ cup	green goddess sauce (see page 249)
1 recipe	spiced eggplant and lentils (see page 128)	6	nasturtium flowers, stemmed, shredded

Heat the peppercorns over low heat in a sauté pan for 2 minutes to bring out the flavor. Do not burn. Add the honey and heat for 5 minutes. Let the honey cool, and rub the honey and pepper mixture all over the racks. Cover the lamb loosely and marinate for 2 hours. Wipe off the marinade, strain, and reserve the strained honey.

Stuff the pasta tubes with the eggplant-lentil mix. Oil a shallow ovenproof gratin dish just large enough to hold the tubes, add them in 1 layer, brush with olive oil, and cover with foil.

Start a charcoal or wood fire, or preheat the broiler or grill.

Grill the racks for 8 minutes on each side. Then turn down the heat and finish the racks on the fat side, brushing the racks with marinade each time you turn them.

Meanwhile, bake the eggplant pasta for 10 minutes covered, then remove the cover and bake for 5 minutes more.

Slice the racks between the ribs into chops, and serve them with the eggplant and lentil filled pasta. Spoon the green goddess sauce over the pasta tubes. Garnish the plates with the nasturtium flowers.

INDIAN-SPICED BUTTERFLIED LEG OF LAMB
WITH ROASTED ONION RELISH

Timing mysteries and guesswork do not exist with this method of cooking a leg of lamb because, since the leg is opened, boned, and flattened out, you can see everything that is going on when it is cooking, and it cooks more or less evenly like a steak.

A 6-pound leg of lamb when butterflied gives you a nearly 4- to 5-pound boned leg. When it is cooked, all you have to do is slice it on a board, and serve it on the board or on a hot platter.

SERVES 6 TO 8

1	6-pound leg of lamb, butterflied	12	mild (Moroccan) black olives, pitted, coarsely chopped
½ cup	Indian spice mix (see page 38)	1 tablespoon	freshly squeezed lime juice
4	medium roasted onions (see page 134), cooking juices saved	¼ teaspoon	ground cardamom
		½ cup	chicken stock (see page 215)
		¼ cup	extra virgin green olive oil
1	small salt-preserved lemon (see page 43); or lemon flesh and zest from 3 lemons, chopped	1 teaspoon	orange- or rose-flower water (or half each)
		¼ cup	olive oil
			Salt
1 tablespoon	fresh rosemary leaves, finely chopped		

Rub the spice mix into the lamb and let it sit refrigerated 6 hours or more.

Chop up the onions, put in a bowl with their saved juices, and add the salted lemon, rosemary, olives, lime juice, cardamom, chicken stock, and extra virgin olive oil. Mix together and taste for salt. Stir in the flavored water(s).

Wipe the marinade off the lamb, rub the sides with the olive oil, season, and grill over a low to medium fire (broil or bake in a 375-degree oven) for about 15 minutes on each side, until it is medium rare. Let sit on the cool side of the fire for 10 minutes to rest, and then carve across the leg in ¼-inch slices. Serve with the sauce passed separately.

VARIATIONS Cooking the lamb in a pan in the oven also gives you pan juices, and some might argue that this lamb needs no other sauce. But if you use the oven method and have the pan juices, the lamb is certainly not ruined by adding the juices (without the fat) to a sage béarnaise sauce or a béarnaise into 1 cup of which is mixed 1 tablespoon of chopped salt-preserved lemon (see page 43), 1 tablespoon chopped fresh mint leaves, and 1 teaspoon of orange-flower water.

BRAISED LAMB SHANK STEW WITH CHICKPEAS AND RED CHILI LINGUINE

Perfectly cooked lamb shanks are a breeze if you: 1) use stock that comes only halfway up the shanks; 2) braise them slowly enough; 3) turn them three or four times while they are cooking. A heavy cooking pan just large enough to hold the shanks one layer deep is essential. To achieve the melting texture that makes them so wonderful, it is important to let them stand, covered with a wet towel (so they do not dry out and form a crust), in a warm place for twenty minutes after they are cooked.

Eat the shanks merely braised, grill them after they have been braised, or take them off the bone to use in stews. I use the shanks for braising and stewing because their gelatinous quality prevents them from drying out, and they are the perfect tender and juicy meat for any lamb stew or ragout.

SERVES 4 TO 6

4	lamb shanks, from the foreleg	2	stems fresh basil, stemmed, stems and leaves saved
½ cup	olive oil	1 teaspoon	ground cumin
15 cloves	garlic, unpeeled	2 tablespoons	canola oil
1	bay leaf	1 recipe	linguine with chickpeas (see page 151)
4 sprigs	fresh thyme		Salt and freshly ground black pepper
1 quart	chicken stock (see page 215)		
2 cups	aromatic vegetable mix (see page 14)		

Preheat the oven to 300 degrees.

Season the lamb shanks heavily and put them in a casserole or heavy pot (without crowding) with the olive oil, unpeeled garlic, bay leaf, and thyme. Brown them evenly over medium heat for 15 minutes, turning every 3 minutes. Remove, wipe out the pan, and put the shanks back in with the stock, vegetable mix, and basil stems. Bring to a simmer, cover the pot, and put it in the oven. Cook until the shanks are very tender, about 2 hours, turning them every 15 minutes.

Remove the shanks when they are done and keep warm and covered with a wet kitchen towel.

Sieve the braising juices into a pot and bring to a boil. The moment the stock boils, push the pot half off the burner, turn down the heat so that one side of the sauce is simmering, and skim off all the fat. Reduce the juices slowly to 4 cups. Keep skimming off any fat and scum and do not let any fat boil back into the sauce (keep the heat no higher than a low simmer).

Meanwhile, remove all the meat from the bones, and cut it into bite-sized pieces. Put the pieces in a bowl with the basil leaves and cumin and gently mix together. Let sit for 10 minutes. Heat the oil in a pan and add the lamb. Toss the lamb in the pan for 5 minutes to toast the cumin. Add the sauce and simmer for 2 minutes. Season.

Serve on hot plates and put the linguine in the center of each plate with the lamb and sauce around.

VARIATIONS We served this stew more than a few times with large pasta tubes filled with mushroom hash (see page 17), or accompanied by stewed thinly sliced elephant garlic, fava beans, black truffles, and curried parsnips—exotic, and very good. Or serve with just chive, sage, or hyssop flowers—all superb with rich meats.

Beef or Veal Stock

The taste of veal stock does not have much character, but its gelatinous structure gives body to all other meat and poultry stocks, and therefore to the finished sauces made from them. Without veal you have to use a lot of chicken wings, beef shanks, or even pig's feet (trotters) to get this structure.

Since good veal bones are not always available, I often use parboiled pork skin or pig's feet (after the trotters are cooked you can eat them grilled with lots of mustard). For a full beef flavor, use oxtail. Beef shin gives the most body to the stock, but half shin and half chuck works well, too.

Put bones and meat back into a cleaned pot and cook for six hours, with the usual constant skimming and a little bit of gentle prodding in the first thirty minutes. This is the only way you can be guaranteed a clear stock.

For brown stock, roast the bones for forty-five minutes in the oven and follow the procedure as in lamb stock.

YIELDS 1 GALLON

5 pounds	beef or veal shank bones, feet, and scraps
1	pig or veal foot
5 quarts	water
4 cups	aromatic vegetable mix (see page 14)
1	herb bundle (see page 16)
1 tablespoon	salt

Put the veal and the pig's foot in a large stock pot that will hold the meat and water to cover it by 6 inches. Bring the water to a simmer while skimming off any scum. Gently move the bones around and skim again, all this for about 45 minutes. Turn off the heat, and let the pot sit for 5 minutes.

Drain the bones and meat in a colander and run cold water over them to completely clean them of all scum. If you don't, the stock will be cloudy and grey and lack clarity of taste.

Clean the pot and put it back on the stove. Return the bones to the pot and cover with water (or stock if you are doing a double stock), going through the same procedure as the first time but without discarding the water. The moment the stock simmers it should be clear, so turn down the heat to low, add the vegetable mix, the herb bundle, and salt. Simmer gently for 6 hours. Turn off the heat and let the stock sit for 15 minutes to let any solids fall to the bottom.

Ladle the stock out into a sieve lined with cheesecloth (or through a very fine strainer) into a container large enough to hold it (another pot, perhaps). Strain the last few inches of stock at the bottom of the pot into another container in case it has solids in it that would cloud the stock. If it does not, then add it to the main body of the stock.

Let the stock cool and then immediately refrigerate, uncovered, until it is cold. Then cover and keep refrigerated for up to 2 days, or freeze in 1- or 2-cup containers for later use.

Quick Beef or Veal Stock

Cook the same way as for poultry stock, but use ground beef or veal, and simmer for 1 hour.

CHAPTER TEN

SAUCES *and* RELISHES

OIL AND VINEGAR

Most recipes for oil and vinegar dressing call for three parts oil to one part vinegar. These proportions make a very acidic sauce that may be fine for things like grilled leeks, but is too strong for most salads. A delicate butter lettuce, for example, demands a five to one ratio. The nature of the salad ingredients also dictates the choice of vinegars and oils as well as the proportions; for example, the endive family and bitter field greens taste best with strong vinegars and a heavy oil such as an Italian green extra virgin olive oil. You can substitute fresh lemon or lime juice for the vinegar.

Always add the salt and freshly ground pepper to the acid first, then stir to dissolve before whisking in the oil. Remember that unless otherwise specified it is very important to emulsify the two liquids to avoid having their disparate tastes and textures in the salad. Only with nonleafy foods like vegetables, fish, and meats do the separate rivers of oil and vinegar look and taste wonderful.

MAKES APPROXIMATELY ¾ CUP

2 tablespoons	vinegar
good pinch	kosher or sea salt
½ teaspoon	freshly ground black pepper
½ cup	extra virgin olive oil

Put the vinegar, salt and pepper in a bowl and stir to dissolve the salt. Gradually add the olive oil and whisk it into the vinegar until an emulsion is formed.

Fresh Tomato, Lemon, and Olive Oil Sauce

This sauce can easily becomes an obsession because it tastes so good and is so easy to make. On warm pasta, pasta salad, grilled fish hot or cold, asparagus hot or cold, meat, and as a snack on grilled garlic bread, it's sublime. For me the explosion of herb perfume that arises when the sauce is poured over hot vegetables or pasta is what summer is all about, even in the middle of winter (if the tomatoes are ripe). The sauce tastes best if made half an hour before you want to use it.

MAKES APPROXIMATELY 2½ CUPS

1 cup	chopped tomatoes (see page 47)
¼ cup	mixed fresh herb leaves, such as basil, marjoram, tarragon, and thyme, coarsely chopped
¼ cup	freshly squeezed lemon juice or good white wine vinegar
2	large shallots, peeled and coarsely chopped
1 cup	extra virgin olive oil
	Sea salt
	Freshly ground black pepper

Put all the ingredients except the salt and pepper in a bowl and stir briefly. Season.

Warm Shrimp Sauce

MAKES APPROXIMATELY 3 CUPS

1 pound	uncooked shrimp
1 cup	lightly salted water
1 recipe	tomato, lemon, and olive oil sauce (see above)

Simmer the shrimp in the salted water for 5 minutes and strain, saving the liquid. Let the shrimp cool, peel them, then chop the shells coarsely and put them in the saved liquid.

Simmer the liquid with the shells for 10 minutes. Strain the shrimp shell liquid into a saucepan and reduce it by half. Discard the shells. Add the liquid to the tomato sauce.

Chop the peeled shrimp into ¼-inch dice and mix it into the sauce.

VARIATIONS You can replace the shrimp with cooked and chopped mussels, crab, or lobster. Or cook shucked oysters the same way as the shrimp until they are firm, chop them coarsely, and use the sauce to pour over linguine. The sauce is not bad either on top of a potato baked in a fire. Meyer lemons, Rangpur limes, or, if you can ever find them, ripe Key limes are also delicious here. And look in Philippino markets for *kalamansi* limes.

MEDITERRANEAN OIL AND VINEGAR SAUCE

This sauce is based on the olive oil and vinegar dressing, but it is meant to be mixed together loosely, not emulsified.

MAKES 1 CUP			
1	salt-preserved lemon (see page 43), seeded, chopped	4	salted anchovy fillets (see page 42), chopped
1 tablespoon	fresh Italian parsley leaves, chopped	1 tablespoon	salted capers, rinsed, soaked 2 hours, drained (see page 44), chopped
1 teaspoon	fresh thyme leaves, chopped	2 tablespoons	mixed fresh herb flowers (if available)
1 tablespoon	fresh tarragon leaves, chopped	4 tablespoons	white wine vinegar
1 tablespoon	fresh chives, chopped	1 teaspoon	freshly ground black pepper
1	shallot, peeled, finely chopped	¾ cup	extra virgin olive oil Sea salt

Put all the ingredients except the salt and oil in a bowl and mix together. Stir in the oil, and taste for salt. It might not need any, depending on the saltiness of the lemons.

VARIATION When using this sauce on fish, add ¼ cup of shellfish essence (see page 188).

ASIAN OIL AND VINEGAR SAUCE

MAKES 1 CUP			
2 tablespoons	Chinese black beans, rinsed, soaked 3 times in water for 10 minutes each time, drained	2	salted anchovy filllets (see page 42), chopped
		¼ cup	rice wine vinegar
		½ cup	peanut or almond oil
2 tablespoons	fresh Italian parsley leaves, chopped	2 tablespoons	sesame oil
¼ cup	fresh cilantro leaves, chopped	pinch	salt
		pinch	freshly ground black pepper
2 tablespoons	fresh chives, chopped		

Put all the ingredients except the oils in a bowl and mix. Stir in the oil and check for seasoning.

FRESH SALSA

The secret to unlocking the complex flavors of the ubiquitous salsa fresca or Mexicana lies in the proportions, but also in cutting the ingredients pretty much into precise ⅛-inch cubes. And the serrano no more than ¹⁄₁₆-inch. Be obsessive about this and you will be rewarded.

SERVES 6 TO 8

4 cups	chopped tomatoes (see page 47)	½ cup	fresh cilantro leaves, chopped
1	red onion, peeled, finely chopped	1 teaspoon	salt
2	fresh serrano chilies, stemmed, seeded, finely chopped	¼ cup	freshly squeezed lime juice
		1 tablespoon	extra virgin olive oil

Mix the tomatoes, onion, chilies, and cilantro in a bowl. Add the salt and lime juice. Mix well. Let the salsa sit for an hour before using. Stir in the oil and serve.

If the sauce is too watery after sitting, drain it before adding the oil and save this delicious liquid for your Bloody Marys, or mix it with olive oil and pour over grilled fish or meat.

VARIATIONS You can make Tomatillo Salsa by using 12 finely chopped tomatillos (outer husks removed and discarded, tomatillos rinsed) instead of the tomatoes, leaving everything else the same, but using fine peanut oil instead of the olive. Or use only 6 tomatillos with 1 English cucumber, peeled, seeded and finely chopped, and the finely grated zest of an orange. Tomatillo salsa is particularly good on grilled or baked oily fish, such as Spanish mackerel, bluefish (my favorite), or shad.

One of my favorite salsas is mango, but in the last 15 years I have definitely gone off using it on fish as I did in my first book. Now I use it on hot grilled or roast pork, duck (Sichuan style spiced and poached), or ham. Make it the same way as the tomato salsa, but substitute 4 ripe mangoes (peeled, sliced, and cut into ½-inch cubes) for the tomatoes and add one red chili (stemmed, seeded, very finely chopped), as well as a cup of fresh mint leaves, blanched, squeezed dry, and finely chopped. Add some chopped ripe Black Mission figs for an even more exotic taste. And almost any tropical fruit can replace the mango, but enhance them all by adding avocado and chopped orange, jasmine, or lemon flowers.

FRESH TOMATO SAUCE

Once tomatoes are boiled for more than a few minutes, they all tend to taste like Campbell's soup, no matter what else you do. This may be praise for Campbell's tomatoes, but why bother to buy fresh tomatoes for a sauce unless the sauce retains their freshness?

Mix this sauce with olive oil to serve cold or finish with butter to serve hot.

MAKES 2 CUPS

4 cups	chopped tomato (see page 47)	1 tablespoon	olive oil
1	onion, peeled, finely chopped	4 tablespoons	unsalted butter
1 tablespoon	fresh herb stems, chopped (tarragon, thyme, basil, marjoram)		Salt and freshly ground white pepper

Put the onion in a nonreactive saucepan with the olive oil, herbs, and ¼ cup water. Cover and sweat for 10 minutes, or until tender. Do not let the onions brown.

Prepare an ice bath.

Add the tomato and cook, uncovered, over high heat, stirring frequently for 3 minutes, or until the tomatoes have just given up their liquid. Puree the tomato mixture, and put it into a metal bowl placed in the ice bath, to stop the cooking. When the puree is cold, put it through a fine sieve.

Hold until needed. Then heat the sauce and whisk in the butter. Season and serve.

HELLFIRE SAUCE

This was one of the many concoctions invented by Steven Vranian, who worked with us at the Santa Fe Bar and Grill in Berkeley, then at Stars San Francisco, and later as chef of Stars in Singapore. He must have played with a lot of chemistry sets as a kid, because he was always coming up with various picklings and hot sauces.

I like this sauce particularly on a grilled fish sandwich, over fries, or on oysters grilled in their shells, or deep-fried in a po' boy sandwich (see page 77).

The sauce keeps refrigerated for up to three months.

You will need cheesecloth.

MAKES APPROXIMATELY 2 CUPS

6	fresh habañero chilies
2 cups	freshly squeezed lime juice
3 tablespoons	kosher salt
4 tablespoons	brandy
1 teaspoon	bitters (Angostura or New Orleans)

Cut the stems off the chilies. Wear gloves or use the food processor, and be careful of your eyes, but in any case, rough-chop the chilies, seeds and all.

Put the lime juice and salt in a glass container (like a preserving jar), and stir to dissolve the salt. Add the chopped chilies, brandy, and bitters. Mix well.

Cover with cheesecloth only. Let sit at room temperature for 5 days. Strain, cover (or bottle), and refrigerate.

KETJAP DIPPING SAUCE

In Indian or Southeast Asian stores you can find a bottled sauce called "ketjap manis." We have all read about how America's favorite sauce was originally from Indonesia, or from the Chinese word *ketsiap*, or from the Malay word *kechap* or *kecap*, which Alan Davidson says means "soy sauce." I find this all endlessly fascinating, and it boggles the mind to think that the first Dutch in Indonesia began the process that ended up in a bottle on every table in every diner in America.

In one of my old books of cooking notes I found I had written "Pepper Catsup—Houston 1883." The list of ingredients is "red jalapeño chilies, chopped onions, white wine vinegar, salt, allspice, horseradish, cloves." The notes say to "seed and chop up the chilies, and sweat them in stainless steel, covered, in the oven with the oil and vinegar. Cook until soft. Puree until smooth. Add salt, allspice, cloves and horseradish. Simmer 10 minutes." In a book called *Practical Housekeeping*, printed in Ohio in 1876, there is a whole chapter called "Catsups and Sauces," which includes catsups of cucumber, currant, cherry, gooseberry, and tomato, all of which when cooked down with spices and lots of sugar essentially become fruit "butters" and are precursors to American barbecue and steak sauces.

But going back to the Asian tradition, I think of the delicious one-minute sauce my cook in Manila would prepare for me, regardless of what was on the menu. She made it also with soy sauce, but both she and I preferred the ketjap manis because it is less salty, a bit sweet, and lighter than many nuclear-powered soy sauces.

If you can't find *kalamansi*, then use ripe (yellowing) limes or Key limes.

MAKES APPROXIMATELY ¾ CUP

½ cup	ketjap manis
¼ cup	fresh *kalamansi* juice
½ tablespoon	light sesame oil

Mix a bit, and dip everything in it.

LEMON-AND-FIG RELISH

MAKES 2 CUPS

8	fresh ripe Mission figs, stemmed, chopped in ⅛-inch pieces	1 tablespoon	orange flower water
2	fresh serrano chilies, stemmed, seeded, finely chopped	1	salt-preserved lemon (see page 43), seeded, chopped into ⅛-inch pieces
½ cup	fresh mint leaves	1 tablespoon	freshly squeezed lime juice
1	fire-roasted onion (see page 134) or medium red onion, peeled, chopped into 1/16-inch dice	2 pinches	sea salt
		1 teaspoon	freshly ground black pepper

Put the figs and chilies in a mixing bowl.

Blanch the mint leaves in boiling water for 1 minute. Cool in ice water, drain, squeeze dry, and finely chop. Add the mint leaves to the figs and chilies.

Add the onion, orange-flower water, salted lemon, lime juice, salt, and pepper to the mixture. Stir well, and let everything sit for 1 hour before serving.

FRESH TOMATO RELISH

MAKES 2 CUPS

4 cups	chopped tomatoes (see page 47)
¼ cup	salted capers, rinsed, soaked 2 hours, drained (see page 44)
2 tablespoons	finely chopped fresh ginger
4 cloves	fresh garlic, peeled, finely chopped
¼ cup	olive oil
2 pinches	sea salt
1 teaspoon	freshly ground white pepper

Heat a nonstick saucepan for a moment, add the chopped tomatoes, and stir them over medium heat until all the liquid evaporates, about 5 minutes, turning up the heat for the last minute.

Prepare an ice bath.

Add the capers, ginger, and garlic and cook another minute. Put the mixture in the bowl set in ice to stop the cooking. When just cool, stir in the oil, salt, and pepper. Let sit 1 hour. Adjust the seasoning and serve at room temperature.

MINT, SAGE, AND ROSEMARY PESTO SAUCE

In 1994, Judy Rogers, the chef and co-owner of my favorite San Francisco daily hang-out (with the best margaritas in California), wrote me a note saying "I love the mint pesto. MAY I STEAL IT?"

All pestos, whether basil, rose petal, mint, artichoke (Jerusalem or globe), cilantro, or nasturtium flower, with nuts or without, can be made (and certainly made faster) in the food processor. However, there are advantages to using a mortar and pestle. The gentler action of this hand-process produces better flavors and brighter colors, each being an indication of the other. In addition, a pesto made in a mortar is less likely to separate while you are making it and will not break later. Please never be tempted to use a blender, which will oxidize and thus mar the delicate flavors and colors of the leaves or vegetables you are using.

Traditional basil pesto contains Parmesan cheese. I prefer ewe's milk cheese, and also the whole family of manchegos—their mild and subtle flavors are a perfect complement to fresh herb pestos.

When making pesto to serve with pasta, hearty vegetable soups, and baked potatoes, use the cheese. For saucing fish dishes, omit the cheese (as here), using breadcrumbs instead of Parmesan.

Do not try to force the proportions. Sometimes a little more or less oil will be just what you need.

MAKES 3 CUPS

2 cups	fresh mint (leaves only)	1 teaspoon	lemon zest
2 tablespoons	fresh sage leaves	1 cup	extra virgin light yellow olive oil
1 tablespoon	fresh rosemary leaves		
2 cloves	garlic, peeled	¼ teaspoon	sea salt
2 tablespoons	fresh white breadcrumbs (see page 32)	1 teaspoon	freshly ground coarse black pepper
1 tablespoon	freshly squeezed lemon juice		

Put the mint, sage, and rosemary in a mortar (or food processor, but then add 2 tablespoons of water as well) with the garlic, breadcrumbs, lemon juice and zest. Grind or process until smooth. Add the olive oil a little at a time, as if making mayonnaise, until the puree is the consistency of creamed butter. Add half the salt and pepper. Taste it, and add more if needed.

VARIATIONS Cilantro pesto mixed with lightly toasted walnuts, salted anchovy (see page 42) and potato; or a parsley and Meyer lemon pesto with tarragon and orange zest.

SIMPLE AND COMPOUND BUTTERS

I have always had an aversion to the premade restaurant sauces sitting around in hot water all day. They lose their freshness, all the delicate perfumes and flavors that take hours to achieve—gone after half an hour in that hot-water bath. At the Santa Fe Bar & Grill, where the kitchen cooking space was taken up by a huge grill (which left no space to make pan sauces), we needed easy sauces that could be made in advance but would not lose their fresh flavors by sitting around all night. And they had to complement a menu that was predominantly grilled items. Butters like ancho chili, sorrel, orange-cilantro, or tomato-rocket were the perfect answer.

Then, with several cooks thinking, the dam of invention suddenly burst, and there was born roasted chili–duck liver butter; red Anaheim chili–sesame; grilled orange–fennel; roasted garlic–red onion; ginger-garlic-chili; ginger-cilantro-tequila; ginger–scallion; roasted peanut–scallion–chili, and so on.

These butters are particularly appropriate for grilled or roasted fish, meat, and poultry, where a liquid sauce would destroy the effect of the crispness (duck skin) or charred surface (grilled lamb chop) by making their cooked surfaces soggy.

Simple butters contain one or two elements, such as anchovies, caviar, a fresh herb, mustard, paprika, or chopped pistachios, while compound butters—such as Bercy (shallots, parsley, and marrow), and the great Montpelier butter—contain a greater number of ingredients, with a more complex result.

The classic "Maître d'Hôtel" butter is a "simple" one, incorporating chopped parsley, lemon juice, salt, and pepper, its fairly direct effect working perfectly with a straightforward dish like grilled sole. This same butter becomes "compound" when you add chopped tarragon leaves and meat stock reduced with Madeira to a syrup. The concoction is called "Colbert Butter" after Jean-Baptiste Colbert, finance minister under Louis XIV—a rich sauce named after a rich man. Its subsequent complexity is appropriate with the complex flavors of a dish like aged beef tenderloin with artichokes and fried soufflé potatoes.

All flavored butters should be left for two hours to develop their flavors before serving.

NASTURTIUM BUTTER

MAKES 1 CUP

6 cups	fresh nasturtium flowers, stemmed
¼ cup	vegetable stock (see page 143)
1 cup	unsalted butter, room temperature (70 degrees)
	Salt and freshly ground white pepper

Prepare an ice bath with a bowl sitting in the iced water.

Put the flowers in 4 quarts of boiling salted water for 5 seconds. Immediately drain, and put in a food processor. Add the vegetable broth and puree, quickly pouring the puree into the bowl sitting in the ice bath to cool the liquid and preserve the fresh color and flavor of the flowers.

When the puree is cool, put it back in the food processor with the butter. Blend until smooth and evenly colored. Taste and adjust for seasoning.

MONTPELIER BUTTER

This butter is so good I could eat it with a spoon. In *New American Classics* (1986) I wrote, "It transforms hot cauliflower; on top of mashed potatoes it is so good that it should be arrested"—and I have not changed my mind since. It is very good at room temperature with cold poached fish, especially salmon, but equally delicious with hot grilled fish. Spooned between slices of cold roast veal or pork with the slices reassembled, left for a day, and then eaten at cool room temperature, it creates a lifelong memory.

This greatest of all butters is traditionally made with a mortar and pestle, but a food processor will do.

MAKES 1½ CUPS

6 leaves	spinach	1 clove	garlic, peeled
½ bunch	watercress leaves	¼ teaspoon	cayenne pepper
2 tablespoons	fresh parsley leaves	3	hard-cooked egg yolks
2 tablespoons	fresh chervil leaves	2	large raw egg yolks
2 tablespoons	chopped fresh chives	¼ pound	unsalted butter, room temperature
1 tablespoon	fresh tarragon leaves		
2	shallots, peeled, chopped	½ cup	extra virgin light yellow olive oil
2	cornichons, rinsed, chopped		
4	salted anchovy fillets (see page 42)	1 teaspoon	white wine vinegar
2 tablespoons	salted capers, rinsed, soaked 2 hours, drained (see page 44)		Salt and freshly ground white pepper

Blanch the spinach, watercress, herbs, and shallots in boiling water for 1 minute. Drain, refresh under cold water, and squeeze dry.

Put the mixture in a mortar or food processor. Add the cornichons, anchovies, capers, garlic, cayenne, salt, and pepper. Work with a pestle or process to a smooth paste.

Add the egg yolks and the butter and process again until thoroughly mixed. Leave the butter in the mortar or put it in a bowl and whisk in the oil *by hand*. The mixture should be glossy and as smooth as velvet. Beat in the vinegar and adjust salt and pepper to taste.

VARIATION For Singapore butter, slightly char some orange peel over a burner, let it cool, and chop it very finely before adding it to the Montpelier butter along with a little charred and finely minced serrano chili (peeled, seeded, and stemmed; start with ½ teaspoon) and 1 teaspoon of the finest light sesame oil.

MAYONNAISE

Whereas flavored butters can be made in food processors, the closer mayonnaise gets to a machine the worse it is. A rewarding cooking and tasting experience is to make mayonnaise in a mortar or in a bowl by hand and then compare it with mayonnaises made in an electric mixer, a food processor, and a blender. Each mayonnaise tastes, feels, looks different. The hand-whisked sauce will be silkier, smoother, lighter, more delicate in taste, and will sit easier in the stomach as well.

Use a light, high-quality olive oil, and have all the ingredients at room temperature. Italian green extra virgin olive oil makes a good mayonnaise, but one that will usually be overpowering. Use it only with strongly flavored foods, such as roasted bell peppers or cold peppered steak.

MAKES APPROXIMATELY 1½ CUPS

3	large egg yolks, room temperature
½ teaspoon	salt
¼ teaspoon	freshly ground white pepper
up to ¼ cup	freshly squeezed lemon juice
1 to 1½ cups	extra virgin light yellow olive oil

Put the yolks, salt, pepper, and half the lemon juice in a bowl and whisk until smooth. Whisk in the oil very slowly at first, increasing the flow at the end. If the mayonnaise gets too thick to beat, add droplets of water and continue adding the oil. (The amount of oil will depend on the consistency of mayonnaise desired.) Whisk in some or all of the remaining lemon juice, depending on how much lemon taste you want, and then season the mayonnaise.

VARIATIONS

+ Green herb mayonnaise: Blanch 1 packed cup mixed herbs (tarragon, parsley, chervil, thyme, marjoram, and basil in equal proportions, for example), 6 spinach leaves, and ¼ cup watercress leaves cooked for 30 seconds in boiling water. Drain, squeeze dry, and finely chop half the herbs. Puree the other half with a tablespoon or so of water. Mix the chopped and pureed herbs into 2 cups of mayonnaise and refrigerate several hours for the flavors to develop. Particularly good on cold poached fish.

+ Chinese black bean mayonnaise: Add ¼ cup Chinese black bean puree to 1 cup mayonnaise; use for cold meats or chilled poached salmon.

+ Indian lime pickle mayonnaise: Puree 1 heaping teaspoon pickle and add it to a cup of mayonnaise; use for sandwiches.

+ Mango chutney mayonnaise: Two tablespoons of chopped chutney to 1 cup of mayonnaise. Particularly good in sandwiches.

GARLIC MAYONNAISE

The most dramatic difference between hand- and machine-made mayonnaise can be tasted when you make garlic mayonnaise in a mortar and pestle (not the smooth chemist's variety but one of semi-rough marble) rather than in a machine. The texture is like velvet, the flavors are subtle, and the result is by far the most digestible.

MAKES 2½ CUPS

4	garlic cloves, peeled
2	egg yolks
¼ cup	fresh white breadcrumbs
½	teaspoon salt
¼ cup	fish or chicken stock, depending on final use (see pages 187, 215)
2 cups	olive oil

Work the garlic, egg yolks, breadcrumbs, salt, and a little stock to a paste in a mortar or food processor. When the paste is smooth, start adding the oil slowly, working it all the time. Add as much oil as the sauce will take without breaking; then add stock to thin it so that it will just pour off a spoon.

VARIATIONS For saucing cold poached red snapper and other white non-oily fish, add sea urchin puree (page 182) and the result is transcendental. Crayfish garlic mayonnaise is not bad; use the cooked shells pounded in the mortar in which you make the mayonnaise, and then sieve out. Put the cooked shelled crayfish tails in the sauce and garnish with chopped hard-cooked egg and chive flowers. Or for smoked–chili garlic mayonnaise, to a cup of garlic mayonnaise add 1 teaspoon chipotle paste, 2 tablespoons chopped cilantro leaves, and lime juice, as well as freshly grated zest of lime to taste. For red pepper–garlic mayonnaise, or *rouille*, mix ⅓ cup red bell pepper puree (see page 39) and 1 teaspoon cayenne (or more to taste) into the initial garlic paste of the garlic mayonnaise recipe to make a sauce that is traditionally served on little toasts floating on fish soup (see page 110), but is also very good on cold meats and fish, or on grilled country-style bread as a snack with drinks. Barbecue garlic mayonnaise: this is so delicious there is nothing I can say really, except mix together 1 cup mayonnaise with ½ cup barbecue sauce and 1 tablespoon dark Antiguan rum, then howl like a coyote after you have had a Sazerac cocktail or two and bitten into a fried-oyster po' boy sandwich (see page 77) slathered in this sauce.

GREEN GODDESS SAUCES

Green goddess mayonnaise and the rémoulade on page 251 are the queen and king of mayonnaise sauces, and are used throughout the book. I love what happens to mayonnaise when it is mixed with sour cream—it becomes less rich, more complicated, and has a light, almost mousse-like texture.

GREEN GODDESS MAYONNAISE

MAKES APPROXIMATELY 1½ CUPS

1 cup	green herb mayonnaise (see variation page 247)
¼ cup	finely chopped fresh chives
1 clove	garlic, peeled, very finely minced
4	salted anchovy fillets (see page 42), minced
½ cup	sour cream

Mix all the ingredients in a bowl. Check for sufficient salt and pepper, adding a little less than you think it needs. Then let the sauce sit for an hour to allow the flavors to combine and check the seasoning again.

GREEN GODDESS OLIVE OIL AND LEMON SAUCE

MAKES 1 CUP

1 cup	mixed herbs (see green herb mayonnaise, page 247)	¼ cup	freshly squeezed lemon juice
¼ cup	finely chopped fresh chives	½ cup	extra virgin olive oil
1 clove	garlic, peeled, very finely minced		Freshly ground black pepper
4	salted anchovy fillets (see page 42), minced		

Process the herbs as in the recipe for green herb mayonnaise (see page 247), put them in a bowl with all the other ingredients, and mix. Season with pepper and salt if necessary.

VARIATION To make green goddess butter, use the same recipe as for the mayonnaise, but omit the mayonnaise and the sour cream, substituting a pound of unsalted butter instead, mixing everything in a food processor, and seasoning it with salt and pepper.

RUSSIAN DRESSING

This sauce needs no explanation to the American public, although here it does have caviar as a surprise ingredient. Caviar was part of the original version; use *payusnaya,* or pressed caviar here since it is full of flavor and the least expensive.

If the sauce is to be served with cold cooked crab or lobster, sieve the liver, the coral, and/or the fat from the crab or lobster shells, and add them to the sauce along with any juices from the shells. This shellfish version is very perishable and must be eaten right away.

MAKES 1½ CUPS	
½ cup	chopped tomatoes (see page 47)
1 cup	mayonnaise (see page 247)
1 teaspoon	prepared horseradish
1 teaspoon	grated white onion
4 ounces	sturgeon caviar

Toss the tomatoes in a hot sauté pan for 3 minutes, or until just dry. Cool and place in a bowl with the other ingredients. Mix well.

MY RÉMOULADE SAUCE

Tartar, ravigote, gribiche, and rémoulade are four familiar mayonnaise sauces with very tricky and clouded pasts. It would take a forensically inclined scholar to sort them out, since over the last century the naming of them seems fairly arbitrary and ever-changing.

Tartar: Both Escoffier and Prosper Montagné (the latter the author of the *Larousse gastronomique*) say that tartar sauce is a mayonnaise with the addition of hard-boiled egg and chives. I feel that tartar sauce should include capers, sour gherkins (in America, sweet pickle), and herbs.

Ravigote: Sometimes a hot, flour-thickened chicken stock sauce with all the tartar ingredients plus shallots, sometimes a cold sauce more like the vinegar and olive oil sauce called gribiche.

Gribiche: Definitely a mayonnaise with a hard-cooked egg base, and the above usual suspects of capers, gherkins, and herbs. Except when it was a vinaigrette, with the same ingredients but with the cooked egg white and yolk chopped finely and mixed in.

Rémoulade: A hard-cooked yolk-based mayonnaise (sometimes), with all the usual suspects and the addition of mustard. Julia Child's first book says that rémoulade is just tartar sauce with anchovy paste added, but ordinary mayonnaise with anchovy (and sometimes tomato) is called "antiboise."

Whatever. I adore them all, so let me take a personal stand and lay down some practical advice: Bring up all this confusion only if you need to liven up the dinner table. Leave tartar simple (mayonnaise with parsley, chives, chopped capers, chopped gherkins, and lemon zest). For ravigote, see gribiche, which should be the vinaigrette type with all the ingredients of the Montpelier butter except the butter.

Here is my take on the superb sauce called rémoulade. Have all the ingredients at room temperature, and the herbs must be fresh.

MAKES APPROXIMATELY 3 CUPS

2 cups	mayonnaise (see page 247)	2 tablespoons	fresh Italian parsley, chopped
3 tablespoons	Dijon mustard		
2	hard-boiled eggs (see page 67), chopped very coarsely	1 tablespoon	fresh tarragon leaves, chopped
		1 tablespoon	fresh chervil leaves, chopped
3	salted anchovy fillets (see page 42), chopped	1 tablespoon	Worcestershire sauce
4	gherkins (cornichons), rinsed, drained, finely chopped	1 teaspoon	your favorite hot sauce
		1 teaspoon	freshly ground black pepper
		1 teaspoon	finely grated lemon zest (or chopped salt-preserved lemons, see page 43)
2 tablespoons	salted capers (see page 44), rinsed, soaked 2 hours, chopped		

Put all the ingredients into a bowl and mix well.

CAUTION Add the gherkins and capers no more than 2 hours before serving. Leaving them in the sauce for too long produces a gasoline taste.

ASPARAGUS SAUCE

I include this sauce here not only because it is delicious, but also because it represents the family of fresh herb and vegetable sauces which, to stay brightly colored and taste fresh and wonderful, face the challenge of preserving these qualities in the cooking process. I use it on vegetables, poached fish or chicken, pasta, and eggs.

I am assuming that the tips (upper 2 to 3 inches) of the asparagus are used for another dish or to garnish whatever this sauce goes on, so they would be boiled in salted water until tender (five to eight minutes), and then tossed in butter or extra virgin olive oil.

MAKES 1 CUP

1 pound	asparagus, green stems only, cut in 1-inch pieces
1 sprig	tarragon
4 ounces	unsalted butter, cut in 1-tablespoon pieces and chilled
	Salt
	Freshly ground white peppercorns

Prepare an ice bath and place a metal bowl in it.

Cook the asparagus pieces in 3 quarts of rapidly boiling salted water. Drain the asparagus when they are tender enough to puree, 5 to 10 minutes depending on the thickness of the pieces.

Puree them in a food processor, and immediately pour the puree into the bowl sitting in the ice bath. Stir the puree until it is completely cold and then put it through a sieve.

To finish the sauce, heat the puree with the tarragon sprig. Whisk in the butter one piece at a time until all of it is melted. Remove the tarragon, season, and serve immediately.

Nasturtium Sauce

This is a sauce for pouring over poached vegetables (fava beans, asparagus, green beans, cauliflower, little onions and so on), or over cooked mussels in a gratin dish (for cooking mussels, see page 181) to be reheated at the last minute. It is also very good on sea urchins baked in their shells, or on any poached white fish.

MAKES 2 TO 3 CUPS

½ cup	nasturtium butter (see page 245), chilled, cut in 1-tablespoon pieces
2 cups	vegetable, fish, or chicken stock, depending on the final use of the sauce (see pages 143, 187, 215)
	Salt

Simmer the stock in a nonreactive pan, and whisk in the butter one piece at a time. Season and use immediately.

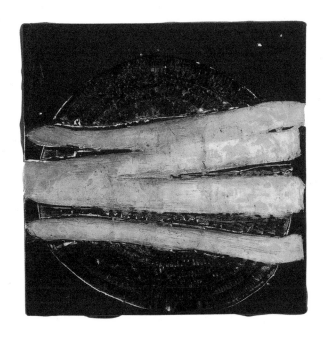

HOLLANDAISE

"Hollandaise" was the first French word I could remember and pronounce, since asparagus with hollandaise sauce was an early passion. It is a pure sauce, and I feel purist about it: lemon juice, salt, pepper or cayenne, butter, and egg yolks are its only proper components.

The sauce is made with five to seven yolks (depending on egg size) per pound of butter, and the question of whether to use clarified or whole butter is an easy one for me. The use of clarified butter in hollandaise comes from the nasty habits of restaurants and hotels (which have endless vats of it on hand): it produces a quicker hollandaise, but the result is oily in texture, less fresh in taste, and harder to digest.

Here are the secrets for a successful hollandaise: First, make a sabayon-like base by beating the yolks with the lemon juice and then cooking the mixture slightly over simmering water, never letting the sauce get too hot and scrambling the eggs. Add the cold butter gradually and keep the sauce warm when finished. If the sauce breaks, start the process again with a couple of new yolks, adding the broken sauce gradually while whisking. A tablespoon of hot water does wonders for critical moments (like the sauce breaking) and texture (if too thick).

Make this sauce with butter imported from France or some of the new American high butterfat ones, and you will soon become an addict.

MAKES 3 CUPS	
5	large egg yolks
3 tablespoons	freshly squeezed lemon juice
½ teaspoon	salt
1 pound	chilled unsalted butter, cut into 1-tablespoon chunks
1 pinch	cayenne

Put the egg yolks, lemon juice, and salt in a stainless-steel, enamel, or other nonreactive bowl over simmering water, and whisk until foamy. Continue to whisk until the yolks thicken and increase in volume like a sabayon (see page 257).

Remove the bowl from the heat and whisk in the butter one piece at a time. After incorporating the first two pieces of butter, return the sauce to the simmering water and continue whisking in the butter. If the eggs look like they are becoming scrambled, remove the bowl from the water and let the egg mixture cool a bit while whisking.

After all the butter has been added, remove the sauce from the heat and season with the cayenne. Taste and adjust salt and lemon juice. Keep the sauce warm and use it within an hour.

VARIATIONS For hollandaise with fish essences: reduce ½ cup fish stock by half and whisk with the yolks initially before continuing with the recipe. Serve with fish, since the addition of the stock unites the flavors of the fish and the sauce. Whipped cream hollandaise: hollandaise folded together with whipped cream. It is lighter and richer, with a less pronounced taste than hollandaise, and perfect with fresh poached fish. Whip ½ cup very cold heavy cream until soft peaks are formed. Fold the cream into the warm hollandaise just before using the sauce. Season the hollandaise heavily, since the cream will dilute the flavors.

RASPBERRY SAUCE

Berry purees can be a base for simple dessert sauces or marinades (for squab, for example), they can be added to butter (for grilled meats), folded into mousses and sabayon sauces, or used to make ethereal soufflés (especially of wild strawberries, see page 261).

Whatever the use, the berries have to be pureed by hand, and the best method is through a fine-mesh nylon or stainless steel sieve, or a food mill fitted with the finest mesh disk. Once berries are subjected to the violence of a food processor (or worse, a blender), their color, flavor, and texture deteriorate. Put through a sieve, berries will produce a puree with body, a very important factor when you plan to add other liquids and do not want a thin sauce. Berries other than raspberries, like strawberries, really need a food mill, since they are difficult to put through a sieve by hand.

MAKES 2 CUPS

2 cups	fresh raspberries
¼ cup	heavy syrup (see page 45)
pinch	salt

Push the raspberries though a sieve by hand, and then mix in the syrup and salt.
Covered and refrigerated the sauce will last 12 hours maximum.

BLUEBERRY SAUCE

Blueberries and huckleberries are the only berries (other than currants and cranberries) that need to be cooked in order to make a sauce. If you puree them raw, they will form an impossible paste.

MAKES 2 CUPS

2 cups	fresh blueberries or huckleberries
¼ cup	heavy syrup (see page 45)
pinch	salt

Put the berries, syrup, and salt in a saucepan and bring to a boil. Simmer for 5 minutes, and then put through a sieve.

CUSTARD

This is the sauce called *crème anglaise* in French (and the basis for that most sublime drink, egg nog).

SERVES 4 TO 6	
½ cup	granulated sugar
6	egg yolks
¼ teaspoon	salt
2 cups	milk
1	1-inch piece vanilla bean

Mix the sugar, yolks, and salt in a bowl and whisk (or use a mixer on medium speed) until pale yellow, about 5 minutes.

Prepare an ice bath with a metal bowl sitting in the iced water.

Heat the milk and vanilla bean together until almost boiling, and pour slowly into the yolk mixture while still whisking. Put the milk and egg mixture in a double boiler and cook over simmering water, stirring constantly, until the custard begins to thicken and coats the spoon.

Remove the custard from the heat and immediately pour into the bowl sitting in the ice. Stir constantly with a spoon to prevent the custard from overcooking (curdling) and forming a skin when it cools. Strain and serve, or cover and refrigerate for up to 3 days.

VARIATIONS To make flavored custards, infuse nuts, fresh ginger, cinnamon sticks, star anise, fennel seeds, or orange or lemon rind into the milk and follow the infusion directions for coconut custard (below).

- ✦ coffee custard: Heat 2 cups of milk with ¼ cup ground espresso coffee until almost boiling; let sit for 30 minutes. Strain and proceed as above.
- ✦ coconut custard: Crack the shell of a fresh coconut and remove the meat from the hard outer shell. Chop the coconut meat fine with a knife or in a food processor. Steep the coconut in 2 cups of warmed milk for at least an hour, or until the milk takes on the coconut's flavor. Then strain the milk, discarding the coconut, and use in the recipe above. Some of the milk may be absorbed by the coconut, so correct the quantity before beginning the recipe.
- ✦ lapsang souchong–chocolate custard: Infuse the milk with 1 tablespoon Lapsang Souchong tea and ¼ cup chocolate sauce.

CARÊME'S CREAM

Antonin Carême was the French chef who gave order to the culinary changeover from the eighteenth to the nineteenth centuries, as Auguste Escoffier did for the change from the nineteenth to the twentieth. Perhaps the most sublime custard of all is this one. Don't be put off by the word "maraschino." This white liqueur has nothing to do with those red cherries.

MAKES 2 CUPS

2 cups	custard (see page 256)
1 tablespoon	white maraschino liqueur

Mix the custard and the maraschino together, let sit for 1 hour, and serve.

VARIATION Fold in ½ cup whipped cream for a richer custard and lighter texture.

CREAMED SABAYON SAUCE

The secret to holding a cold sabayon sauce so that it does not collapse and separate is to whisk it in a bowl sitting in ice and water without stopping until it is quite cold. After that it will hold in a covered container in the refrigerator for up to four days.

Have a bowl (big enough to contain the bowl of sabayon) filled with ice and water next to the stove.

MAKES 4 CUPS

6	egg yolks
½ cup	sugar
pinch	salt
1 cup	champagne or white wine
1 cup	heavy cream

Combine the yolks, sugar, and salt in a stainless-steel mixing bowl. Whisk together for 2 minutes and then add the champagne.

Put the bowl over simmering water (but not in it) and whisk the mixture with an up-and-down motion (to incorporate as much air as possible into the mixture) until the egg mixture is thick and pale yellow, or for about 10 minutes. Then put the cooking bowl in the ice-water bath, and whisk the sabayon vigorously again until it is cold.

Whip the cream and fold it into the sabayon. Cover and keep chilled for up to 4 days.

VARIATION Savory sabayon sauce: this is the same sauce, served hot or cold, but with no sugar. It is made with shellfish or lobster essence (see page 188) in place of half the wine, and is used to sauce hot or cold fish dishes. One of my favorites is a sabayon made with mussel and shellfish essence, with a tablespoon of coarse cracked black or white pepper folded in at the last moment.

CHAPTER ELEVEN

DESSERTS

STRAWBERRIES IN OLD BURGUNDY

STRAWBERRIES IN RED CURRANT SAUCE

WILD STRAWBERRY SOUFFLÉ

ELIZABETH DAVID'S SYLLABUB

ROBERT MAY'S BLACK FRUIT FOOL

THE DREAM OF EDOUARD NIGNON

WARM FRUIT STEW

THE CLAUDE TROISGROS PEAR, PEAR, PEAR

FIGS WITH WILD THYME HONEY IN RED WINE AND LAPSANG SOUCHONG CUSTARD

MERINGUES WITH LONGANS (DRAGON'S EYE "LYCHEES")

NEW ENGLAND SUMMER PUDDING

COOKED CREAM WITH SUGARED APRICOTS AND HOT HUCKLEBERRY SAUCE

"BURNT" PASSION FRUIT CURD

WHITE PEACH AND JASMINE ICE

TWENTY-MINUTE BLUEBERRY TART

TART PASTRY

TREACLE TART

CARAMELIZED POUND CAKE NAPOLEON WITH WHITE "MANGO" NECTARINES
AND STRAWBERRY ICE CREAM

ROSE WATER–ROSEMARY POLENTA POUND CAKE

BLACK BOTTOM PIE

HOT CHOCOLATE

KUMQUAT "FANTASY" CREAM

STRAWBERRIES IN OLD BURGUNDY

On a wine tour though France in June of 1976, every meal ended with summer strawberries. I believe in gorging in the surfeit of the season, but after two weeks of those berries I started to dread the end of each meal.

We were at Paul Bocuse when, at the end of the meal, I was gazing again at the magnificent desserts, while waiting with dread for the inevitable berries. But when he spooned the strawberries into the big glass of what was left of my old La Tache, I sighed with relief and enjoyed strawberries all over again—so much, in fact, that had they been the wild ones, I think I would have passed out.

You can also use young wine with strawberries, adding a grinding of black pepper, and I prefer Zinfandel or Pinot Noir, although the other reds work too. If the wine is more than twenty years old, it is permissible to add a teaspoon of sugar.

STRAWBERRIES IN RED CURRANT SAUCE

This technique works absolute miracles with strawberries all the year round, so when red currants are in season, make this syrup and freeze it to cheer yourself up in winter.

SERVES 4 TO 6

2 cups	fresh red currants, stemmed
1 cup	light sugar syrup (see page 45)
2 cups	fresh strawberries, hulled

Put the red currants in simmering sugar syrup, and cook 1 minute. Turn off the heat, let the currants sit 30 minutes, and then put them and the syrup though a nylon sieve.

Pour the warm, but not hot, currant sauce over the strawberries, cover, and let sit for 30 minutes, but no longer, in the refrigerator.

WILD STRAWBERRY SOUFFLÉ

To preserve the fresh taste of red fruits when I make their soufflés, I use egg whites only. For the same reason, I use tin-lined metal charlotte molds, which allow the soufflés to cook as fast as possible.

For me the most memorable red fruit soufflé is made with a puree of wild strawberries, but by all means, use cloudberries (*Rubus chamaemorus*), the greatest berries of them all, if you can find them.

SERVES 4

1 cup	wild strawberry puree (see page 25 for berry purees)
2 tablespoons	butter, softened
1½	cups sugar
4	egg whites at room temperature

Preheat the oven to 400 degrees.

Butter four 4-inch charlotte molds. Using ½ cup of the sugar, coat the entire surface of each mold, discarding any sugar that does not adhere to the butter.

Whip the egg whites in a clean bowl to soft peaks. Gradually beat in the remaining sugar and continue to beat for about 5 minutes until the whites are glossy and stand in stiff peaks. Quickly but gently fold in the wild strawberry puree and spoon the mixture into the prepared soufflé molds, filling each mold no more than three-quarters full. Make a ½-inch-deep moat around the inner edge of each charlotte with your finger.

Bake in the middle of the oven until risen 3 to 4 inches above the edge of the mold, and lightly browned, 15 to 20 minutes.

VARIATIONS Instead of wild strawberries use raspberries, or a puree of pears soaked in Armagnac, and garnish with rose water mascarpone or chocolate custard. Or make passion fruit puree soufflés and serve with white peach and jasmine ice (see page 273), or use watermelon puree or fresh ginger and serve with a yellow peach sauce; or use fresh, young green coconut and serve with mangosteen and lychee sorbet.

ELIZABETH DAVID'S SYLLABUB

In London, in 1969, I bought Elizabeth's *Syllabubs and Fruit Fools*, and read about some of the giants of English food writing and cookery, such as Robert May, Elizabeth Raffald, Sir Kenelm Digby, and Hannah Glasse. At the same time I was reading about Max Beerbohm, in Lord David Cecil's *Max*, and the syllabubs served at his wedding (at breakfast no less).

These syllabubs are glorious things, as Elizabeth wrote, "simple and sumptuous. The skill demanded is minimal; the presentation is basic and elegant." And since they must be prepared a day or two in advance, they are perfect for entertaining.

SERVES 2	
½ cup	Manzanilla sherry
2 tablespoons	brandy
1	lemon, finely zested, juiced
¼ cup	sugar
1½ cups	double cream (see page 27)
pinch	freshly grated nutmeg
pinch	salt

Put the sherry, brandy, and lemon zest and juice in a bowl and let sit overnight. Strain, saving the liquid only.

Put the sugar in a nonreactive bowl with the strained sherry, and stir until the sugar is dissolved. Add the cream, nutmeg, and salt. Whisk the mixture for 5 minutes, or until it thickens enough to hold a soft peak on the whisk. It can become overbeaten in seconds, so be careful.

Spoon the syllabub into small (4-ounce) glasses, filling them to the top. Refrigerate until needed.

VARIATIONS These are perfection when made with the juice of Meyer lemons, or using the whole ripe fruit (seedless) chopped up. Quinces are divine cooked with water and sugar, pureed and mixed with double cream (see page 27). Then there is the most famous of all fools, gooseberry: cook 2 pounds pink or green ripe gooseberries in a double boiler with ½ pound sugar. When soft, puree and strain off the liquid, reducing it and adding it back to the berries before whisking the puree into the cream.

ROBERT MAY'S BLACK FRUIT FOOL

Robert May worked as a chef for the Countess of Kent, a woman whose great love of food is evident in her 1653 book, *A True Gentlewoman's Delight*. May's own book, *The Accomplisht Cook* (1660), is one that has inspired me for over thirty years—along with John Evelyn's *Acetaria: A Discourse of Sallets* (1969), which served as a guide for my vegetable garden in Massachusetts before I became a professional chef.

This fruit mixture was called "black tart stuff" by Robert May, the name being one commonly given to open-tart fillings that are "rich and wonderful without being as heavy and cloying as mincemeat" (Elizabeth David). It is important to cook the prunes separately from the raisins, since the very sweet, cloying, and slightly sulfurous liquid from the raisins will ruin the pure flavors of the prunes in wine.

SERVES 4

½ pound	large prunes		¼ cup	currants or little raisins
½ cup	red wine		¼ teaspoon	salt
¼ cup	ruby port		2 cups	heavy cream
4 tablespoons	dark brown sugar		½ cup	herb flowers or rose petals
¼ pound	large raisins (preferably Spanish Moscatels)			

Preheat the oven to 300 degrees.

Put the prunes in a nonreactive ovenproof casserole with the wine, port, brown sugar, and enough water (2 to 3 cups) to cover them. Cover and cook at 300 degrees for 2 hours, or until they are completely soft and have absorbed most of the liquid.

Meanwhile, put the raisins and currants in another casserole with water to cover them, cover, and put the casserole in the oven with the prunes for their last hour of cooking.

Remove the prunes and take out the pits. Puree them with all their liquid through a food mill or sieve. Drain the raisin-currant mixture, puree it also, and mix into the prune puree with the salt. Discard the liquid.

Put the fool into a chilled glass bowl just large enough to hold it with 2 inches to spare. Pour the cream on top. Garnish with herb flowers or rose petals, and serve with shortbread.

THE DREAM OF EDOUARD NIGNON

Author of *Eloges de la cuisine Française* (1933) and *Les Plaisirs de la table* (1926), Nignon was a chef and author with a mad and wonderful style. A bit of a Luddite, he deplored the then-current lack of "meditation and patience" that makes for "grande cuisine." "Down with chemistry! Down with speed!" was his tirade.

For this dream you will need a 12-inch ring mold.

SERVES 6 TO 8

2 tablespoons	butter		24	almond macaroons, crushed into coarse crumbs
3 tablespoons	sugar (for the mold)			
8	egg whites		1 cup	fresh strawberries, hulled
5 tablespoons	vanilla sugar (see page 44)		1 cup	fresh raspberries
			1 cup	sweetened whipped cream
pinch	salt			

Generously butter the inside of the mold and dust it with the sugar, shaking out what does not stick to the butter.

Preheat the oven to 375 degrees.

Make a meringue, as on page 268, with the egg whites, vanilla sugar, and pinch of salt. Fold in the crumbed macaroons. Put the soufflé mixture in the mold, and tap the mold twice lightly on the counter.

Put the mold in the oven and immediately reduce the heat to 350 degrees. Cook for 35 minutes, or until a thin skewer inserted in the center of the soufflé comes out clean. Take the mold out of the oven, let sit for 10 minutes, and then turn it out on a round flat platter a couple of inches larger than the mold.

Meanwhile, chop the strawberries coarsely and put them in a bowl with the raspberries. Add a pinch of salt. Stir vigorously for 1 minute to break up the raspberries, and then fold in the whipped cream.

Put the berry cream in the center hole of the soufflé and serve immediately.

VARIATION I would call it my dream if I added stewed rhubarb to the berry mix.

WARM FRUIT STEW

One of my favorite modernizations of a timeless classic dish (and one that you can cook in ten minutes) is this inevitable crowd-pleaser of fruit warmed slightly in sugar syrup and served with ice cream.

It is a dish for all seasons, using whatever ripe fruit is available, such as mangoes, papayas, figs, peaches, plums, nectarines, all kinds of berries including ripe green and pink gooseberries, cherries, and so on. But it does seem to reach its apotheosis with summer berries. If you include raspberries, throw them in only for the last minute of cooking.

SERVES 4

1 cup	strawberries, rinsed, cut in half		1 tablespoon	sweet butter, cut into cubes or softened
1 cup	blueberries, rinsed			Salt
1 cup	blackberries		2 teaspoons	fresh lemon juice
¼ cup	light syrup (see page 45)		1 pint	vanilla ice cream

Put the strawberries, blueberries, and blackberries in a frying pan and add the syrup. Cook over medium heat for 2 minutes, shaking the pan gently to coat the berries with syrup. Add the butter, a pinch of salt, and the lemon juice, and continue to cook, swirling the berries and butter around in the pan, another minute, or until the butter is melted.

Spoon the fruit compote onto four plates and place scoops of ice cream in the center of each serving.

VARIATIONS To make an uncooked compote out of tropical fruits, peel and cut up a ripe mango and a ripe papaya. Put in a bowl and add 1 cup of warm medium sugar syrup (see page 45) and the juices/pulp of two ripe passion fruits. Mix in a pinch of salt and chill for 1 hour. Serve with coconut ice cream, or plain in a hollowed-out meringue. For a warm compote put all the fruit in the syrup as above and cook in the same way as the berry compote, then serve on polenta pound cake (see page 227).

For other fruit compotes, use white "mango" and "honeydew" nectarines, or three different kinds of yellow and white peaches. In 1983, at Phelps Vineyards, we poached fresh apricots in sweet Riesling from the vineyard, and served them to great effect with a hazelnut sabayon.

THE CLAUDE TROISGROS PEAR, PEAR, PEAR

I don't remember why I named this after Claude, but probably because he invented it. I certainly didn't, but now I don't know if I have changed the original or not.

It is better (more refined at least) than the green apple sorbet doused with Calvados that they serve at La Coupole in Paris, but only just.

The best white pear brandy that I know is made by Etter in Switzerland.

SERVES 4

2	ripe Comice pears, peeled, peelings saved
½ cup	light sugar syrup (see page 45)
¼ cup	finest white pear brandy
1 cup	pear sorbet (see as for white peach ice on page 273)
pinch	salt
¼ cup	pink rose petals, shredded

Put the peelings in the syrup and simmer in a small nonreactive saucepan for 20 minutes. Strain into a bowl and chill the syrup.

Cut the pears in half lengthwise, remove the cores and stems, and slice them ⅛ inch thick along the length of the halves. Stir 2 tablespoons of the brandy and the salt into the chilled syrup. Add the pear slices, cover, and chill for 30 minutes.

Put a scoop of the ice in the center of four large shallow soup plates. Spoon the pears around, and pour the remaining brandy over the pears. Garnish with the rose petals.

VARIATIONS Try poaching the pears in Muscat wine and serving them with cardamom-flavored ricotta (1 teaspoon ground cardamom per cup of ricotta). At an AMFAR benefit in Napa Valley in 1998, I served these pears with creamed blue cheese in the center of the plate, some chestnut honey poured over the cheese, and a black Muscat sorbet on top of that.

Figs with Wild Thyme Honey in Red Wine and Lapsang Souchong Custard

The flavors of wild California, Provence, and refined China are in this dessert, so an orange-flower water or green Chartreuse custard sauce would also work well.

The figs taste even better if made the day before.

SERVES 4

16	whole dried figs	2 tablespoons	Lapsang Souchong tea leaves
1 bottle (750 ml)	red wine, fruity Zinfandel type	1 recipe	custard (see page 256)
4 sprigs	fresh thyme	1 cup	heavy cream
½ cup	sugar	1 teaspoon	rose water
¼ cup	wild thyme honey, or other good honey, like leatherwood		

Put the figs and red wine in a nonreactive saucepan, and soak for 1 hour. Add the thyme, sugar, and honey, and simmer until the figs are tender, about 1 hour. Strain, reserving the figs, and boil down the cooking liquid until it is reduced to cup. Stem the figs and put them back in the reduced wine sauce and let them cool.

Put the tea leaves in a bowl and pour ¼ cup boiling water over them. Steep for 5 minutes. Add the custard to the bowl, stir, and let marinate 1 hour. Strain the custard and discard the tea leaves.

To serve, whip the cream and fold it into the custard. Put the figs on plates. Pour the wine syrup over the figs, sprinkle the figs with the rose water, and then spoon some Lapsang Souchang custard cream on top of the figs.

VARIATION Poach the dried figs in sweet wine like a Muscat, and serve with Roquefort cheese mashed with a quarter of its volume of double cream (see page 27) or fresh ricotta. Or use fresh figs, cover them in cardamom-flavored honey (1 teaspoon ground cardamom to 1 cup honey) and bake them for 15 minutes at 400 degrees. Serve at room temperature with a cold, sweetened black-pepper sabayon.

MERINGUES WITH LONGANS (DRAGON'S EYE "LYCHEES")

Longans (*Dimocarpus longan*) aren't lychees at all, but they have a place in my heart, nonetheless. The opening day ceremony for the Peak Café in Hong Kong in 1990 was under a dragon eye tree, a site chosen by the Shinto priest because my company was called Freedragon and the site of the restaurant is the birthplace of Hong Kong's dragons. That this fruit's local name is "dragon's eye" and that it is said to promote a healthy sexual appetite certainly did nothing to deter our enthusiasm for the site.

The longan looks like a fresh lychee, but the taste is perfumed beyond any lychee. Pop a whole one in your mouth, as I did every morning in Hong Kong, and you might believe that the old Chinese saying is true!

I find the big meringues—like the superb pavlovas from Australia (filled with tropical fruits and cream), or the *vacherins* of France (filled with ice creams)—a bit difficult to make, so I make free-form round meringue shells and hollow them out. It helps to draw a circle on the parchment paper on which you will cook the meringues, turn the paper over, and spoon the meringue into the outline of the circle.

Southeast Asia has many dishes that use the flesh of half-ripe green coconuts, which are filled with coconut water and in which the white flesh is still gelatinous. One of my favorite things in the world is the fresh coconut milk made by pureeing the flesh together with the water from these young coconuts.

On a steamy hot day, a bowl of the fresh coconut milk mixed with the unripe coconut flesh, dark palm sugar, tapioca, and shaved ice is perfectly soothing and settles everyone down.

SERVES 4

4	egg whites, room temperature	1 cup	green coconut water
1 cup	fine sugar	1 cup	fresh young green coconut meat
pinch	salt	16	fresh longans, peeled, seeded, cut in half
1/4 teaspoon	ground cardamom	½ cup	dark palm sugar, dissolved in ½ cup water
6 cups	water		
½ cup	large pearl tapioca		
1 cup	unsweetened coconut milk (canned)		

Preheat the oven to 160 degrees.

Draw 4-inch rounds on parchment paper and turn the paper over onto a baking sheet.

Whip the egg whites to soft peaks with half the sugar and a pinch of salt in a clean bowl. Gradually beat in the remaining sugar and the cardamom, and continue to beat until the whites are glossy and stand in stiff peaks, about 10 minutes by hand or 5 minutes with an electric mixer.

Spoon, or form with a pastry bag, the meringue into the circles making 3-inch high peaks. Bake for 3 to 4 hours or more until the meringue is crusty on the outside but still soft on the inside. Do not let the meringues take on any color. When they are done, leave the oven door open for another hour before taking them out to cool in a place with no drafts. Better still, let them cool in the turned-off oven overnight.

Boil the water in a pan, add the tapioca, and cook over low heat for 45 minutes, stirring every 10 minutes. Remove from the heat, cover, and let stand 1 hour. Then put the tapioca in a bowl filled with ice water, stir for 1 minute, and drain well.

Simmer the coconut milk until reduced by half, and then chill. Puree the coconut water with the green coconut meat, and mix the puree into the chilled, reduced coconut milk. Add a pinch of salt, then add the tapioca, and mix the whole thing well.

Mix the peeled fruit with the palm sugar syrup. Hold the meringues upside-down, hollow out their centers from the bottom with a teaspoon, and fill the cavities with the coconut-tapioca puree. Put the meringues on individual plates, place the longans around the meringues, and spoon the palm sugar syrup over the meringues.

VARIATIONS Instead of the tropical fruit, I love to use stewed rhubarb. Simmer 1 cup dark brown sugar, 1 pound rhubarb cut in ½-inch lengths, and ¼ cup water gently in a nonreactive pan for 10 minutes. Strain, reduce the liquid by half (5 to 10 minutes), chill, and pour back over the rhubarb. Or use stewed fresh Morello cherries, cooked the same way as the rhubarb. Or stuff the meringues with star anise–flavored mascarpone, and use a passion fruit sauce.

NEW ENGLAND SUMMER PUDDING

I am always surprised that this dessert never became as popular in America as in England. It is a natural any time you have lots of summer berries. But we did make it a lot in New England. And since it must rest overnight before serving, it is a perfect dessert for entertaining.

Use whatever mixed berries you can find, but the berries must be sieved. Regardless of what other recipes may say, the texture will be ruined if the seeds are left in and some berries left whole.

Elderberries (*Sambucus nigra*) grow with abandon in Rhode Island, where they are probably *Sambucus canadensis,* and in the South, where they are probably *Sambucus mexicana.* But use whichever. All are delicious when cooked with other berries, if a bit odd by themselves.

SERVES 6 TO 8

2 cups	fresh strawberries, hulled		1 cup	light sugar syrup (see page 45)
2 cups	fresh raspberries			
1 cup	fresh red currants, stemmed		pinch	salt
			10–15	slices day-old dense white bread (sliced ¼-inch thick)
1 cup	elderberries (if you have them)			
2 cups	fresh blueberries, logan-berries, or ollalieberries		2 cups	custard (see page 256)

Coarsely chop the strawberries and put them and the other berries in a nonreactive saucepan. Add the syrup and salt and cook over high heat for 5 minutes, or until the berries are just beginning to give up their juices. Remove from the heat and cool. Pass the berries through a food mill or sieve. Discard the seeds.

Line a 2-quart pudding mold or other deep bowl with cheesecloth. Dip both sides of some of the bread slices in the berry puree and arrange very neatly and snugly around the sides and bottom of the mold. Soak the remaining slices in the berry puree and layer, alternating with the remaining berry puree, and ending with soaked bread to completely cover the top.

Place a plate that fits just inside the top of the mold on top of the pudding. Put the mold in a pan to catch the overflow of berry juice, and weight the plate. Refrigerate the pudding overnight.

To serve, unmold the pudding onto a serving platter, slice, and serve with the custard.

Cooked Cream with Sugared Apricots and Hot Huckleberry Sauce

We developed this version of *panna cotta* at Stars in San Francisco, calling it French Sweet Cream, though why "French" I have no idea.

SERVES 4 TO 6

2 cups	sour cream	1 tablespoon	freshly squeezed lemon juice
1 cup	heavy cream		
½ cup	mascarpone	½ cup	cooked huckleberry (or blueberry) sauce (see page 255)
½ cup	sugar		
½ teaspoon	salt		
1 level tablespoon	gelatin	2	large Australian sugar-preserved apricots, finely chopped
3 tablespoons	water		
1½ teaspoons	pure real vanilla extract		

Put the creams, mascarpone, sugar, and salt in a metal bowl and mix together well. Let sit 30 minutes.

In a small saucepan, place the gelatin in the water and let it sit 10 minutes. Stir for a minute over low heat to completely dissolve.

Meanwhile, put the bowl of creams over (but not in) simmering water, and warm the creams for 3 minutes, stirring constantly. Add and mix in the gelatin, the vanilla, and the lemon juice. Continue cooking until the mixture is just warm to the touch.

Put the cream mixture through a fine strainer and divide it among four 6-ounce high ramekins or baba molds. Refrigerate for 4 hours, or until set.

To unmold the creams, put the ramekins in hot water for several seconds and then invert them onto plates. Sprinkle the creams and the plate surface with the chopped apricots. Warm the huckleberry sauce and spoon over the creams. Eat immediately, as the creams will start to melt on contact with the hot berry sauce.

VARIATIONS Use chocolate and caramel sauces; tropical fruit or any other fruit compotes (see pages 265); strawberries in red wine (see page 260) and Sichuan peppercorns; cooked figs (see page 267) or figs stewed in chocolate and rum, or even in green Chartreuse; or quinces stewed in rosemary sugar syrup and then macerated in white pear brandy.

"Burnt" Passion Fruit Curd

The only thing better than lemon curd is this one made with passion fruit.

4	eggs	¼ cup	heavy cream
2	egg yolks	1 cup	sugar
1 cup	ripe, fresh passion fruit juice (6 large fruits, pulp removed, pureed in a blender 1 minute, sieved)	pinch	salt
		½ cup	unsalted butter, at room temperature, cut into 1-tablespoon pieces
2 tablespoons	freshly squeezed lime juice	¼ cup	superfine sugar

Put all the ingredients except the butter and superfine sugar in a metal, nonreactive bowl and beat together well until the sugar is completely dissolved.

Prepare an ice bath in a bowl slightly bigger than the bowl used to beat the ingredients.

Put the bowl with the egg mixture over simmering water (but not in it) and cook while beating for 10 minutes, or just until the curd thickens, being careful not to let the egg mixture curdle. Beat in the butter. Transfer the bowl to the ice bath, and beat the curd for 5 minutes, or until cold.

Spoon the curd into cold, small shallow gratin dishes, cover, and refrigerate 2 hours.

Preheat the broiler to maximum heat.

When ready to serve, spread ⅟₁₆ inch of sugar evenly over the surface of each dish. Put the dishes under the broiler close to the flame until the sugar caramelizes. Serve immediately.

WHITE PEACH AND JASMINE ICE

After recently tasting the amazing Kahili white pineapples, I decided to introduce Hawaii to Escoffier's white peaches with pineapple ice and raspberry sauce (*Pêches Rose Chéri*), thirty years after first making the dish at Chez Panisse.

After poaching the peaches, I took my leis of pikake (jasmine) and pakalana flowers and put them into the syrup. Then, casually dipping my finger in the syrup and tasting the astonishing result, and inspired by the hauntingly beautiful flavors, I decided I should do something with this syrup alone (not just use it to store peaches). I turned the syrup into a sorbet. News that an outsider had shown Hawaiians how to cook Hawaiian was all over the radio and TV the next day.

SERVES 6

5	ripe white peaches
6 cups	medium sugar syrup (see page 45)
½ cup	freshly squeezed lime juice
½ cup	fresh jasmine flowers
½ teaspoon	salt

Prepare a large ice bath (see page 19).

Put the syrup in a nonreactive pan and bring to a simmer. Put the peaches in the syrup for 3 minutes, remove, and plunge them into the ice bath for 2 minutes.

Peel off the skin of all the peaches and put the skins back into the simmering syrup. Remove the pits, smash them in half, remove the peach kernels, and put them in the syrup also. Simmer the syrup for 30 minutes. Take the syrup off the heat, wait 5 minutes for it to cool slightly, and add the jasmine flowers. Let them steep for 1 hour. Strain the syrup, add the lime juice, and chill.

Chop the peaches and mix with 1 cup of the syrup.

Freeze the ice in an ice cream machine according to the manufacturer's instructions and serve with the peaches.

VARIATION Try Kahili pineapple mixed with mangosteen and passion fruit juices served in ice bowls in which yellow ginger flowers have been frozen.

Twenty-Minute Blueberry Tart

I love this tart since it needs no embellishment, and if you have frozen tart shells in the freezer, you are only twenty minutes away from a perfect dessert.

SERVES 6

1	tart shell (see below)
1 quart	fresh blueberries or 1½ quarts huckleberries
½ cup	red currant jelly
¼ cup	water

Preheat the oven to 400 degrees.

Bake the tart shell until it is golden (15 minutes) and put on a rack to cool.

Meanwhile, spill the berries out on a tray and pick out and discard any squashed or unripe ones, stems, and leaves. Put the cleaned berries in a bowl.

Heat the jelly and water in a little saucepan, stirring until there are no lumps, but only for 5 minutes at the most. Pour the jelly syrup through a sieve over the bowl of berries, and immediately toss the bowl up and down and around to coat the berries, or stir very gently with a rubber spatula. Pour the berries into the shell, mounded up in the center. Serve immediately.

Tart Pastry

MAKES ONE 9- TO 10-INCH ROUND TART SHELL, ¼-INCH THICK

2 cups	all-purpose flour, plus additional as needed
¼ cup	sugar
½ teaspoon	salt
½ pound	unsalted butter, cut in small pieces
¼ cup	cold water
	Flour for dusting

Combine the 2 cups of flour with the sugar and salt in a bowl. Mix the butter quickly into the flour by hand or with the paddle attachment of a mixer until the butter is in small pieces, the size of corn kernels. Add the water and blend together, gathering the mass into a ball. Wrap the dough in plastic wrap and refrigerate (or freeze) until needed.

Place the pastry on a lightly floured table. If the dough is cold and hard, beat it gently with a rolling pin to soften it. Shape it into a flattened circle. Dust the top with flour, turn over, dust again, and roll out the dough into a 14- or 15-inch round to make a tart shell. Wrap and refrigerate.

The shell can be double wrapped (in non-smelling plastic and then foil) and frozen for up to a month.

TREACLE TART

This tart is worth the effort to find the treacle, also called golden syrup. If you don't want to make it, go to St. John restaurant when you are next in London and have it there. It's one tart I can never resist, especially if covered in thick, rich Jersey or Guernsey cream.

SERVES 6 TO 8

1½ cups	golden syrup (Tate & Lyle)		¼ cup	heavy cream
½ cup	white breadcrumbs (see page 32)		pinch	salt
1 teaspoon	freshly grated lemon zest		1	10-inch unbaked tart shell (see page 274)
1 teaspoon	freshly squeezed lemon juice		½ cup	double cream (see page 27)

Preheat the oven to 375 degrees.

Pour the syrup in a medium saucepan and bring to a boil. Turn off the heat, add the breadcrumbs, and mix well. Let sit for 5 minutes, then stir in the zest, lemon juice, heavy cream, and salt.

Pour the mixture into the tart shell, put the tart in the oven, and bake for 10 minutes. Turn the oven down to 325 degrees and bake another 30 minutes, or until the filling has bubbled up and the crust is deep gold.

Take out and let cool. Do not refrigerate. Serve with the double cream.

CARAMELIZED POUND CAKE NAPOLEON WITH WHITE "MANGO" NECTARINES AND STRAWBERRY ICE CREAM

I have always loved strawberry shortcakes, especially when the shortcakes are hot and buttered and are served with lots of whipped cream and raspberry, blackberry, or blueberry sauces. But I find the cakes themselves, even at their best, a bit much to eat.

So I came up with the idea of using toasted and caramelized thin slices of cake, thereby cutting way down on the starch in the dish while emphasizing the fruit.

In my first book, I used plums (ripe Simka, Santa Rosa, and Queen Anne), but now I would use the superb new nectarines that have recently come on the market, like "mango" and "honeydew."

The napoleon must be assembled at the very last moment so that the cake does not become soggy. Taking only a few minutes to assemble once you have done the set up, this dish is an ideal and very easy showstopper.

SERVES 4

12	slices polenta pound cake (see page 277), 3½ by 2 inches, cut ⅛-inch thick		¼ cup	water
			2 cups	creamed sabayon sauce (see page 257)
½ cup	caramel (see page 45)		2 tablespoons	sifted or sieved confectioners' sugar
12	ripe "mango" or "honey dew" nectarines, pitted		1 pint	best-quality fresh strawberry ice cream
¼ cup	granulated sugar			
pinch	salt			

Preheat the oven to 425 degrees.

Put the cake slices on a wire baking rack on a baking tray. Heat the caramel and brush lightly onto each side of each slice. Put the tray in the oven and bake for 10 minutes. Take the tray out and let the cake slices cool thoroughly.

Prepare an ice bath (see page 19).

Slice the nectarines ¼-inch thick and put them in a sauté pan. Add the sugar, salt, and water and cook over medium heat until the fruit is tender and beginning to fall apart. Transfer the hot nectarines to a metal bowl and put the bowl in the ice bath to cool the fruit, stirring occasionally.

When you are ready to serve the napoleon, put a cooled cake slice on each plate, spoon some of the nectarines onto it, and then spoon some of the sabayon on the fruit. Then place another slice of cake on the sabayon and repeat the process of alternating fruit and sabayon, ending with the last piece of cake as a top.

Sprinkle the top piece with the confectioner's sugar and serve with a couple of scoops of strawberry ice cream alongside.

VARIATIONS Try with gingerbread instead of the pound cake, and try using hazelnut or chestnut ice cream (stir ½ cup nut puree into a pint of vanilla), or rose petal ice cream (chop up ½ cup pink petals and mix into a pint of vanilla ice cream) instead of the strawberry.

Rose Water–Rosemary Polenta Pound Cake

SERVES 6 TO 8; ONE 9-INCH LOAF CAKE

½ pound	unsalted butter, softened	1½ teaspoons	rose water
½ cup	plus 2 tablespoons fine cornmeal	½ teaspoon	pure vanilla extract
		½ teaspoon	cream of tartar
1 teaspoon	finely grated lemon zest	¼ teaspoon	baking soda
1½ teaspoons	fresh rosemary leaves, finely chopped	½ cup	sour cream
		1 cup	sifted cake flour
1 cup	sugar	¼ teaspoon	salt
4	eggs, separated		

Preheat the oven to 325 degrees. Use one tablespoon of the butter to butter a 9-inch loaf pan and dust with 2 tablespoons of the cornmeal. Shake out the pan.

Beat the remaining butter, lemon zest, rosemary, and sugar in a bowl until light and fluffy, about 10 minutes. Beat in the egg yolks one at a time. Add the rose water, vanilla, cream of tartar, baking soda, and sour cream and mix well. Sift the remaining cup of cornmeal together with the flour and salt, and add the mixture to the batter. Mix until just incorporated.

Whip the egg whites until stiff but not dry and fold into the batter.

Bake until a thin skewer stuck in the center of the cake comes out clean, 50 to 60 minutes. Cool on a rack for 15 minutes and then unmold the cake.

Hot Chocolate

This chocolate is served at Angelina in Paris, on the rue de Rivoli around the corner from the Place Vendôme and the Ritz. It is divine.

SERVES 2 TO 4

1 cup	heavy cream
4 ounces	very best quality bittersweet chocolate
1 tablespoon	superfine sugar
pinch	salt
1 cup	milk

Put the cream, chocolate, sugar, and salt in a metal bowl set over barely simmering water.

When the cream is hot to the touch (but never boiling), gently whisk the chocolate into the cream until it is thoroughly mixed. Take the bowl off the heat and whisk the mixture for 2 to 3 minutes.

The mixture can be stored covered in the refrigerator for up to a week, but don't add the milk until ready to serve. Then heat the milk (without boiling) and whisk in the chocolate mixture until it is hot and frothy. Serve immediately in demitasse cups.

BLACK BOTTOM PIE

Needs no comment. Or rather, I can't think of any that would do justice to this perfect pie. Except to say that I would change the phrase "as American as apple pie" to "as American as black bottom pie."

SERVES 6 TO 8

The Crust:		Rum-Flavored Layer:	
35	crisp ginger cookies, ginger snap type (1¾ cups when ground)	4	egg whites
		pinch	salt
6 tablespoons	melted butter	½ cup	superfine sugar
		2 tablespoons	dark rum
Basic Filling:		Topping:	
3½ cups	milk	2 tablespoons	confectioners' sugar
1 tablespoon	gelatin soaked in ⅔ cup warm water	1 cup	heavy cream
		1 ounce	coarsely grated semisweet chocolate
1 cup	sugar		
2 tablespoons	cornstarch		
2 pinches	salt		
8	egg yolks, beaten (save the whites)		
Chocolate Layer:			
3 ounces	unsweetened baking chocolate		
1 teaspoon	pure vanilla extract		

Preheat the oven to 325 degrees. Soak the gelatin in the water and keep warm.

MAKE THE CRUST: Roll out the cookies or break them up in a food processor until they are coarse crumbs. Put them in a bowl and mix in the melted butter. Line a 9-inch pie pan, sides and bottom, with the buttered crumbs, pressing them flat and firm. Bake the pie shell 10 minutes in the oven to set the crust. Take it out of the oven and let cool.

MAKE THE FILLING: Put the milk in a large saucepan, heat it to boiling and immediately turn off the heat. Mix the sugar, cornstarch, and salt together in a bowl, then add the egg yolks and beat until smooth. Slowly add the milk whisking all the time. Put the mixture back into the saucepan and cook until the mixture coats the back of a spoon, about 10 minutes. Let cool for 5 minutes. Add one third of the gelatin water mixture. Divide the custard into one third and two thirds, putting each in a separate bowl.

MAKE THE CHOCOLATE LAYER: Melt the unsweetened chocolate in a bowl over hot water, and then add two thirds of the custard. Stir in the vanilla and half of the remaining gelatin. Put this chocolate custard in the pie shell.

MAKE THE RUM LAYER: Beat the egg whites with the pinch of salt while slowly adding the sugar until the whites just make a firm peak. Mix the rum into the remaining third of the custard, add the remaining third of the gelatin, and then fold the whites into the custard.

Spread this rum-custard mix over the chocolate layer in the pie, cover, and refrigerate for at least 2 hours and up to overnight.

When ready to serve, whip the sugar with the cream and pile over the top of the pie. Sprinkle with the grated semisweet chocolate.

KUMQUAT "FANTASY" CREAM

If Edouard Nignon could dream about macaroon soufflés with strawberries (see page 264), then I can and have dreamt about this cream served with almost anything, or just by itself.

One morning in San Francisco in 1990, exhausted from a long charity banquet for 400 people the night before and wandering through the pastry kitchen on my way upstairs to the main kitchen, I stopped to taste the cream being prepared for tiramisu. "Stop right there!" I cried. "Cancel the old dessert. We have a new one."

We filled little thin-walled chocolate cups with this cream, put them on a bed of caramel custard sauce, then topped the cups with chopped hazelnuts and white chocolate shavings. These chocolate cups are much too hard to do at home, so if you cannot buy them, use the cream on savarins, baba, or napoleons like on the pound cake on page 277.

I love kumquats, and the variety you will probably find is *Fortunella margarita*, with oval fruit; but if you see the round one, *Fortunella japonica*, buy it. It is sweeter. You can eat the whole kumquat except for the seeds and stem.

SERVES 4 TO 6

6	egg yolks		16	kumquats, stemmed
½ cup	sugar		½ cup	medium syrup
2 tablespoons	Grand Marnier			(see page 45)
pinch	salt		½ tablespoon	fresh rosemary leaves,
1 pound	fresh mascarpone cream			finely chopped

Prepare an ice bath (see page 19).

Put the egg yolks, sugar, Grand Marnier, and salt in a metal bowl, and beat for 2 minutes. Put the bowl over (not touching) barely simmering water and beat for another 5 to 10 minutes, or until the mixture is thick and doubled in volume.

Put the bowl in the ice bath and continue beating for 5 minutes, or until cool, incorporating as much air as possible.

Add the mascarpone, and whip until thick. Do not overbeat or the mascarpone will separate. Refrigerate the cream until needed.

Put the kumquats in a saucepan with the syrup, bring to a simmer, and cover. Cook over low heat for 15 minutes, or until the fruit is very tender. Add the rosemary and let cool. When the kumquats are cool enough to handle, drain them and reserve the syrup. Then remove the seeds and chop the kumquats coarsely (⅛-inch pieces). If there is a lot of liquid left, reduce it until it is a thick syrup, and pour it back over the chopped fruit.

SOURCES AND RESOURCES

BAKING AND PASTRY

King Arthur Flour Baker's Catalogue
P.O. Box 1122, Norwich, VT 05055
(800) 827-6836
www.kingarthurflour.com

CAVIAR

Caviar Assouline
505 Vine St., Philadelphia, PA 19106
(800) 521-4491
www.caviarassouline.com

Caviarteria
502 Park Ave., New York, NY 10022
(212) 759-7410
www.caviarteria.com

Petrossian
419 West 13th St., New York, NY 10014
(800) 828-9241
www.petrossian.com
Caviar and truffles (and a wide variety of
smoked fish).

Urbani USA
2924 Fortieth Ave., Long Island City, NY
11101
(800) 281-2330
www.urbani.com

CHEESE AND BUTTER

Artisan Cheese
2413 California St., San Francisco, CA
94115
(415) 929-8610

Cato Corner Farm
178 Cato Corner Rd., Colchester, CT
06415
(860) 537-3884
catocornerfarm@mindspring.com

Cowgirl Creamery
P.O. Box 594, 80 Fourth St.,
Point Reyes Station, CA 94956
(415) 663-9335
www.cowgirlcreamery.com
Cottage cheese, crème fraîche, mascarpone, and fromage blanc.

Cypress Grove
4600 Dows Prairie Rd., McKinleyville,
CA 95519
(707) 839-3168
www.cypressgrovechevre.com

Dallas Mozzarella Company
2944 Elm St., Dallas, TX 75226
(214) 741-4072
www.mozzco.com
Wide variety of hand-pulled mozzarella
cheese.

Murray's Cheese Shop
257 Bleecker St., New York, NY 10014
(888) 692-4339
www.murrayscheese.com
Farmhouse cheese and very good crème
fraîche.

Organic Valley CROPP Cooperative
507 West Main St., La Farge, WI 54639
(888) 444-6455
www.organicvalley.com
High fat content, salted Amish butter.

Point Reyes Farmstead Cheese Company
P.O. Box 9, Point Reyes Station, CA
94956
(415) 663-8880
www.pointreyescheese.com
One of the first sources I used at Chez
Panisse for local ingredients.

Redwood Hill Farm
5480 Thomas Rd., Sebastopol, CA 94572
(707) 823-8250
www.redwoodhill.com
Known for their goat cheeses, and
especially the California *crottins.*

Rogue River Valley Creamery
P.O. Box 3606, Central Point, OR 91502
(541) 665-1155
www.roguegoldcheese.com
Cheddar and jack, but best known for
their Oregon blue cheese.

Vermont Shepherd
875 Patch Rd., Putney, VT 05346
(802) 387-4473
www.vermontshepherd.com

EQUIPMENT

J. B. Prince
www.jbprince.com
Molds and utensils.

Sur la Table
www.surlatable.com

Williams Sonoma
www.williams-sonoma.com

FARMERS' MARKETS

www.ams.usda.gov/farmersmarkets

FISH AND SHELLFISH

Farm 2 Market
P.O. Box 124, Trout Town Rd.,
Roscoe, NY 12776
(800) 633-4326
www.farm-2-market.com
Live lobsters, mussels, oysters, and clams.

The Fresh Fish Company
P.O. Box 192885
San Francisco, CA 94119
(415) 777-5900
www.portseafood@cs.com

Fresh Fish 4 U
12765 South Saginaw, Suite 303, Grand
Blanc, MI 48439
(877) 479-3474
www.freshfish4U.com
Fresh-water fish.

Fulton Street Lobster and Seafood
126 Dupond St., Plainview, NY 11803
(516) 349-9091
www.fultonstreet.com
Cooked and raw seafood platters.

Garden and Valley Isle Seafood
225 North Nimitz, Hway. 3, Honolulu,
HI 96817
(808) 524-4847
www.gvisfd.com
Hawaiian and Pacific Rim seafood and
fish.

James Hook Lobster Company
15-17 Northern Ave., Boston, MA 02210
(617) 423-5500
www.jameshooklobster.com
Fresh lobsters delivered daily.

J. J. Brenner
13053 Brenner Oyster Rd., Shelton, WA
98584
(253) 929-1562
www.jjbrenner.com
A grower and shipper of fresh oysters
and clams.

Legal Seafoods
33 Everett St., Allston, MA 02134
(800) 328-3474
www.legalseafoods.com
Fresh-caught lobsters.

Max & Me Atlantic Smoked Salmon
4723 Durham Rd., Lilthtown, PA 18901
(800) 503-3663
www.maxandme.com
Smoked fish, especially salmon.

Pacific Seafood Company
15501 South East Piazza, Clackamas, OR
97015
(503) 657-1101
www.pacseafood.com
Fresh crab.

Pearl
5878 Marine Way, P.O. Box 1792
Sechelt, B.C., V0N 3A0, Canada
(604) 740-0465
www.pearlsea.com
A wide variety of oysters, ranging in sizes
and styles, shipped frozen or fresh.

Spanish Table
www.tablespan.com
Cuttlefish and squid ink.

Washington State Browne Trading
Company
260 Commercial St., Portland, ME 04101
(800) 944-7848
www.browne-trading.com
Smoked fish and caviar.

FOIE GRAS, POULTRY, RABBIT, AND DUCK FAT

Cabbage Hill Farm
115 Crow Hill Rd., Mt. Kisco, NY 10549
(914) 241-2658
www.cabbagehillfarm.org
Nice range of meats, especially turkeys.

Citarella
2135 Broadway, New York, NY 10023
(212) 874-0383
www.citarella.com

D'Artagnan
280 Wilson Ave., Newark, NJ 07105
(800) 327-8246
www.dartagnan.com
Fresh, natural meats.

Hudson Valley Foie Gras
80 Brooks Rd., Ferndale, NY 12734
(845) 292-2500
www.hudsonvalleyfoiegras.com
Foie gras and prepared duck products.

Joie de Vivre
P.O. Box 875, Modesto, CA 95353
(209) 869-0788
www.frenchselections.com

Urbani USA
2924 Fortieth Ave., Long Island City, NY
11101
(800) 281-2330
www.urbani.com

FRUITS, VEGETABLES, AND NUTS

Frieda's
4465 Corporate Center Dr.,
Los Alimidas, CA 90720
(800) 421-9477
www.friedas.com
Wide variety of specialty produce.

The Chino Farm
Rancho Sante Fe, CA
(858) 756-3184
Fresh huitlacoche.

Coastal Organics
660 Eastwood Dr., Oxnard, CA 93030
(805) 983-3064

Greenleaf Produce
1955 Gerald Ave., San Francisco, CA
94124
(415) 647-2991
Hard-to-find tropical fruit such as fresh
green almonds, passion fruit, longans,
and kumquats.

Indian Rock Produce
P.O. Box 317, Quakertown, PA 18951
(800) 882-0512
www.indianrockproduce.com
Fresh produce and dried fruit.

Perfect Puree
975 Vintage Ave., St. Helena, CA 94574
(800) 566-3707
www.perfectpuree.com
A wide variety of vegetables and essential
purees including berries and domestic
and exotic fruits.

Todd Farm
Through the Montgomery Curb Market,
Madison Ave., Montgomery, AL 36109
information (334) 263-6445
shipping (334) 361-1569
Fresh corn, black-eyed peas, and great
lady peas.

Thompson & Morgan
Poplar Lane, Ipswich, Suffolk IP8 3BU,
England
011-44-1473-688-821
www.thompson-morgan.com
Edible flowers seeds, vegetables, and
potato plants.

Windrose Farm
5750 El Pharo Rd., Paso Robles, CA
93446
(805) 239-3757
windrose@tcsn.net
The best dried beans and a hundred or
so heirloom tomatoes.

World Variety Produce
P.O. Box 21127, Los Angeles, CA 90021
(800) 588-0151
www.melissas.com
Tropical fruit.

Virginia Gold Orchard
100 Asian Pear Way, Natural Bridge, VA
24578
(540) 291-1481
www.virginiagoldorchard.com
Perfect Asian pears.

GAME

Broken Arrow Ranch
P.O. Box 530, Ingram, TX 78025
(800) 962-4263
www.brokenarrowranch.com
Free-range venison, antelope, and wild
boar.

Polarica
105 Quint St., San Francisco, CA 94124
(415) 647-1300
www.polarica.com
Fish, game, and pasta.

Urbani USA
2924 Fortieth Ave., Long Island City, NY
11101
(800) 281-2330
www.urbani.com
Ostrich, buffalo, bear, and kangaroo.

HONEY

Crescent Valley Apiaries
HC 65, Box 51, Bovina Center, NY 13470
(607) 832-4317
Thyme honey harvested when it flowers,
unfiltered and unheated.

Esperya USA
1715 West Farms Rd., Bronx, NY 10460
(718) 860-2949
www.esperya.com
Luigi Manias's honey, along with Italian
ingredients.

Rainforest Honey Company
Box 1123, Sooke, B.C., VOS 1NO,
Canada
(877) 554-6639
Unfiltered, unheated Leatherwood honey
from Tasmania.

GENERAL GROCERS

Balducci's
www.balducci.com
All types of specialty and hard-to-find
gourmet foods.

Dean and Deluca
www.deananddeluca.com
Specialty foods like oils, olives, and
foie gras.

INFORMATION

www.slowfood.com
The website of the international Slow
Food movement.

www.albc-usa.org
The website of the American Livestock
Breeds Conservancy.

MEAT

Calhoun's Country Hams
19 South East St., Culpepper, VA 22701
(877) 825-8319
www.calhounhams.com
Virginia ham.

Summerfield Farms
10044 James Monroe Hway., Culpepper,
VA 22701
(800) 898-3276
Free-range veal, lamb, dry-aged beef,
Kobe beef.

OILS AND VINEGAR

Francvin
P.O. Box 696, New York, NY 10156
(212) 679-4674
www.lesmoulinsdores.com

Holmquist Hazelnut Orchards
9821 Holmquist Rd., Lynden, WA 98264
(360) 988-9240
www.holmquisthazelnuts.com
Italian hazelnuts and the oil made
from them.

SEA SALT AND FLEUR DE SEL

Dean & DeLuca
2526 East 36th Street North Circle,
Wichita, KS 67219
(877) 826-9246
www.deananddeluca.com

Hawaiian Specialty Salt
P.O. Box 5766, Helo, Hawaii 96720
(808) 334-3929
www.hawaiisalt.com
Unrefined sea salt.

SEEDS

Seed Savers Exchange
3076 Northwinn Rd., Decorah, IA 52101
(563) 382-5990
www.seedsavers.com
All types of seeds, especially heirloom
varieties.

SPICES AND OTHER
ETHNIC SUPPLIES

Asia Foods
www.asiafoods.com
Asian ingredients, spices, and specialty
cookware.

Esperya
www.esperya.com
Italian ingredients and spices.

Ethnic Grocer
www.ethnicgrocer.com
All types of foods and spices.

Kalustyan
www.kalustyan.com
All types of Indian foods, both dried and
fresh, especially spices and seasonings.

Katagiri
www.katagiri.com
Japanese ingredients.

Manicaretti
www.manicaretti.com
Artisanal Italian oils and pasta.

Mexican Grocer
www.mexgrocer.com
Authentic Mexican gourmet supplies
and spices.

Penzeys
www.penzeys.com
Spices, seasonings, and marinades.

South African Foodshop
www.southafricanfoodshop.com
African spices and hard-to-find specialty
ingredients indigenous to southern
Africa.

Spanish Table
www.tablespan.com

Sultans Delight
www.sultansdelight.com
Mediterranean and Middle Eastern
foods.

Thai Grocer
www.thaigrocer.com

Tienda
www.tienda.com
Spanish specialty foods.

World of Spice
www.worldofspice.com
England's best source for spices and
flavors.

World Merchants
www.worldspice.com
For spices, chilies, and leaf tea.

TEA

32-29 Green Point Ave., Long Island
City, NY 11101
(888) 832-5433
www.serendipitea.com
Hundreds of teas.

TRUFFLES

Urbani USA
2924 Fortieth Ave., Long Island City, NY
11101
(800) 281-2330
www.urbani.com

Sainte Alvere Truffle Market
www.sainte-alvere.com

WILD RICE

White Earth Land Recovery Project
32033 East Round Lake Rd., Ponsford,
Minnesota 56575
(888) 779-3577
www.welrp.org
Rice harvested by the Ojibway tribe on
the White Earth Reservation—truly wild.

METRIC CONVERSION CHART

WEIGHT EQUIVALENTS

The metric weights given in this chart are not exact equivalents, but have been rounded up or down slightly to make measuring easier.

AVOIRDUPOIS	METRIC
¼ oz	7 g
½ oz	15 g
1 oz	30 g
2 oz	60 g
3 oz	90 g
4 oz	115 g
5 oz	150 g
6 oz	175 g
7 oz	200 g
8 oz (½ lb)	225 g
9 oz	250 g
10 oz	300 g
11 oz	325 g
12 oz	350 g
13 oz	375 g
14 oz	400 g
15 oz	425 g
16 oz (1 lb)	450 g
1½ lb	750 g
2 lb	900 g
2¼ lb	1 kg
3 lb	1.4 kg
4 lb	1.8 kg

VOLUME EQUIVALENTS

These are not exact equivalents for American cups and spoons, but have been rounded up or down slightly to make measuring easier.

AMERICAN	METRIC	IMPERIAL
¼ t	1.2 ml	--
½ t	2.5 ml	--
1 t	5.0 ml	--
½ T (1.5 t)	7.5 ml	--
1 T (3 t)	15 ml	--
¼ cup (4 T)	60 ml	2 fl oz
⅓ cup (5 T)	75 ml	2½ fl oz
½ cup (8 T)	125 ml	4 fl oz
⅔ cup (10 T)	150 ml	5 fl oz
¾ cup (12 T)	175 ml	6 fl oz
1 cup (16 T)	250 ml	8 fl oz
1¼ cups	300 ml	10 fl oz (½ pt)
1½ cups	350 ml	12 fl oz
2 cups (1 pint)	500 ml	16 fl oz
2½ cups	625 ml	20 fl oz (1 pint)
1 quart	1 liter	32 fl oz

OVEN TEMPERATURE EQUIVALENTS

OVEN MARK	F	C	GAS
Very cool	250–275	130–140	½–1
Cool	300	150	2
Warm	325	170	3
Moderate	350	180	4
Moderately hot	375–400	190–200	5–6
Hot	425–450	220–230	7–8
Very hot	475	250	9

cannellini beans with, 180
celery root with, 62
Bloody Mary, 51
chorizo steaks with, 228
seafood shooters with, 57
blue cheese, 14
blue corn enchiladas with huitlacoche
and squash flowers, 38, 155
blueberries
in sauce, 255
in stew, 265
in summer pudding, 270
tart, 274
blueberry sauce, 255
Bocuse, Paul, 20, 196, 260
boiling in salted water, 21
boning, 22, 165, 166
Bonne cuisine du Comte de Nice, La
(Médecin), 80, 182
Botany of Desire, The (Pollan), 8
Boulestin, Marcel, 121, 169
bouquet garni. See herb bundle
braised beef cheeks with a mustard and
breadcrumb crust, 222
braised beef short ribs, 221
braised chicken in a casserole with
chestnuts and sausages, 194–95
braised lamb shank stew with chickpeas
and red chili linguine, 232
braised pig trotters with ginger and
ginger flowers, 224
braised rabbit with prunes Catalan
style, 211
inspiration for, 133
braised sweetbreads, 45–46
braising, 24
brandade. See creamed puree of salt cod
brandy, 209, 211, 241, 262, 266
bread, 31–32
breadcrumbs, 32
brining
dry brine or duck salt marinade, 22
pork brining, 23
wet brine, 22–23
British Cookery (Grigson), 123
broad beans. *See* fava beans
brouillade, 34
browning, 24
brunoise, 14
buckwheat groats. *See* kasha
burgundy, 260
"burnt" passion fruit curd, 272

butternut squash, in white truffle oil, 129
butters, 27
ancho, 192
clarified, 27, 218
Colbert, 245
flavored, 78
garlic-and-parsley, 68
green goddess, 178–79, 249
Indian spiced, 136
Maitre d'Hôtel, 245
Montpelier, 78, 130, 136, 137, 165,
219, 220, 246
mushroom, 130
nasturtium, 245
salted *vs.* unsalted, 27
shellfish, 189
simple and compound, 245–46
Singapore, 246

cabbage
in coleslaw, 87
Savoy, 130
cannellini beans
bacon with, 225
baked, 132
lobster with, 180
cannelloni with salt cod and fresh
tomato sauce, 148
canola oil, 27–28, 29
capellini
baked whole lobster with, 178–79
mussels with, 150
capellini with mussels and JT's
"Américaine," 150
capers, 44
in English autumn salad, 91
in Mediterranean oil and vinegar
sauce, 238
in Montpelier butter, 246
in parsley and onion salad, 90
in rémoulade sauce, 251
in tomato relish, 243
capon, roasted, 196
caramel, 45
in pound cake, 276
caramelized pound cake napoleon with
white "mango" nectarines and
strawberry ice cream, 276
caramelized sugar and ginger sauce, 227
duck with, 204
Carême, Antonin, 17, 36, 208, 257
Carême's cream, 257

Carnet d'Anna, Le (de Pomiane),
113, 224
Carnet d'epicure, Le (Escoffier), 20
Casa Armas (Manila), 184
casserole of whole foie gras, 213
casseroles
braised chicken, 194–95
sweetbread, 46–47
of whole foie gras, 213
*Catalan Cookery Book, A: A Collection
of Impossible Recipes* (Davis), 133
cataplana, 181–82
cauliflower with white truffle sauce,
140–41
caviar
osetra, 169
in oyster soup, 111
pressed, 60, 250
salmon with, 169
in sauce with lobster and oysters, 179
sevruga, 61, 169, 179
steelhead salmon, 58
celery root
blood sausage with, 62
oven-roasted, 137
Chamberlain, Samuel, 71
Chapel, Alain, 20
Chappellet Vineyards, 137
Charles Gaines's grilled corn, 125
charlotte molds, 261
Chartreuse, 64
cheesecloth, 48, 96
cheeses
blue, 14
Crescenza, 65
Fontina, 82
Gorgonzola, 94
chervil, 168
chestnuts
braised chicken with, 194–95
cornmeal crêpes stuffed with, 214
foie gras with, 213
preserved duck legs with, 203
Chez Denis (Paris), 35
Chez Panisse (Berkeley), 17, 35, 37,
50, 64, 80, 91, 133, 135, 140, 174, 273
chicken, 192–99
braised in a casserole, 194–95
breast of, 192
in club sandwich, 73
in Cobb salad, 99
grilled poussin, 199

ART CREDITS

Full captions for Donald Sultan's paintings are as follows:

Page 2: *Five Lemons and Tangerine April 21, 1986* (detail). Oil, spackle, and tar on tile, 12½" x 12½". Private collection.

Page 5: *Three Melons and a Pineapple July 2, 1996.* Oil, spackle, and tar on tile over wood, 12" x 12". Private collection.

Page 6: *Radishes June 20, 1989.* Tar, spackle, and oil on tile over wood, 12" x 12". Collection of Park International, Bedford, New York.

Page 9: *White Asparagus June 5, 1984.* Oil, spackle, and tar on tile, 12¾" x 12¾". Private collection.

Page 10: *Red, Orange, Yellow, Green Peppers January 30, 1998.* Oil, spackle, and tar on tile over masonite, 48" x 48". Collection of the Baldwin Gallery.

Page 52: *Pears and Lemon August 9, 1984* (detail). Oil, spackle, and tar on tile, 12½" x 12¾". Collection of Joseph Helman.

Page 61: *Five Pears, an Apple, and a Lemon December 14, 1984.* Oil, spackle, and tar on tile, 12" x 12". Private collection.

Page 84: *Peppers March 13, 1988.* Oil, spackle, and tar on tile over wood, 12" x 12". Private collection.

Page 97: *Geranium June 16, 1989.* Oil, spackle, and tar over wood, 12" x 12". Private collection.

Page 100: *Squash December 1988* (detail). Oil, spackle, and tar on tile over wood, 12" x 12". Collection of Bob Feldman.

Page 103: *Three Carrots February 10, 1994.* Oil, spackle, and tar over masonite, 13" x 13". Private collection.

Page 116: *Beans September 27, 1996* (detail). Oil, spackle, and tar on tile, 12" x 12". Courtesy of Gana Art Gallery, Seoul, Korea.

Page 124: *Carrots May 21, 1984.* Oil, spackle, and tar on tile, 12" x 12". Private collection.

Page 144: *Red Fruit and Eggs June 23, 1998* (detail). Oil, spackle, and tar on tile over wood, 12" x 12". Private collection.

Page 159: *Three Walnuts October 5, 1993.* Oil, spackle, and tar on tile over masonite, 48" x 48". Private collection.

Page 162: *Fish July 26, 1990.* Oil, spackle, and tar on tile over wood, 12" x 12". Collection of Bob Feldman.

Page 190: *Bird August 3, 1988.* Oil, spackle, and tar on tile over wood, 12" x 12". Private collection.

Page 216: *Steer January 14, 1983.* Plaster, butyl rubber, and pastel on tile over masonite, 96" x 96". Collection of Douglas Cramer.

Page 219: *Steer October 7, 1982.* Chalk and tar on tile over masonite, 98¼" x 97¾". Collection of Toby Schieber.

Page 234: *Lemons August 26, 1984.* Oil paint, spackle, and tar on tile, 12¾" x 12¾". Private collection.

Page 253: *Asparagus April 20, 1984.* Oil, tar, and spackle on tile, 12" x 12". Collection of Joseph Helman.

Page 258: *Apples and Oranges March 7, 1986* (detail). Oil, spackle, and tar on tile, 12½" x 12½". Collection of the artist.

Page 269: *Grapes, Apples, and Pears December 2, 1997.* Tar, oil, and spackle on tile over masonite, 48" x 48". Collection of Lynch Bages, France.